The Logic of Strategy

The Logic of Strategy

Edited by

CRISTINA BICCHIERI
RICHARD JEFFREY
BRIAN SKYRMS

New York   Oxford

Oxford University Press

1999

Oxford University Press

Oxford   New York
Athens   Auckland   Bangkok   Bogotá   Buenos Aires   Calcutta
Cape Town   Chennai   Dar es Salaam   Delhi   Florence   Hong Kong   Istanbul
Karachi   Kuala Lumpur   Madrid   Melbourne   Mexico City   Mumbai
Nairobi   Paris   São Paulo   Singapore   Taipei   Tokyo   Toronto   Warsaw

and associated companies in
Berlin   Ibadan

Published by Oxford University Press, Inc.   .
198 Madison Avenue, New York, New York 10016

Oxford is a registered trademark of Oxford University Press

Library of Congress Cataloging-in-Publication Data
The logic of strategy / edited by Cristina Bicchieri, Richard Jeffrey, Brian Skyrms.
p.   cm.   .
Includes bibliographical references.
ISBN 0-19-511715-8
1. Strategy (Philosophy).   2. Game theory.   I. Bicchieri, Cristina.
II. Jeffrey, Richard C.   III. Skyrms, Brian.
B105.S68 L64 - 1998
160—dc21   9850190

9 8 7 6 5 4 3 2 1

Printed in the United States of America
on acid-free paper

Contents

Contents

Introduction:
What Is the Logic of Strategy?

The analysis of strategic interaction between rational decision makers is the business of game theory. In a broad sense, game theory is the logic of strategy, but a logician would not classify this subject as a branch of logic. The game theory of von Neumann and Morgenstern and Nash speaks the language of mathematics, but not specifically the language of logic. More recently, however, it has become increasingly evident that traditional game theory carried with it tacit assumptions, which are best made clear within frameworks provided by various branches of philosophical logic: the logic of subjunctive conditionals and the logics of belief and knowledge operators. This realization began with explicit investigation of the role of assumptions of common knowledge in game theory—as a result of pioneering work by Schelling, Lewis, Harsanyi, and Aumann. More recently, the literature on refinements of the Nash equilibrium concept in extensive form games has put the spotlight on counterfactual conditions about off-the-equilibrium path behavior. Binmore puts it this way: "Suppose that a perfectly rational person made the following sequence of irrational moves, then . . . ." The validity of such well-established methods as solution of extensive form games of perfect information by backward induction rests on such esoteric considerations.

It is this narrower sense of the logic of strategy that is the theme of this volume. Both game theorists and philosophers are contributing to the development of this area. Here, we collect essays on the forefront of research on the logic of strategy.

Our first selection is by a philosopher who invented the "selection function" semantics for counterfactual conditions used in modern philosophical logic. In "Knowledge, Belief, and Counterfactual Reasoning in Games," Robert Stalnaker uses this and other tools from philosophical logic to develop a framework within which assumptions underlying strategic reasoning and the conceptual foundations of game theory can be explicitly formulated. He uses this framework to evaluate solution concepts such as various kinds of rationalizability in games.

The second essay, "Consequentialism, Non-Archimedean Probabilities and Lexicographic Expected Utility," is by Peter Hammond, an economist who is well known for his development of consequentialist foundations of expected utility theory. Hammond is engaged in a project of generalizing the consequentialist approach to game theory. In extensive form games the question of how rational players update on events of zero probability takes on special significance—a problem that is also discussed in the preceding essay. It is tempting to use a framework in which the putative zeros are really infinitesimals and updating is by standard Bayesian conditioning. Here Hammond develops consequentialist foundations for such a framework.

In "Solutions Based on Ratifiability and Sure Thing Reasoning," William Harper, a philosopher who is one of the architects of causal decision theory, introduces a refinement of the Nash equilibrium concept based on Richard Jeffrey's notion of "ratifiability" and an extension of L. J. Savage's "sure thing" reasoning. Harper then uses the Stalnaker framework of the first essay to analyze his refinement.

André Fuhrmann and Isaac Levi discuss the proper application of a "minimal revision" interpretation of conditions originally proposed by the philosopher Frank Ramsey. They argue in "Undercutting the Ramsey Test for Conditionals" that the assertability conditions of an important class of conditionals is not given by Ramsey's test, but rather by an inductive extension of that test. These considerations are related to the literature on "nonmonotonic logic" in theoretical computer science, and clearly have implications for the issues regarding the interpretation of conditionals in game theory raised in the foregoing essays.

In "Aumann's 'No Agreement' Theorem Generalized," the focus shifts from conditionals to common knowledge. In a famous paper Robert Aumann proved that a group of agents whose current probabilities are common knowledge and who have a common prior must still agree, even if they received private information in the meantime. Aumann's model has the agents updating by conditioning on their private information. Matthias Hild, Richard Jeffrey, and Mathias Risse generalize the theorem to less structured models of learning.

Aumann's account of common knowledge bases the semantics for the knowledge operator, "Agent X knows that . . . ," on a partition. The agent knows that she is in a certain cell of her knowledge and knows every proposition which corresponds to a superset of that cell. This gives this knowledge operator the logical structure of the necessity operator in what is known as an S-5 system of modal logic. In both S-5 and the weaker S-4 systems, the "KK principle"—if you know a proposition then you know that you know it—is valid. In "Rational Failures of the KK Principle" Timothy Williamson develops epistemic models which allow for violations of this principle.

In our next selection, Hyun Song Shin and Timothy Williamson explore weakening Aumann's definition of common knowledge in a different way. They replace knowledge with belief. Then they investigate the question that forms the title of their talk: "How Much Common Belief Is Necessary for a Convention?"

In "Sophisticated Bounded Agents Play the Repeated Dilemma," Michael Bacharach, Hyun Song Shin, and Mark Williams investigate the effect of bounds on the length of sentences of the form "1 knows that 2 knows that 1 knows that . . ." that players can understand. They show that such "bounded rationality" can explain cooperation in finitely repeated Prisoner's Dilemma.

The essay with the most philosophical title—"Can Free Choice Be Known?"—is the contribution of Itzhak Gilboa, an economist. It is not primarily an essay on free will, but rather an argument that the rational decision maker cannot have her own acts in her probability space.

In our concluding essay, "Symmetry Arguments for Cooperation in the Prisoner's Dilemma," Cristina Bicchieri and Mitchell Green discuss some of the most famous, or infamous, arguments in the literature on rational choice. They use the Stalnaker models introduced in the first essay to provide a rather different view of the kind of case discussed by Gilboa in the preceding piece.

Cristina Bicchieri
Richard Jeffrey
Brian Skyrms

References

Aumann, R. J. (1976) "Agreeing to Disagree," *Annals of Statistics* 4, 1236–39.

Aumann, R. J. (1987) "Correlated Equilibrium as an Expression of Bayesian Rationality," *Econometrica* 55, 1–18.

Aumann, R. J. (1995) "Backward Induction and Common Knowledge of Rationality," *Games and Economic Behavior* 8, 6–19.

Binmore, K. (1987–88) "Modeling Rational Players I and II," *Economics and Philosophy* 3, 179–214.

Gibbard, A. and Harper, W. L. (1978) "Counterfactuals and Two Kinds of Expected Utility," in *Foundations and Applications of Decision Theory*, ed. C. A. Hooker, J. J. Leach, and E. F. McClennen. Reidel: Dordrecht.

Harsanyi, J. C. (1967) "Games of Incomplete Information Played by Bayesian Players, I, II, III," *Management Science* 14, 159–82, 320–34, 486–502.

Lewis, D. K. (1969) *Convention.* Harvard University Press: Cambridge, Mass.

Lewis, D. K. (1973) *Counterfactuals.* Oxford University Press: Oxford.

Schelling, T. C. (1960) *The Strategy of Conflict.* Harvard University Press: Cambridge, Mass.

Stalnaker, R. C. (1968) "A Theory of Conditionals," in *Studies in Logical Theory: Essays in Honor of Carl G. Hempel*, ed. N. Rescher. Blackwell: Oxford.
Stalnaker, R. C. (1972) "Letter to David Lewis," in *Ifs*, ed. W. L. Harper, R. C. Stalnaker, and G. Pearce. Reidel: Dordrecht.

Contributors

Michael Bacharach — *Institute of Economics and Statistics, Oxford*

Cristina Bicchieri — *Department of Philosophy, Carnegie Mellon University*

André Fuhrmann — *Department of Philosophy, University of Konstanz*

Itzhak Gilboa — *Department of Managerial Economics and Decision Sciences, J. L. Kellogg Graduate School of Managment, Northwestern University*

Mitchell S. Green — *Department of Philosophy, University of Virginia*

Peter J. Hammond — *Department of Philosophy, University of Western Ontario*

William Harper — *Department of Economics, Stanford University*

Matthias Hild — *Christ's College, Cambridge*

Richard Jeffrey — *Department of Philosophy, Princeton University*

Isaac Levi — *Department of Philosophy, Columbia University*

Mathias Risse — *Department of Philosophy, Princeton University*

Hyun Song Shin — *University College, Oxford*

Brian Skyrms — *Department of Philosophy, University of California, Irvine*

Robert Stalnaker — *Department of Linguistics and Philosophy, MIT*

Mark Williams — *Exeter College, Oxford*

Timothy Williamson — *University College, Oxford*

The Logic of Strategy

CHAPTER 1

Knowledge, Belief, and Counterfactual Reasoning in Games

Robert Stalnaker

1. Introduction

Deliberation about what to do in any context requires reasoning about what will or would happen in various alternative situations, including situations that the agent knows will never in fact be realized. In contexts that involve two or more agents who have to take account of each others' deliberation, the counterfactual reasoning may become quite complex. When I deliberate, I have to consider not only what the causal effects would be of alternative choices that I might make, but also what other agents might believe about the potential effects of my choices and how their alternative possible actions might affect my beliefs. Counterfactual possibilities are implicit in the models that game theorists and decision theorists have developed—in the alternative branches in the trees that model extensive form games and the different cells of the matrices of strategic form representations—but much of the reasoning about those possibilities remains in the informal commentary on and motivation for the models developed. Puzzlement is sometimes expressed by game theorists about the relevance of what happens in a game "off the equilibrium path": of what would happen if what is (according to the theory) both true and known by the players to be true were instead false. My aim in this essay is to make some suggestions for clarifying some of the concepts involved in counterfactual reasoning in strategic contexts, both the reasoning of the rational agents being modeled and the reasoning of the theorist who is doing the modeling, and to bring together some ideas and technical tools developed by philosophers and logicians that I think might be relevant to the analysis of strategic reasoning, and more generally to the conceptual foundations of game theory.

There are two different kinds of counterfactual possibilities—causal and epistemic possibilities—that need to be distinguished. They play different but interacting roles in a rational agent's reasoning about what he and others will and should do, and I think equivocation between them is responsible for some of the puzzlement about counterfactual reasoning. In deliberation, I reason both about how the world might have been different if I or others did different things than we are going to do, and also about how my beliefs, or others' beliefs, might change if I or they learned things that we expect not to learn. To take an often cited example from the philosophical literature to illustrate the contrast between these two kinds of counterfactual suppositions; compare *If Shakespeare didn't write Hamlet, someone else did*, with *If Shakespeare hadn't written Hamlet, someone else would have.*[1] The first expresses a quite reasonable disposition to hold onto the belief that someone wrote Hamlet should one receive the unexpected information that Shakespeare did not; the second expresses a causal belief, a belief about objective dependencies, that would be reasonable only if one held a bizarre theory according to which authors are incidental instruments in the production of works that are destined to be written. The content of what is supposed in the antecedents of these contrasting conditionals is the same, and both suppositions are or may be counterfactual in the sense that the person entertaining them believes with probability one that what is being supposed is false. But it is clear that the way in which it is being supposed is quite different in the two cases.

This contrast is obviously relevant to strategic reasoning. Beliefs about what it is rational to do depend on causal beliefs, including beliefs about what the causal consequences would be of actions that are alternatives to the one I am going to choose. But what is rational depends on what is believed, and I also reason about the way my beliefs and those of others would change if we received unexpected information. The two kinds of reasoning interact, since one of the causal effects of a possible action open to me might be to give unexpected information to another rational agent.[2]

It is obvious that a possible course of events may be causally impossible even if it is epistemically open, as when you have already committed yourself but I have not yet learned of your decision. It also may happen that a course of events is causally open even when it is epistemically closed in the sense that someone believes, with probability one, that it will not happen. But can it be true of a causally open course of events that someone not only believes, but also *knows* that it will not occur? This is less clear; it depends on how we understand the concept of knowledge. It does not seem incoherent to suppose that you know that I am rational, even though irrational choices are still causally possible for me. In fact, the concept of rationality seems applicable to actions only when there are options open to an agent. If we are to make sense of assumptions of knowledge and common knowledge of rationality, we need to allow for the possibility that an agent may know what he or another agent is going to do, even when it remains true that the agent could have done otherwise.

To clarify the causal and epistemic concepts that interact in strategic reasoning, it is useful to break them down into their component parts. If, for example, there is a problem about exactly what it means to assume that there is common knowledge of rationality, it ought to be analyzed into problems about exactly what rationality is, or about what knowledge is, or about how common knowledge is defined in terms of knowledge. The framework I will use to represent these concepts is one that is designed to help reveal the compositional structure of such complex concepts: it is a formal semantic or model theoretic framework—specifically, the Kripkean "possible worlds" framework for theorizing about modal, causal, and epistemic concepts. I will start by sketching a simple conception of a model, in the model theorist's sense, of a strategic form game. Second, I will add to the simple conception of a model the resources to account for one kind of counterfactual reasoning, reasoning about belief revision. In these models we can represent concepts of rationality, belief, and common belief, and so can define the complex concept of common belief in rationality, and some related complex concepts, in terms of their component parts. The next step is to consider the concept of knowledge, and the relation between knowledge and belief. I will look at some different assumptions about knowledge, and at the consequences of these different assumptions for the concepts of common knowledge and common knowledge of rationality. Then to illustrate the way some of the notions I discuss might be applied to clarify some counterfactual reasoning about games, I will discuss some familiar problems about backward induction arguments, using the model theory to sharpen the assumptions of those arguments, and to state and prove some theorems about the consequences of assumptions about common belief and knowledge.

2. Model Theory for Games

Before sketching the conception of a model of a game that I will be using, I will set out some assumptions that motivate it, assumptions that I think will be shared by most, though not all, game theorists. First, I assume that a game is a *partial* description of a set or sequence of interdependent Bayesian decision problems. The description is partial in that, while it specifies all the revelant utilities motivating the agents, it does not give their degrees of belief. Instead, qualitative constraints are put on what the agents are assumed to believe about the actions of other agents; but these constraints will not normally be enough to determine what the agents believe about each other, or to determine what solutions are prescribed to the decision problems. Second, I assume that all of the decision problems in the game are problems of individual decision making. There is no special concept of rationality for decision making in a situation where the outcomes depend on the actions of more than one agent. The acts of other agents are, like chance events, natural disasters, and acts of God, just facts about an uncertain world that agents have beliefs and degrees of belief about. The utilities of other agents are relevant to an agent only as information that, together with beliefs about the rationality of those agents, helps to predict their actions. Third, I assume that in cases where degrees of belief are undetermined, or only partially determined, by the description of a decision problem, then no action is prescribed by the theory unless there is an action that would be rational for every system of degrees of belief compatible with what is specified. There are no special rules of rationality telling one what to do in the absence of degrees of belief, except this: Decide what you believe, and then maximize expected utility.

A model for a game is intended to represent a completion of the partial specification of the set or sequence of Bayesian decision problems that is given by the definition of the game, as well as a representation of a particular play of the game. The class of all models for a game will include all ways of filling in the relevant details that are compatible with the conditions imposed by the definition of the game. Although a model is intended to represent one particular playing of the game, a single model will contain many possible worlds, since we need a representation not only of what actually happens in the situation being modeled but also of what might or would happen in alternative situations that are compatible with the capacities and beliefs of one or another of the agents. Along with a set of possible worlds, models will contain various relations and measures on the set that are intended to determine all the facts about the possible worlds that may be relevant to the actions of any of the agents playing the game in a particular concrete context.

The models considered in this paper are models for finite games in normal or strategic form. I assume, as usual, that the game Γ itself consists of a structure $\langle N, \langle C_i, u_i \rangle_{i \in N} \rangle$, where N is a finite set of players, C_i is a finite set of alternative strategies for player i, and u_i is player i's utility function taking a strategy profile (a specification of a strategy for each player) into a utility value for the outcome that would result from that sequence of strategies. A model for a game will consist of a set of possible worlds (a state space), one of which is designated as the actual world of the model. In each possible world in the model, each player has certain beliefs and partial beliefs, and each player makes a certain strategy choice. The possible worlds themselves are simple, primitive elements of the model; the information about them—what the players believe and do in each possible world—is represented by several functions and relations given by a specification of the particular model. Specifically, a model for a game Γ will consist of a structure $\langle W, \mathbf{a}, \langle S_i, R_i, P_i \rangle_{i \in N} \rangle$, where W is a nonempty set (the possible worlds), $\mathbf{a}$ is a member of W (the actual world), each S_i is a function taking possible worlds into strategy choices for player i, each R_i is a binary relation on W, and each P_i is an additive measure function on subsets of W.

The R relations represent the qualitative structure of the players' beliefs in the different possible worlds in the following way: The set of possible worlds that are compatible with what player i believes in world w is the set $\{x: w\, R_i\, x\}$. It is assumed that the R relations are *serial*, *transitive*, and *Euclidean*.[3] The first assumption is simply the requirement that all players must have consistent beliefs (that there must be at least one possible world compatible with what any player believes in that world). The other two constraints encode the assumption that players know their own minds: They are necessary and sufficient to ensure that players have introspective access to their beliefs: If they believe something, they believe that they believe it, and if they do not, they believe that they do not.

The S functions encode the facts about what the players do—what strategies they choose—in each possible world. It is assumed that if $x R_i y$, then $S_i(x) = S_i(y)$. Intuitively, this requirement is the assumption that players know, at the moment of choice, what they are doing—what choice they are making. Like the constraints on the structure of the R relations, this constraint is motivated by the assumption that players have introspective access to their own states of mind.

The measure function P_i encodes the information about the player's *partial* beliefs in each possible world in the following way: Player i's belief function in possible world w is the relativization of P_i to the set $\{x: w R_i x\}$. That is, for any proposition ϕ, $P_{i,w}(\phi) = P_i(\phi \cap \{x: w R_i x\})/P_i(\{x: w R_i x\})$. The assumptions we are making about R_i and P_i will ensure that $P_i(\{x: w R_i x\})$ is nonzero for all w, so that this probability will always be defined.

The use of a single measure function for each player, defined on the whole space of possible worlds, to encode the information required to define the player's degrees of belief is just a technical convenience, an economical way to specify the many different belief functions that represent the player's beliefs in different possible worlds. No additional assumptions about the players' beliefs are implicit in this form of representation, since our introspection assumptions already imply that any two different belief states for a single player are disjoint, and any set of probability measures on disjoint sets can be represented by a single measure on the union of all the sets. This single measure will contain some extraneous information that has no representational significance—different total measures will determine the same set of belief functions—but this artifact of the model is harmless.[4]

In order to avoid complications that are not relevant to the conceptual issues I am interested in, I will be assuming throughout this discussion that our models are finite, and that the measure functions all assign nonzero probability to every nonempty subset of possible worlds.

We need to impose one additional constraint on our models, a constraint that is motivated by our concern with counterfactual reasoning. A specification of a game puts constraints on the causal consequences of the actions that may be chosen in the playing of the game, and we want these constraints to be represented in the models. Specifically, in a strategic form game, the assumption is that the strategies are chosen independently, which means that the choices made by one player cannot influence the beliefs or the actions of the other players. One could express the assumption by saying that certain counterfactual statements must be true in the possible worlds in the model: if a player had chosen a different strategy from the one he in fact chose, the other players would still have chosen the same strategies, and would have had the same beliefs that they in fact had. The constraint we need to add is a closure condition on the set of possible worlds—a requirement that there be enough possible worlds of the right kind to represent these counterfactual possibilities.

For any world w and strategy s for player i, there is a world $f(w, s)$ meeting the following four conditions

(1) For all $j \neq i$, if $w\,R_j\,x$, then $f(w, s)\,R_j\,x$.
(2) If $w\,R_i\,x$, then $f(w, s)\,R_i\,f(x, s)$.
(3) $S_i(f(w, s)) = s$.
(4) $P_i(f(w, s)) = P_i(w)$.

Intuitively, $f(w, s)$ represents the counterfactual possible world that, in w, is the world that would have been realized if player i, believing exactly what he believes in w about the other players, had chosen strategy s.

Any of the (finite) models constructed for the arguments given in this paper can be extended to (finite) models satisfying this closure condition. One simply adds, for each $w \in W$ and each strategy profile c, a world corresponding to the pair (w, c), and extending the Rs, Ps, and Ss in a way that conforms to the four conditions.[5]

Because of our concern to represent counterfactual reasoning, it is essential that we allow for the possibility that players have false beliefs in some possible worlds, which means that a world in which they have certain beliefs need not itself by compatible with those beliefs. Because the epistemic structures we have defined allow for false belief, they are more general than the partition structures that will be more familiar to game theorists. An equivalence relation meets the three conditions we have imposed on our R relations, but in addition must be reflexive. To impose this additional condition would be to assume that all players necessarily have only true beliefs. But even if an agent in fact has only true beliefs, counterfactual reasoning requires an agent to consider possible situations in which some beliefs are false. First, we want to consider belief-contravening, or epistemic, counterfactuals: how players would revise their beliefs were they to learn they were mistaken. Second, we want to consider deliberation that involves causal counterfactuals: a player considers what the consequences would be of his doing something he is not in fact going to do. In both cases, a player must consider possible situations in which either she or another player has a false belief.

Even though the R relations are not, in general, equivalence relations, there is a relation definable in terms of R that does determine a partition structure: say that two worlds x and y are *subjectively indistinguishable* for player $i (x \approx_i y)$ if player i's belief state in x is the same as it is in y. That is, $x \approx_i y$ if and only if $\{z: x\,R_i\,z\} = \{z: y\,R_i\,z\}$. Each equivalence class determined by a subjective indistinguishability relation will be divided into two parts: the worlds that are compatible with what the player believes, and the worlds that are not. In the regular partition models, all worlds are compatible with what the player believes in the world, and the two relations, R_i and $\approx_i$, will coincide.

To represent counterfactual reasoning, we must also allow for possible worlds in which players act irrationally. Even if I am resolved to act rationally, I may consider in deliberation what the consequences would be of acting in ways that are not. And even if I am certain that you will act rationally, I may consider how I would revise my beliefs if I learned that I was wrong about this. Even models satisfying some strong condition, such as common belief or knowledge that everyone is rational, will still be models that contain counterfactual possible worlds in which players have false beliefs, and worlds in which they fail to maximize expected utility.

The aim of this model theory is generality: to make, in the definition of a model, as few substantive assumptions as possible about the epistemic states and behavior of players of a game in order that substantive assumptions can be made explicit as conditions that distinguish some models from others. Of course the definition inevitably includes a range of idealizing and simplifying assumptions, made for a variety of reasons. Let me just mention a few of the assumptions that have been built into the conception of a model, and the reasons for doing so.

First, while we allow for irrational action and false belief, we do assume (as is usual) that players all have coherent beliefs that can be represented by a probability function on some nonempty space of possibilities. So, in effect, we make the outrageously unrealistic assumption that players are logically omniscient. This assumption is made only because it is still unclear, either conceptually or technically, how to understand or represent the epistemic situations of agents that are not ideal in this sense. This is a serious problem, but not one I will try to address here.

Second, as I have said, it is assumed that players have introspective access to their beliefs. This assumption could be relaxed by imposing weaker conditions on the R relations, although doing so would raise both technical and conceptual problems. It is not clear how one acts on one's beliefs if one does not have introspective access to them. Some may object to the introspective assumption on the ground that a person may have unconscious or inarticulate beliefs, but the assumption is not incompatible with this: if beliefs can be unconscious, so can beliefs about beliefs. It is not assumed that one knows how to say what one believes.

Third, some have questioned the assumption that players know what they do. This assumption might be relaxed with little effect; what is its motivation? The idea is simply that in a static model for a strategic form game, we are modeling the situation at the moment of choice, and it seems reasonable to assume that, at that moment, the agent knows what choice is being made.

Fourth, it is assumed that players know the structure of the game—the options available and the utility values of outcomes for all of the players. This assumption is just a simplifying assumption made to avoid trying to do too much at once. It could easily be relaxed with minimal effect on the structure of the models, and without raising conceptual problems. That is, one could consider models in which different games were being played in different possible worlds, and in which players might be uncertain or mistaken about what the game was.

Finally, as noted, we assume that models are finite. This is again just a simplifying assumption. Relaxing it would require some small modifications and add some mathematical complications but would not change the basic story.

In any possible-worlds model, one can identify *propositions* with subsets of the set of possible worlds, with what economists and statisticians call "events." The idea is to identify the content of what someone may think or say with its truth conditions, that is, with the set of possible worlds that would realize the conditions that make what is said or thought true. For any proposition ϕ and player i, we can define the proposition that i fully believes that ϕ as the set $\{x \in W: \{y \in W: x R_i y\} \subseteq \phi\}$, and the proposition that i believes that ϕ to at least degree r as the set $\{x \in W: P_{i,x}(\phi) \geq r\}$. So we have the resources to interpret unlimited iterations of belief in any proposition, and the infinitely iterated concept of *common belief* (all players believe that ϕ, and all believe that all believe that ϕ, and all believe that all believe that ϕ, and . . . , etc.) can be defined as the intersection of all the propositions in this infinite conjunction. Equivalently, we can represent common belief in terms of the *transitive closure* R^*, of the set all the R relations. For any proposition ϕ, it is, in possible world x, common belief among the players that ϕ if and only if ϕ is true in all possible worlds compatible with common belief, which is to say if and only if $\{y: x R^* y\} \subseteq \phi$.

If rationality is identified with maximizing expected utility, then we can define, in any model, the propositions that some particular player is rational, that all players are rational, that all players believe that all players are rational, and of course that it is common belief among the players that all players are rational. Here is a sequence of definitions, leading to a specification of the proposition that there is common belief that all players are rational.[6]. First, the *expected utility* of an action (a strategy choice) s for a player i in a world x is defined in the familiar way:

$$eu_{i,x}(s) = \sum_{e \in C_{-i}} P_{i,x}([e]) \times u_i((s, e))$$

Second, we define the set of strategies that maximize expected utility for player i in world x:

$$r_{i,x} = \{s \in C_i: eu_{i,x}(s) \geq eu_{i,x}(s') \text{ for all } s' \in C_i\}$$

Third, the proposition *that player i is rational* is the set of possible worlds in which the strategy chosen maximizes expected utility in that world:

$$A_i = \{x \in W: S_i(x) \in r_{i,x}\}$$

Fourth, the proposition *everyone is rational* is the intersection of the A_i':

$$A = \cap_{i \subset N} A_i$$

Fifth, the proposition *there is common belief that everyone is rational* is defined as follows:

$$Z = \{x \in W: \{y \in W: x \, R^* \, y\} \subseteq A\}$$

Any specification that determines a proposition relative to a model can also be used to pick out a class of models—all the models in which the proposition is true in that model's actual world. So for any given game, we can pick out the class of models of that game that satisfy some intuitive condition, for example, the class of models in which the proposition Z, that there is common belief in rationality, is true (in the actual world of the model). A class of models defined this way in turn determines a set of strategy profiles for the game: a profile is a member of the set if and only if it is realized in the actual world of one of the models in the class of models. This fact gives us a way that is both precise and intuitively motivated of defining a solution concept for games, or of giving a proof of adequacy for a solution concept already defined. The solution concept that has the most transparent semantic motivation of this kind is rationalizability: we can define rationalizability semantically as the set of strategies of a game that are realized in (the actual world of) some model in which there is common belief in rationality.[7] Alternatively, we can give a direct nonsemantic definition of the set of strategies—the set of strategies that survive the iterated elimination of strictly dominated strategies—and then prove that this set is *characterized* by the class of models in which there is common belief in rationality: A set of strategies is characterized by a class of models if the set includes exactly the strategies that are realized in some model in the class.[8]

3. Belief Revision

There are many ways to modify and extend this simple conception of a model of a game. I will consider here just one embellishment, one that is relevant to our concern with counterfactual reasoning. This is the addition of some structure to model the players' policies for revising their beliefs in response to new information. We assume, as is usual, that rational players are disposed to revise their beliefs by conditionalization, but there is nothing in the models we have defined to say how players would revise their beliefs if they learned something that had a prior probability of 0, something incompatible with the initial state of belief. A belief revision policy is a way of determining the sets of possible worlds that define the posterior belief states that would be induced by such information. The problem is not to generate such belief revision policies out of the models we already have—that is impossible. Rather, it is to say what new structure needs to be added to the model in order to represent belief revision policies, and what formal constraints the policies must obey.

Since we are modeling strategic form games, our models are static, and so there is no representation of any actual change in what is believed. But even in a static situation, one might ask how an agent's beliefs are disposed to change if he learns that he was mistaken about something he believed with probability one, and the answer to this question may be relevant to his decisions. These dispositions to change beliefs, in contrast to the potential changes that would display the dispositions, are a part of the agent's prior subjective state, the only state represented in the worlds of our models.

I said at the start that one aim in constructing this model theory was to clarify, in isolation, the separate concepts that interact with each other in strategic contexts and that are the components parts of the complex concepts used to describe those contexts. In keeping with this motivation, I will first look at a pure and simple abstract version of belief revision theory, for a single agent in a single possible world, ignoring degrees of belief, and assuming nothing about the subject matter of the beliefs. After getting clear about the basic structure, I will say how to incorporate it into our models, with many agents, many possible worlds, and probability measures on both the prior and posterior belief states. The simple theory that I will sketch is a standard one that has been formulated in a number of essentially equivalent ways by different theorists.[9] Sometimes the theory is formulated syntactically, with prior and posterior belief states represented by sets of sentences of some formal language, but I will focus on a purely model theoretic formulation of the theory in which the agent's belief revision policy is represented by a set of possible worlds—the prior belief state—and a function taking each piece of potential new information into the conditional belief state that corresponds to the state that would be induced by receiving that information. Let B be the set representing the prior state, and let B' be the set of all the possible worlds that are compatible with any new information that the agent could possibly receive. Then if ϕ is any proposition that is a subset of B', $B(\phi)$ will be the set that represents the posterior belief state induced by information ϕ.

There are just four constraints that the standard belief revision theory imposes on this belief revision function:

(1) For any ϕ, $B(\phi) \subseteq \phi$.
(2) If ϕ is nonempty, then $B(\phi)$ is nonempty.
(3) If $B \cap \phi$ is nonempty, then $B(\phi) = B \cap \phi$.
(4) If $B(\phi) \cap \psi$ is nonempty, then $B(\phi \,\&\, \psi) = B(\phi) \cap \psi$.

The first condition is simply the requirement that the new information received is believed in the conditional state. The second is the requirement that consistent information results in a consistent conditional state. The third condition requires that belief change be conservative in the sense that one should not give up any beliefs unless the new information forces one to give something up: if ϕ is compatible with the prior beliefs, the conditional belief state will simply add ϕ to the prior beliefs. The fourth condition is a generalization of the conservative condition. Its effect is to require that if two pieces of information are received in succession, the second being compatible with the posterior state induced by the first, then the resulting change should be the same as if both pieces of information were received together.

Any belief revision function meeting these four conditions can be represented by an ordering of all the possible worlds, and any ordering of a set of possible worlds will determine a function meeting the four conditions. Let Q be any binary transitive and connected relation on a set B'. Then we can define B as the set of highest ranking members of B', and for any subset ϕ of B' we can define $B(\phi)$ as the set of highest ranking members of ϕ:

$$B(\phi) = \{x \in \phi: y\,Q\,x \text{ for all } y \in \phi\}$$

It is easy to show that this function will satisfy the four conditions. On the other hand, given any revision function meeting the four conditions, we can define a binary relation Q in terms of it as follows:

$$x\,Q\,y \text{ iff } y \in B(\{x, y\})$$

It is easy to show, using the four conditions, that Q, defined this way, is transitive and connected, and that $B(\phi) = \{x \in \phi: y\,Q\,x \text{ for all } y \in \phi\}$. So the specification of such a Q relation is just an alternative formulation of the same revision theory.

Now to incorporate this belief revision theory into our models, we need to give each player such a belief revision policy in each possible world. This will be accomplished if we add to the model a binary relation Q for each player. We need just one such relation for each player if we take our assumption that players know their own states of mind to apply to belief revision policies as well as to beliefs themselves. Since the belief revision policy is a feature of the agent's subjective state, it is reasonable to assume that in all possible worlds that are subjectively indistinguishable for a player he has the same belief revision policies.

Subjective indistinguishability (which we defined as follows: $x \approx_i y$ if and only if $\{z: x\,R_i\,z\} = \{z: y\,R_i\,z\}$) is an equivalence relation that partitions the space of all possible worlds for each player, and the player's belief revision function will be the same for each world in the equivalence class. (The equivalence class plays the role of B' in the simple belief revision structure.) What we need to add to the game model is a relation Q_i for each player that orders all the worlds within each equivalence class with respect to epistemic plausibility, with worlds compatible with what the player believes in the worlds in that class having maximum plausibility. So Q_i must meet the following three conditions:

(q1) $x \approx_i y$, if and only if $x\,Q_i\,y$ or $y\,Q_i\,x$.
(q2) Q_i is transitive.
(q3) $x\,R_i\,y$ if and only if $w\,Q_i\,y$ for all w such that $w \approx_i x$.

For any proposition ϕ, we can define the conditional belief state for player i in world x, $B_{i,x}(\phi)$ (the posterior belief state that would be induced by learning ϕ),[10] in terms of Q_i as follows:

$$B_{i,x}(\phi) = \{w \in \phi: \text{for all } y \in \phi \cap \{z: z \approx_i x\},\ y\,Q_i\,w\}$$

Once we have added to our models a relation Q_i for each player that meets these three conditions, the R relations become redundant, since they are definable in terms of Q.[11] For a more economical formulation of the theory, we drop the R_i when we add the Q_i, taking condition (q1) above as the new definition of subjective indistinguishability, and condition (q3) as the definition of R_i. Formulated this way, the models are now defined as follows.

A model is a structure $\langle W, \mathbf{a}, \langle S_i, Q_i, P_i \rangle_{i \in N} \rangle$. W, $\mathbf{a}$, P_i, and S_i are as before. Each Q_i is a binary reflexive transitive relation on W meeting in addition the following condition: Any two worlds that are Q_i related (in either direction) to a third world are Q_i related (in at least one direction) to each other. One can then prove that each R_i, defined as above, is serial, transitive, and euclidean. So our new models incorporate and refine models of the simpler kind.

To summarize, the new structure we have added to our models expresses exactly the following two assumptions:

(1)   In each possible world each player has a belief revision policy that conforms to the conditions of the simple AGM belief revision theory sketched above, where (for player i and world x) the set B is $\{y: x\, R_i\, y\}$, and the set B' is $\{y: y \approx_i x\}$

(2)   In each world, each player has a correct belief about what his own belief revision policy is.

Each player's belief revision structure determines a ranking of all possible worlds with respect to the player's degree of epistemic success or failure in that world. In some worlds, the player has only true beliefs; in others, he makes an error, but not as serious an error as he makes in still other possible worlds. Suppose I am fifth on a standby waiting list for a seat on a plane. I learn that there is only one unclaimed seat, and as a result I feel certain that I will not get on the plane. I believe that the person at the top of the list will certainly take the seat, and if she does not, then I am certain that the second in line will take it, and so on. Now suppose in fact that my beliefs are mistaken: the person at the top of the list turns the seat down, and the next person takes it. Then my initial beliefs were in error, but not as seriously as they would be if I were to get the seat. If number two gets the seat, then I was making a simple first-degree error, while if I get the seat, I was making a fourth-degree error.

It will be useful to define, recursively, a sequence of propositions that distinguish the possible worlds in which a player's beliefs are in error to different degrees:

E_i^1 is the proposition that player i has at least some fale belief, that is, makes at least a simple first degree error.

$$E_i^1 = \{x \in W: \text{ for some } y \text{ such that } y \approx_i x, \text{ not } y\, Q_i\, x\}$$
$$(= \{x \in W: \text{ not } x\, R_i\, x\})$$

E_i^{k+1} is the proposition that player i makes at least a $k+1$ degree error:

$$E_i^{k+1} = \{x \in E_i^k: \text{for some } y \in E_i^k \text{ such that } y \approx_i x, \text{ not } y \, Q_i \, x\}$$

The belief revision structure provides for epistemic distinctions between propositions that are all believed with probability one. Even though each of two propositions has maximum degree of belief, one may be believed *more robustly* than the other in the sense that the agent is more disposed to continue believing it in response to new information. Suppose, to take a fanciful example, there are three presidential candidates: George, a Republican from Texas; Bill, a Democrat from Arkansas; and Ross, an independent from Texas. Suppose an agent believes, with probability one, that George will win. She also believes, with probability one, that a Texan will win and that a major party candidate will win, since these follow, given her other beliefs, from the proposition that George will win. But one of these two weaker beliefs may be more robust than the other. Suppose the agent is disposed, on learning that George lost, to conclude that Bill must then be the winner. In this case, the belief that a major party candidate will win is more robust than the belief that a Texan will win.

The belief revision structure is purely qualitative, but the measure functions that were already a part of the models provide a measure of the partial beliefs for conditional as well as for prior belief states. The Q relations, like the R relations, deliver the sets of possible worlds relative to which degrees of belief are defined. The partial beliefs for conditional belief state, like those for the prior states, are given by relativizing the measure function to the relevant set of possible worlds. Just as player i's partial beliefs in possible world x are given by relativizing the measure to the set $B_{i,x} = \{y: x \, R_i \, y\}$, so the partial beliefs in the conditional belief state for player i, world x, and condition ϕ are given by relativizing the measure to the set $B_{i,x}(\phi) = \{y \in \phi: \text{for all } z \in \phi \text{ such that } z \approx_i x, z \, Q_i \, y\}$.

So with the help of the belief revision function we can define *conditional* probability functions for each player in each world:

$$P_{i,x}(\phi/\psi) = P_i(\phi \cap B_{i,x}(\psi))/P_i(B_{i,x}(\psi))$$

In the case where the condition ψ is compatible with i's prior beliefs—where $P_{i,x}(\psi) > 0$—this will coincide with conditional probability as ordinarily defined. (This is ensured by the conservative condition on the belief revision function.) But this definition extends the conditional probability functions for player x in world i to any condition compatible with the set of worlds that are subjectively indistinguishable for x in i.[12]

These extended probability functions are equivalent to *lexicographic probability systems* as discussed in Blume, Brandenburger, and Dekel (1991a, 1991b) and Brandenburger (1992). In general, a lexicographic probability system (LPS) is an ordered sequence of probability distributions $(p_1, \dots, p_k)$ defined on some state space. An LPS has *full support* if every point in the space receives nonzero probability from at least one of the distributions in the sequence. It has *disjoint support* if each point receives nonzero probability from at most one of the distributions in the sequence.

The conditional probability functions defined above determine LPSs for each player i and world x in the following way: The relevant state space for the LPS for player i and world x is $\{w \in W: x \approx_i w\}$. The jth distribution in the sequence $p_j(w)$ will be $P_{i,x}(w/E_i^j)$. This LPS has full and disjoint support.

In the application discussed in the papers by Blume, Brandenburger, and Dekel cited above, the space on which the LPSs for player i are defined is the set of strategy profiles, C_{-i}, for players other than i. Since these partial profiles partition the space of possible worlds in our model, each of our conditional probability functions for player i induces a probability distribution on the coarser space, C_{-i}. These induced LPSs also have full support: this is ensured by the independence condition that we imposed on models, which implies that for all players i, worlds x and profiles $c_{-i} \in C_{-i}$, there is $w \approx_i x$ such that $S_{-i}(w) = c_{-i}$. Full support is essential for the proof of a theorem stated below, and proved in an appendix.

Unlike the fine-grained LPSs defined on worlds, the coarser LPSs defined on C_{-i} need not have disjoint support, since a profile may be realized in more than one possible world.

The belief revision theory and the extended probability functions give us the resources to introduce a refinement of the concept of rationality. Say that an action is *perfectly rational* if it not only maximizes expected utility but also satisfies a tie-breaking procedure that requires that certain *conditional* expected utilities be maximized as well.[13] The idea is that in cases where two or more actions maximize expected utility, the agent should consider, in choosing between them, how he should act if he learned he was in error about something. If two actions are still tied, the tie-breaking procedure is iterated—the agent considers how he should act if he learned that he was making an error of a higher degree. Here is a sequence of definitions leading to a definition of perfect rationality.

Given the extended conditional probability functions, the definition of conditional expected utility is straightforward:

$$eu_{i,x}(s/\phi) = \sum_{e \in C_{-i}} P_{i,x}([e]/\phi) \times u_i((s, e))$$

Second, we define, recursively, a sequence of sets of strategies that maximize expected utility and also satisfy the succession of tie-breaking rules:

$$r_{i,x}^0 = r_{i,x} = r_{i,x} \text{ (that is, } \{s \in C_i: eu_{i,x}(s) \geq eu_{i,x}(s') \text{ for all } s' \in C_i\})$$
$$r_{i,x}^{k+1} = \{s \in r_{i,x}^k: eu_{i,x}(s/E^{k+1}) \geq eu_{i,x}(s'/E^{k+1}) \text{ for all } s' \in r_{i,x}^k\}$$
$$r_{i,x}^+ = \cap r_{i,x}^k \text{ for all } k \text{ such that } E^k \cap \{y: x \approx_i y\} \text{ is nonempty}$$

The set $r_{i,x}^+$ is the set of strategies that are prefectly rational for player i in world x. So the proposition that player i is perfectly rational is defined as follows:

$$A_i^+ = \{x \in W : S_i(x) \in r_{i,x}^+\}$$

I want to emphasize that this refinement is defined wholly within individual decision theory. The belief revision theory that we have imported into our models is a general, abstract structure, as appropriate for a single agent facing a decision problem to which the actions of other agents are irrelevant as it is for a situation in which there are multiple agents. It is sometimes said that while states with probability zero are relevant in game theory, they are irrelevant to individual decision making,[14] but I see no reason to make this distinction. There is as much or as little reason to take account, in one's deliberation, of the possibility that nature may surprise one as there is to take account of the possibility that one may be fooled by one's fellow creatures.

Perfect rationality is a concept of individual decision theory, but in the game model context this concept may be used to give a model theoretic definition of a refinement of rationalizability. Say that a strategy of a game Γ is *perfectly rationalizable* if and only if the strategy is played in some model of Γ in which the players have common belief that they all are perfectly rational. As with ordinary correlated rationalizability, one can use a simple algorithm to pick out the relevant class of strategies and can prove a characterization theorem that states that the model theoretic and algorithmic definitions determine the same class of strategies. Here is the theorem:

> *Strategies that survive the elimination of all weakly dominated strategies followed by the iterated elimination of strictly dominated strategies are all and only those that are realized in a model in which players have common belief that all are perfectly rational.*[15]

Before going on to discuss knowledge, let me give two examples of games to illustrate the concepts of perfect rationality and perfect rationalizability.

First, consider the following very simple game: Alice can take a dollar for herself alone, ending the game, or instead leave the decision up to Bert, who can decide whether the two players get a dollar each or whether neither gets anything. The strategic form for the game is shown in Figure 1.1.

Figure 1.1

Both strategies for both players are rationalizable, but only Tt is perfectly rationalizable. If Alice is certain that Bert will play t, then either of her strategies would maximize expected utility. But only choice T will ensure that utility is maximized also on the condition that her belief about Bert's choice is mistaken. Similarly, Bert may be certain that Alice will not give him the chance to choose, but if he has to commit himself to a strategy in advance, then if he is perfectly rational, he will opt for the choice that would maximize expected utility if he did get a chance to choose.

Second, consider the following pure common interest game, where the only problem is one of coordination. It is also a perfect information game. One might think that coordination is no problem in a perfect information game, but this example shows that this is not necessarily true.

Alice can decide that each player gets two dollars, ending the game, or can leave the decision to Bert, who may decide that each player gets one dollar, or may give the decision back to Alice. This time, Alice must decide whether each player gets three dollars, or neither gets anything. The strategic form for the game is shown in Figure 1.2.

Now suppose Bert believes, with probability one, that Alice will choose T; what should he do? This depends on what he thinks Alice would do on the hypothesis that his belief about her is mistaken. Suppose that, if he were to be surprised by Alice choosing L on the first move, he would conclude that, contrary to what he previously believed, she is irrational, and is more likely to choose L on her second choice as well. Given these belief revision policies, only choice t is perfectly rational for him. But why should Alice choose T? Suppose she is sure that Bert will choose t, which, as we have just seen, is the only perfectly rational choice for him to make if his beliefs about Alice are as we have described. Then Alice's only rational choice is T. So it might be that Alice and Bert both know each others' beliefs about each other, and are both perfectly rational, but they still fail to coordinate on the optimal outcome for both. Of course, nothing in the game requires that Bert and Alice should have

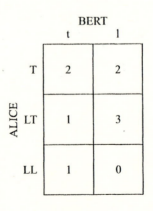

Figure 1.2

these beliefs and belief revision policies, but the game is compatible with them and with the assumption that both Bert and Alice are perfectly rational.

Now one might be inclined to question whether Bert really believes that Alice is fully rational, since he believes she would choose L on her second move, if she got a second move, and this choice, being strictly dominated, would be irrational. Perhaps if Bert believed that Alice was actually disposed to choose L on her second move then he would not believe she was fully rational; but it is not suggested that he believes this. Suppose we divide Alice's strategy T into two strategies, TT and TL, that differ only in Alice's counterfactual dispositions: the two strategies are "T, and I *would* choose T again on the second move if I were faced with that choice," and "T, but I *would* choose L on the second move if I were faced with that choice." One might argue that only TT, of these two, could be fully rational, but we may suppose that Bert believes, with probability one, that Alice will choose TT, and not TL. But were he to learn that he is wrong—that she did not choose TT (since she did not choose T on the first move)—he would conclude that she instead chooses LL. To think there is something incoherent about this combination of beliefs and belief revision policy is to confuse epistemic with causal counterfactuals; it would be like thinking that because I believe that if Shakespeare had not written *Hamlet* it would have never been written by anyone, I must therefore be disposed to conclude that *Hamlet* was never written were I to learn that Shakespeare was in fact not its author.

4. Knowledge

As has often been noted, rationalizability is a very weak constraint on strategy choice, and perfect rationalizability is only slightly more restrictive. Would it make any difference if we assumed, not just common *belief* in rationality, or perfect rationality, but common *knowledge* as well? Whether it makes a difference, and what difference it makes, will depend on how knowledge is analyzed, and on what is assumed about the relation between knowledge and belief. I will consider a certain analysis of knowledge with roots in the philosophical literature about the definition of knowledge, an analysis that can be made precise with the resources of the belief revision structure that we have built into our models. But before getting to that analysis, I want to make some general remarks about the relation between knowledge and belief.

Whatever the details of one's analysis of knowledge and belief, it is clear that the central difference between the two concepts is that the first, unlike the second, can apply only when the agent is in fact correct in what he believes: the claim that i knows that ϕ, in contrast with the claim that i believes that ϕ, entails that ϕ is true. Everyone knows that knowledge is different from belief—even from the extreme of belief, probability one—in this way, but sometimes it is suggested that this difference does not matter for the purposes of decision theory, since the rationality of a decision is independent of whether the beliefs on which it is based are in fact correct. It is *expected* utility, not the value of the actual payoff that I receive in the end, that is relevant to the explanation and evaluation of my actions, and expected utility cannot be influenced by facts about the actual world that do not affect my beliefs. But as soon as we start looking at one person's beliefs and knowledge about another's beliefs and knowledge, the difference between the two notions begins to matter. The assumption that Alice believes (with probability one) that Bert believes (with probability one) that the cat ate the canary tells us nothing about what Alice believes about the cat and the canary themselves. But if we assume instead that Alice *knows* that Bert *knows* that the cat ate the canary, it follows, not only that the cat in fact ate the canary, but that Alice knows it, and therefore believes it as well.

Since knowledge and belief have different properties, a concept that conflates them will have properties that are appropriate for neither of the two concepts taken separately. Because belief is a subjective concept, it is reasonable to assume, as we have assumed, that agents have introspective access to what they believe, and to what they do not believe. But if we switch from belief to knowledge, an external condition on the cognitive state is imposed, and because of this the assumption of introspective access is no longer tenable, even for logically omniscient perfect reasoners whose mental states are accessible to them. Suppose Alice believes, with complete conviction and with good reason, that the cat ate the canary but is, through no fault of her own, factually mistaken. She *believes*, let us suppose, that she knows that the cat ate the canary, but her belief that she knows it cannot be correct. Obviously, no amount of introspection into the state of her own mind will reveal to her the fact that she lacks this knowledge. If we conflate knowledge and belief, assuming in general that i knows that ϕ if and only if i's degree of belief for ϕ is one, then we get a concept that combines the introspective properties appropriate only to the internal, subjective concept of belief with the success properties appropriate only to an external concept that makes claims about the objective world. The result is a concept of knowledge that rests on equivocation.

The result of this equivocation is a concept of knowledge with the familiar partition structure, the structure often assumed in discussions by economists and theoretical computer scientists about common knowledge, and this simple and elegant structure has led to many interesting results.[16] The assumption that knowledge and common knowledge have this structure is the assumption that there can be no such thing as false belief, that while ignorance is possible, error is not. And since there is no false belief, there can be no disagreement, no surprises, and no coherent counterfactual reasoning.[17]

It is sometimes suggested that if one were to analyze knowledge simply as true belief, then the result would be a concept of knowledge with this partition structure, but this is not correct. The conjunctive concept, true belief, will *never* determine a partition structure unless it is assumed that it is necessary that *all* beliefs are true, in which case the conjunctive concept would be redundant. For suppose there might be a false belief, that it might be that some person i believed that ϕ but was mistaken. Then it is false that i truly believes that ϕ, and so if true belief satisfied the conditions of the partition structure, it would follow that i truly believes that he does not truly believe that ϕ, from which (since he believes ϕ) he could infer that ϕ is false. The point is that to assume negative introspection for true belief is to assume that a believer can distinguish, introspectively, her true beliefs from her false beliefs, which implies (at least if she is consistent) that she will not have any false beliefs.

While it can never be reasonable to equate knowledge and belief in general, we can specify the contingent conditions under which knowledge and belief will coincide. If we assume about a particular situation that *as a matter of fact*, a person has no false beliefs, then (and only then) we can conclude that, in that situation, knowledge and belief coincide. To get this conclusion, we need make no assumptions about knowledge beyond the minimal one that knowledge implies true belief. The assumption we need to make is that full belief is a state that is subjectively indistinguishable from knowledge: that fully believing that ϕ is the same as fully believing that one knows that ϕ.

If we make the idealizing assumption about a particular game situation being modeled that no one has any false beliefs, and that it is common belief that no one has any false beliefs, then we can have the benefits of the identification of knowledge and belief without the pernicious consequences that come from equivocating between them. What we cannot and need not assume is that it is a *necessary* truth—true in all possible worlds in the model—that no one has any false beliefs. Even if players *actually* have only true beliefs, there will inevitably be *counterfactual* possible worlds in the model in which players have false beliefs. These counterfactual possible worlds must be there to represent the causal possibilities that define the structure of the game, and to represent the belief revision policies of the players. If we assumed that it was a necessary truth that there was no false belief, then it would be impossible for one player to believe that a second player was rational in any model for any game in which irrational options were available to the second player.

In terms of this idealizing assumption about knowledge and belief, we can define a refinement of rationalizability, which I have called *strong rationalizability*. Here is the model theoretic definition: For any game Γ a strategy profile is strongly rationalizable if and only if it is realized in a model in which there is no error, common belief that all players are rational, and common belief that there is no error.[18] The set of strategy profiles characterized by this condition can also be given an algorithmic definition, using an iterated elimination procedure intermediate between the elimination of strictly dominated and of weakly dominated strategies.[19] We can also define a further refinement, *strong perfect rationalizability*: just substitute "perfect rationality" for "rationality" in the condition defining strong rationalizability. A minor variation of the algorithm will pick out the set of strategy profiles characterized by these conditions.

Knowledge and belief coincide on this demanding idealization, but suppose we want to consider the more general case in which a person may know some things about the world, even while being mistaken about others. How should knowledge be analyzed? The conception of knowledge that I will propose for consideration is a simple version of what has been called, in the philosophical literature on the analysis of knowledge, the *defeasibility analysis*. The intuitive idea behind this account is that "if a person has knowledge, then that person's justification must be sufficiently strong that it is not capable of being *defeated* by evidence that he does not possess" (Pappas and Swain, 1978, 27). According to this idea, if evidence that is unavailable to you would give you reason to give up a belief that you have, then your belief rests in part on your ignorance of that evidence, so even if that belief is true, it will not count as knowledge.

We can make this idea precise by exploiting the belief revision structure sketched above and the notion of robustness that allowed us to make epistemic distinctions between propositions believed with probability one. The analysis is simple: i knows that ϕ if and only if i believes that ϕ (with probability one), *and that belief is robust with respect to the truth*. That is, i knows that ϕ in a possible world x if and only if ϕ receives probability one from i in x, and also receives probability one in every conditional belief state for which the condition is true in x. More precisely, the proposition that i knows that ϕ is the set $\{x \in W$: for all ψ such that $x \in \psi$, $B_{i,x}(\psi) \subseteq \phi\}$.

Let me illustrate the idea with the example discussed above of the presidential candidates. Recall that there are three candidates, George, Bill, and Ross, and that the subject believes, with probability one, that George will win. As a reuslt she also believes with probability one that a Texan will win, and that a major party candidate will win. But the belief that a major party candidate will win is more robust than the belief that a Texan will win, since our subject is disposed, should she learn that George did not win, to infer that the winner was Bill. Now suppose that, to everyone's surprise, Ross wins. Then even though our subject's belief that a Texan would win turned out to be true, it does not seem reasonable to say that she *knew* that a Texan would win, since she was right only by luck. Had she know more (that George would lose), then that information would have undercut her belief. On the other hand, if Bill turned out to be the winner, then it would not be unreasonable to say that she knew that a major party candidate would win, since in this case her belief did not depend on her belief that it was George rather than Bill who would win.

The defeasibility conception of knowledge can be given a much simpler definition in terms of the belief revision structure. It can be shown that the definition given above is equivalent to the following: The proposition i knows that ϕ is the set $\{x$: $\{y$: $x \, Q_i \, y\} \subseteq \phi\}$. This exactly parallels the definition of the proposition that i believes that ϕ: $\{x$: $\{y$: $x \, R_i \, y\} \subseteq \phi\}$. On the defeasibility analysis, the relations that define the belief revision structure are exactly the same as the relations of epistemic accessibility in the standard semantics for epistemic logic.[20] And common knowledge (the infinite conjunction, everyone knows that ϕ, everyone knows that everyone knows that ϕ, . . .) exactly parallels common belief: the propositions *there is common knowledge that* ϕ is $\{x$: $\{y$: $xQ^*y\} \subseteq \phi\}$, where Q^* is the transitive closure of the Q_i relations.

The defeasibility analysis provides us with two new model theoretic conditions that can be used to define solution concepts: first, the condition that there is common knowledge of rationality; second, the condition that there is common knowledge of perfect rationality. The conditions are stronger (respectively) than the conditions we have used to characterize rationalizability and perfect rationalizability but weaker than the conditions that characterize the concepts I have called strong rationalizability and strong perfect rationalizability. That is, the class of models in which there is common belief in (perfect) rationality properly includes the class in which there is common knowledge, in the defeasibility sense, of (perfect) rationality, which in turn properly includes the class in which there is no error, common belief that there is no error, and common belief in (perfect) rationality. So the defeasibility analysis gives us two distinctive model theoretic solution concepts, but, surprisingly, the sets of strategy profiles characterized by these new model theoretic conditions are the same as those characterized, in one case, by the weaker condition and, in the other case, by the stronger condition. That is, the following two claims are theorems:

(1) *Any strategy realized in a model in which there is common belief in (simple) rationality is also realized in a model in which there is common* knowledge *(in the defeasibility sense) of rationality.*

(2) *Any strategy profile realized in a model in which there is common knowledge of* perfect *rationality is also realized in a model meeting in addition the stronger condition that there is common belief that no one has a false belief.*

Proofs are sketched in the appendix.

5. Backward Induction

To illustrate how some of this apparatus might be deployed to help clarify the role in strategic arguments of assumptions about knowledge, belief, and counterfactual reasoning, I will conclude by looking at a puzzle about backward induction reasoning, focusing on one notorious example: the finite iterated Prisoners' Dilemma. The backward induction argument purports to show that if there is common belief, or perhaps common knowledge, that both players are rational, then both players will defect every time, from the beginning. Obviously, rational players will defect on the last move and, since they know this on the next to the last move, they will defect then as well, and so on back through the game. This kind of argument is widely thought to be paradoxical, but there is little agreement about what the paradox consists in. Some say that the argument is fallacious, others that it shows an incoherence in the assumption of common knowledge of rationality, and still others that it reveals a self-referential paradox akin to semantic paradoxes such as the liar. The model theoretic apparatus we have been discussing gives us the resources to make precise the theses that alternative versions of the argument purport to prove, and to assess the validity of the arguments. Some versions are clearly fallacious, but others, as I will show, are valid.

The intuitive backward induction argument applies directly to games in extensive form, whereas our game models are of static strategic form games.[21] But any extensive form game has a unique strategic form, and proofs based on the idea of the intuitive backward induction argument can be used to establish claims about the strategic form of the game. A backward induction argument is best seen as an argument by mathematical induction about a class of games that is closed with respect to the subgame relation—in the case at hand, the class of iterated Prisoners' Dilemmas of length n for any natural number n.

The conclusions of the backward induction arguments are conditional theses: if certain conditions obtain, then players will choose strategies that result in defection every time. The conditions assumed will correspond to the constraints on models that we have used to characterize various solution concepts, so the theses in question will be claims that only strategy profiles that result in defection every time will satisfy the conditions defining some solution concept. If, for example, the conditions are that there is common belief in rationality, then the thesis would be that only strategies that result in defection every time are rationalizable. It is clear that a backward induction argument for this thesis must be fallacious since many cooperative strategies are rationalizable. Philip Pettit and Robert Sugden (1989) have given a nice diagnosis of the fallacy in this version of the argument. What if we make the stronger assumption that there is common *knowledge* of rationality, or of perfect rationality? Suppose, first, that we make the idealizing assumption necessary for identifying knowledge with belief: that there is no error and common belief that there is no error, and common belief that both players are rational. Are all *strongly* rationalizable strategy pairs in the iterated Prisoners' Dilemma pairs that result in defection every time? In this case the answer is positive, and the theorem that states this conclusion is proved by a backward induction argument.

To prove this backward induction theorem, we must first prove a lemma that is a general claim about multistage games—a class of games that includes iterated games. First, some notation and terminology. Let Γ be any game that can be represented as a multistage game with observed action (a game that can be divided into stages where at each stage all players move simultaneously, and all players know the result of all previous moves). Let $\Gamma^{\#}$ be any subgame—any game that begins at the start of some later stage of Γ. For any strategy profile c of Γ that determines a path through the subgame $\Gamma^{\#}$, let $c^{\#}$ be the profile for $\Gamma^{\#}$ that is determined by c, and let $C^{\#}$ be the set of all strategy profiles of Γ that determine a path through $\Gamma^{\#}$. By "an SR model," I will mean a model in which there is (in the actual world of the model) no error, common belief that there is no error, and common belief that all players are rational. Now we can state the multistage game lemma:

> If profile c is strongly rationalizable in Γ, and if c determines a path through $\Gamma^{\#}$, then $c^{\#}$ is strongly rationalizable in $\Gamma^{\#}$.

This is proved by constructing a model for $\Gamma^{\#}$ in terms of a model for Γ, and showing that if the original model is an SR model then so is the new one. Let M by any SR model for Γ in which c is played in the actual world of the model. Let $\Gamma^{\#}$ be any subgame that contains the path determined by c. We define a model $M^{\#}$ for $\Gamma^{\#}$ in terms of M as follows: $W^{\#} = \{x \in W : S(x) \in C^{\#}\}$. The $Q_i^{\#}$ and $P_i^{\#}$ are simply the restrictions of the Q_i and P_i to $W^{\#}$. The $S_i^{\#}$ are defined so that, for each $x \in W^{\#}$, $S^{\#}(x)$ is the profile for the game $\Gamma^{\#}$ that is determined by the profile $S(x)$. (That is, if $S(x) = e$, then $S^{\#}(x) = e^{\#}$.)

To see that $M^{\#}$ is an SR model for $\Gamma^{\#}$, note first that if there is no error and common belief that there is no error in the original model, then this will also hold for the model of the subgame: if $\{x: \mathbf{a}\, R^{*}\, x\} \subseteq \{x: x\, R_{i}\, x$ for all $i\}$, then $\{x: \mathbf{a}\, R^{\#*}\, x\} \subseteq \{x: x\, R_{i}^{\#}\, x$ for all $i\}$. This is clear, since $\{x: \mathbf{a}\, R^{\#*}\, x\} \subseteq \{x : \mathbf{a}\, R^{*}\, x\} \cap W^{\#}$, and $\{x: x\, R_{i}^{\#}\, x$ for all $i\} = \{x: x\, R_{i}\, x$ for all $i\} \cap W^{\#}$. Second, because of the fact that players know all previous moves at the beginning of each stage, they can make their strategy choices conditional on whether a subgame is reached. (More precisely, for any player i and pair of strategies s and s' for i that are compatible with $\Gamma^{\#}$ being reached, there is a strategy equivalent to this: s if $\Gamma^{\#}$ is reached, s' if not.) This implies that for any world w, player i, and subgame such that it is compatible with i's beliefs that that subgame be reached, a strategy will be rational for i only if the strategy determined for the subgame is rational, conditional on the hypothesis that the subgame is reached. This ensures that rationality is preserved in all worlds when the model is modified. So $c^{\#}$ is strongly rationalizable in $\Gamma^{\#}$.

An analogous result about strong *perfect* rationalizability can be shown by essentially the same argument.

One further observation before turning to the backward induction theorem itself: for any game Γ, if profile c is compatible with common belief in (the actual world of) an SR model for Γ, then c itself is strongly rationalizable. It is obvious that if $S(x) = c$ and $\mathbf{a}\, R^{*}\, x$, then the same model, with x rather than $\mathbf{a}$ as the actual world, will be an SR model if the original model was.

Now the backward induction theorem:

> *Any strongly rationalizable strategy profile in a finite iterated Prisoners' Dilemma is one in which both players defect every time.*[22]

The proof is by induction on the size of the game. For the base case—the one-shot PD—it is obvious that the theorem holds, since only defection is rational. Now assume that the theorem holds for games of length k. Let Γ be a game of length $k + 1$, and Γ^{-} be the corresponding iterated PD of length k. Let M be any SR model of Γ, and let c be any strategy profile that is compatible with common belief (that is, c is any profile for which there exists an x such that $S(x) = c$, and $\mathbf{a}\, R^{*}\, x$). By the observation just made, c is strongly rationalizable, so by the multistage game lemma, c^{-} (the profile for Γ^{-} determined by c) is strongly rationalizable in Γ^{-}. But then by hypothesis of induction, c^{-} is a profile in which both players defect every time. So c (in game Γ) is a profile in which both players defect every time after the first move. But c is any profile compatible with common belief in the actual world of the model, so it follows that in the model M it is common belief that both players will choose strategies that result in defection every time after the first move. Given these beliefs, any strategy for either player that begins with the cooperative move is strictly dominated, relative to that player's beliefs. Since the players are both rational, it follows that they choose a strategy that begins with defection, and so one that results in defection on every move.

Our theorem could obviously be generalized to cover some other games that have been prominent in discussions of backward induction such as the centipede game and (for strong *perfect* rationalizability) the chain store game. But it is not true, even in perfect information games, that the strong or strong and perfect rationalizability conditions are always sufficient to support backward induction reasoning. Recall the perfect information, pure coordination game discussed above in which Alice and Bert failed to coordinate on the backward induction equilibrium, even though the conditions for strong perfect rationalizability were satisfied. In that example, the strategy profile played was a perfect, but not subgame perfect, equilibrium.[23]

As I noted at the end of the last section, it can be shown that the set of strongly and perfectly rationalizable strategy profiles is characterized also by the class of models in which there is common knowledge (in the defeasibility sense) of perfect rationality. So we can drop the strong idealizing assumption that there is no error, and still get the conclusion that if there is common knowledge (in the defeasibility sense) of perfect rationality, then players will choose strategies that result in defection every time.

Pettit and Sugden, in their discussion of the paradox of backward induction, grant that the argument is valid when it is common knowledge rather than common belief that is assumed (though they do not say why they think this, or what they are assuming about knowledge). They suggest that there is nothing surprising or paradoxical about this, since the assumption of common *knowledge* of rationality is incompatible with the possibility of rational deliberation, and so is too strong to be interesting. Since knowledge logically implies truth, they argue, the argument shows that "as a matter of logical necessity, both players *must* defect and presumably therefore that they know they must defect" (Pettit and Sugden, 1989, 181). I think this remark rests on a confusion of epistemic with causal possibilities. There is no reason why I cannot both *know* that something is true, and also entertain the counterfactual possibility that it is false. It is of course inconsistent to suppose, counterfactually or otherwise, the conjunction of the claim that ϕ is false with the claim that I know that ϕ is true, but it is not inconsistent for me, knowing (in the actual world) that ϕ is true, to suppose, counterfactually, that ϕ is false. As Pettit and Sugden say, the connection between knowledge and truth is a matter of logical necessity, but that does not mean that if I know that I will defect, I therefore *must* defect "as a matter of logical necessity." One might as well argue that lifelong bachelors are powerless to marry, since it is a matter of logical necessity that lifelong bachelors never marry.

The semantic connection between knowledge and truth is not, in any case, what is doing the work in this version of the backward induction argument: it is rather the assumption that the players believe in common that neither of them is in error about anything. We could drop the assumption that the players' beliefs are all actually true, assuming not common knowledge of rationality, but only common belief in rationality and common belief that no one is in error about anything. This will suffice to validate the induction argument.

Notice that common belief that there will not, in fact, be any surprises does not imply the belief that there could not be any surprises. Alice might think as follows: "Bert expects me to defect, and I will defect, but I could cooperate, and if I did, he would be surprised. Furthermore, I expect him to defect, but he could cooperate, and if he did, I would be surprised." If these "could"s were epistemic or subjective, expressing uncertainty, then this soliloquy would make no sense, but it is unproblematic if they are counterfactual "could"s used to express Alice's beliefs about her and Bert's capacities. A rational person may know that she will not exercise certain of her options, since she may believe that it is not in her interest to do so.

It is neither legitimate nor required for the success of the backward induction argument to draw conclusions about what the players would believe or do under counterfactual conditions. In fact, consider the following "tat for tit" strategy: defect on the first move, then on all subsequent moves, do what the other player did on the previous move, until the last move; defect unconditionally on the last move. Our backward induction argument does not exclude the possibility that the players should each, in the actual world, adopt this strategy, since this pair of strategies results in defection every time. This pair is indeed compatible with the conditions for strong and perfect rationalizability. Of course, unless each player assigned a very low probability to the hypothesis that this was the other player's strategy, it would not be rational for him to adopt it, but he need not rule it out. Thus Pettit and Sugden are wrong when they say that the backward induction argument can work only if it is assumed that each player would maintain the beliefs necessary for common belief in rationality "regardless of what the other does" (Pettit and Sugden, 1989, 178). All that is required is the belief that the beliefs necessary for common knowledge of rationality will in fact be maintained, given what the players in fact plan to do. This requirement need not be *assumed*: it is a consequence of what is assumed.

6. Conclusion

The aim in constructing this model theory was to get a framework in which to sharpen and clarify the concepts used both by rational agents in their deliberative and strategic reasoning and by theorists in their attempts to describe, predict, and explain the behavior of such agents. The intention was, first, to get a framework that is rich in expressive resources but weak in the claims that are presupposed or implicit in the theory, so that various hypotheses about the epistemic states and behavior of agents can be stated clearly and compared. Second, the intention was to have a framework in which concepts can be analyzed into their basic components, which can then be considered and clarified in isolation before being combined with each other. We want to be able to consider, for example, the logic of belief, individual utility maximization, belief revision, and causal-counterfactual structure separately, and then put them together to see how the separate components interact. The framework is designed to be extended both by considering further specific substantive assumptions, for example, about the beliefs and belief revision policies of players, and by adding to the descriptive resources of the model theory additional structure that might be relevant to strategic reasoning or its evaluation, for example, temporal structure for the representation of dynamic games, and resources for more explicit representation of counterfactual propositions. To illustrate some of the fruits of this approach, we have stated some theorems that provide model theoretic characterizations of some solution concepts, and have looked closely at one familiar form of reasoning—backward induction— and at some conditions that are sufficient to validate this form of reasoning in certain games, and at conditions that are not sufficient. The focus has been on the concepts involved in two kinds of counterfactual reasoning whose interaction is essential to deliberation in strategic contexts and to the evaluation of the decisions that result from such deliberation: reasoning about what the consequences would be of actions that are alternatives to the action chosen, and reasoning about how one would revise one's beliefs if one were to receive information that one expects not to receive. We can become clear about why people do what they do, and about what they ought to do, only by getting clear the relevance of what they could have done, and might have learned, but did not.

Appendix*

Proofs of three theorems

Theorem I
The set of strategies that survive elimination of weakly dominated strategies followed by iterated elimination of strictly dominated strategies is characterized by the class of models in which there is common belief in perfect rationality.

First, we show that for any strategy in the set, there exists a model of the appropriate kind. Suppose s is such a strategy, for player j. Here is the construction of $M = \langle W, \mathbf{a}, \langle S_i, Q_i, P_i \rangle_{i \in N} \rangle$: Let D be the set of strategy profiles made up only of strategies that survive the iterated elimination procedure, and let D' be a copy of this set. Then $W = D' \cup C$. (That is, the set of worlds will contain two distinct worlds corresponding to each profile in D, and one world for each profile that is not in D.) $\mathbf{a}$—the actual world of the model—will be any member x of D' such that $x_j = s$. S is defined in the obvious way: $S_i(x) = x_i$ for all $x \in W$ and $i \in N$.

---

*I thank Pierpaolo Battigalli for pointing out an error in an earlier version of the proof for theorem I.

The definitions of the relations Q_i and the measure functions P_i will presuppose the following two results from decision theory: Suppose we have a decision problem with states S_i to S_n, and alternative actions A_i to A_m.

(1) *If A_i is not strictly dominated, then there is a probability distribution over S_i to S_n to which A_i is a best response.* (Where an action is strictly dominated if there is some alternative strategy or probability mix of alternative actions, that is a strictly better response to every state.)

(2) *If A_i is not weakly dominated, then there is a fully mixed probability distribution over S_i to S_n to which it is a best response.*

From these facts it follows, first, that for any strategy $s \in D_i$, there will be a probability distribution $m[s]$ over D_{-i} to which s is a best response, and, second, that for any strategy $s \in C_i$, there will be a fully mixed probability distribution $m'[s]$ over C_{-i} to which, if $s \in D_i$, then s is a best response. Let m and m' be two functions that, for each i, take D_i and C_i, respectively into probability distributions over D_{-i} and C_{-i} that meet these conditions. We will use these functions to define the Q relations and the measure functions in our model in the following way. For all $x, y \in W$ and $i \in N$, $x Q_i y$ iff (1) $x_i = y_i$ and (2) at least one of the following three conditions is met:

(a) $y \in D'$, and $m[y_i](y_{-i}) > 0$.
(b) $x \in C$.
(c) $x \in D'$, and $m[x_i](x_{-i}) = 0$.

This definition divides each subjective indistinguishability class into an inner and an outer set. Worlds meeting condition (a) are in the inner set, and so are compatible with player i's beliefs in any world in which he plays the same strategy. All remaining worlds in which that strategy is played are in the outer set, grouped together in the belief revision structure. It should be clear that the definition ensures that the Qs are all transitive, reflexive and weakly connected.

Now we define P_i, for each i, as follows:

(a) If $y \in D'$ and $m[y_i](y_{-i}) > 0$, then $P_i(y) = m[y_i](y_{-i})$.
(b) if $y \in D'$ but $m[y_i](y_{-i}) = 0$, or if $y \in C$, and y is the duplicate of such a world in C, then $P_i(y) = 1/2 \times m'[y_i](y_{-i})$.
(c) If y is one of the remaining worlds in C, then $P_i(y) = m'[y_i](y_{-i})$.

First, because all of the probability distributions determined by the second function, m', are fully mixed, this definition ensures that, for all i and x, $P_i(x) > 0$. Second, it can be verified that the properties of the probability distributions will ensure that, for each i and for each $x \in D'$, $S(x_i)$ will maximize expected utility, and will also maximize conditional expected utility on the hypothesis of error. This implies that all players are perfectly rational in all worlds in D'. Third, note that for any i and any $x \in D'$, $\{y: x R^* y\} \subseteq D'$. So, since $\mathbf{a} \in D'$, this is a model in which there is common belief in perfect rationality.

The model we have constructed may not satisfy the independence condition, but it can be extended to a model that does so by adding some additional worlds, and this can be done without affecting either the beliefs or the perfect rationality of the players in the original worlds. First, replace W with $W \times C$, identifying the worlds of the original model with the pairs $\langle w, c \rangle$ such that $S(x) = c$. Extend the measure functions and the R relations as in note 5. Then extend the Q relations so as to ensure that all of the new worlds added have lower priority than any of the original worlds. The result will be that in the extended model, players belief revision policies in all worlds compatible with common belief will have three levels: first the inner worlds in D', second the old outer worlds in D' and C, and third the new worlds added to satisfy the independence condition. If E is the set of added worlds that are subjectively indistinguishable from one of the original worlds, then the measure function can be adjusted to ensure that for any i and any profile $c \in C$, $P_i([c] \cap E) = m'_i(c_{-i})$, and so that perfect rationality is maintained in all worlds compatible with common belief.

This completes the argument that there exists a model for any strategy surviving the iteration algorithm. Now we show the other half of the characterization claim: that *only* strategies surviving the iteration algorithm can be satisfied in a model in which there is common belief in perfect rationality. We note first the following fact.

Let E be any subset of C, the profiles of Γ; let E_i be the set of strategies for player i that are part of some profile in E, and let E_{-i} be the set of profiles for players other than i containing only strategies that are part of some member of E. Suppose E satisfies these two conditions: (1) every strategy in E_i is admissible (not weakly dominated relative to C_{-i}), and (2) no strategy in E_i is strictly dominated relative to E_{-i}. Then $E \subseteq D$. For suppose, for reductio, that there were some player i and strategy s in E_i that was eliminated by the elimination procedure that defines D. Assume that s is one of the strategies that is eliminated at the earliest stage at which, for some j, some member of E_j is eliminated. Then since by (1) s is not weakly dominated in the whole game, it must be strictly dominated relative to the set of profiles of strategies not yet eliminated at that stage, which includes all of the profiles in E_{-i}. So s is strictly dominated relative to E_{-i}, contrary to condition (2).

Now let M be an arbitrary model in which there is common belief in perfect rationality, and for each i let E be the set of strategy profiles played in some world in $\{y: \mathbf{a} \, R^* \, y\}$. Now, first, it is clear that no strategy in E_i is strictly dominated relative to E_{-i}, for that would be possible only if player i were irrational. But, second, no strategy in E is weakly dominated in the whole game, because that is incompatible with the player being perfectly rational. (*Remark*: It is at this point that we appeal, implicitly, to the independence condition. To be justified in claiming that weakly dominated strategies cannot be perfectly rational, we need the assumption that for every world x, player i, and strategy profile for the other players c_{-i}, there is a world y such that $x \approx_i y$, and $S_{-i}(y) = c_{-i}$. This follows from the independence condition.) So by the fact noted just above, it follows that $E \subseteq D$, from which it follows that only strategies in D are played in **a**. (*Remark*: **a** need not itself be a member of $\{y: \mathbf{a}\, R^*\, y\}$, but since players necessarily know what strategy they themselves are playing, any strategy played in **a** will be played in some member of $\{y: \mathbf{a}\, R^*\, y\}$.)

Theorem II

The set of rationalizable strategies is characterized by the class of models in which there is common knowledge (in the defeasibility sense) of rationality.

This theorem says that the set of strategies that is characterized by one class of models (those in which there is common belief in rationality) is also characterized by a different class of models which is a proper subclass of the first class. The proof is given by taking an arbitrary model of the larger class and showing how to modify it so that it becomes a model of the more restrictive class in which the same strategy profile is realized. We begin with an arbitrary model for any game Γ in which there is common belief that everyone is rational, and turn it into a model in which there is common knowledge, in the defeasibility sense, that everyone is rational.

Let the given model be $M = \langle W, \mathbf{a}, \langle S_i, Q_i, P_i \rangle_{i \in N} \rangle$, and assume that $\{x: \mathbf{a}\, R^*\, x\} \subseteq A$. ($A$ is the set of worlds in which all players maximize expected utility.) The modified model $M^{\#} = \langle W, \mathbf{a}, \langle S_i, Q_i^{\#}, P_i \rangle_{i \in N} \rangle$ will keep everything the same, except for the Q relations, which will be redefined. But the Q's will be modified in a way that does not affect the R relations, which are defined in terms of the Q's. Recall that the models with the belief revision structure (Q-models) are refinements of the simple models with which we began (R-models). So each Q-model determines a unique R-model. Say that two Q-models of a game Γ are *R-equivalent* if they determine the same R-model. It should be evident that any two R-equivalent models are equivalent with respect to the simple rationality of any player in any world, since simple rationality depends only on the beliefs and partial beliefs of the players, and not on the ways that they would revise those beliefs

Now define the Q relations of the new model as follows. For all $x, y \in W$, and $i \in N$, $x\, Q_i'\, y$ iff one of the following three conditions is met:

(1) $x\, R_i\, y$.
(2) Neither $x\, R_i\, y$ nor $y\, R_i\, x$, but $x \approx_i y$ and $y \in \{\mathbf{a}\} \cup \{w: \mathbf{a}\, R^*\, w\}$.
(3) Neither $x\, R_i\, y$ nor $y\, R_i\, x$, but $x \approx_i y$ and $x \notin \{\mathbf{a}\} \cup \{w: \mathbf{a}\, R^*\, w\}$.

First, this definition ensures that the relations are transitive, reflexive, and weakly connected, as required. Second, it ensures that the new model is R-equivalent to the original model, and so that players are rational in the same worlds. Third, we show that $\{w: \mathbf{a}\, Q^{\#*}\, w\} \subseteq A$: By the definition of $Q_i^{\#}$, it can be seen that for any i, if $x \in \{\mathbf{a}\} \cup \{w: \mathbf{a}\, R^*\, w\}$ and $x\, Q_i^{\#}\, y$, then $y \in \{\mathbf{a}\} \cup \{w: \mathbf{a}\, R^*\, w\}$. So $\{w: \mathbf{a}\, Q^{\#*}\, w\} \subseteq \{\mathbf{a}\} \cup \{w: \mathbf{a}\, R^*\, w\}$. But in the original model, $\{\mathbf{a}\} \cup \{w: \mathbf{a}\, R^*\, w\} \subseteq A$, so it follows that $\{w: \mathbf{a}\, Q^{\#*}\, w\} \subseteq A$. That is, in the new model, there is common knowledge, in the defeasibility sense, that everyone maximizes utility.

Theorem III
The set of strongly and perfect rationalizable strategy profiles is characterized by the set of models in which there is common knowledge (in the defeasibility sense) that all are rational.

This theorem, like theorem II, says that the set of profiles that is characterized by one class of models is also characterized by a different class of models—a class of which the first is a proper subclass. Again, the proof is given by taking an arbitrary model from the larger class and showing how to modify it so that it becomes a model of the more restrictive class in which the same strategy profile is realized. In this case, we begin with a model for any game Γ in which there is common knowledge, in the defeasibility sense, that all players are perfectly rational, and, while conserving this property, turn it into a model in which there is also common knowledge that there is no error.

Let the given model be $M = \langle W, \mathbf{a}, \langle S_i, Q_i, P_i \rangle_{i \in N} \rangle$, and assume that $\{x \colon \mathbf{a}\, Q^* x\} \subseteq A^+$. ($A^+$ is the set of worlds in which all players are perfectly rational.) The modified model $M^\# = \langle W, \mathbf{a}, \langle S_i, Q_i^\#, P_i^\# \rangle_{i \in N} \rangle$, will keep the same W, $\mathbf{a}$, and S functions while modifying the Qs and Ps. I will describe the intuitive idea of the change, and then give the formal definition. The idea is that, in the modified model, players are slightly more cautious or skeptical than they are in the original model (in all possible worlds that are compatible with common knowledge). Possible worlds in which a player makes an error (in the original model) are made compatible with that player's beliefs but given a very low probability—so low that all positive differences between the expected utilities of different strategies are preserved. This will ensure that the players will be perfectly rational in exactly the same possible worlds.

To define the procedure more precisely, it will be convenient to modify the model in stages. At each stage, we will make the players more cautious only with respect to first-degree errors. A finite number of modifications of the kind to be defined will result in a model that meets the appropriate conditions. Here are the definitions for the new Qs and Ps. First, for all $x, y \in W$, and all $i \in N$, if $x\, Q_i\, y$, then $x\, Q_i^\#\, y$, and in addition for all $x \in E_i^1 \cap \{w \colon \mathbf{a}\, Q^* w\}$ and all z such that $x \approx_i z$, $z\, Q_i^\#\, x$. Second, $P_i^\#(y) = \varepsilon \times P_i(y)$ for all $y \in E_i^1 \cap \{w \colon \mathbf{a}\, Q^* w\}$; for all other y, $P_i^\#(y) = P_i(y)$. The factor ε is a positive number chosen to be small enough so that, for all i and x, all positive differences between i's expected utilities in x for any two strategies remain the same in the new model as they are in the original model (That is, for any $x \in W$, $i \in N$, and $s, s' \in C_i$, if $eu_{i,x}(s) > eu_{i,x}(s')$, then $eu_{i,x}^\#(s) > eu_{i,x}^\#(s')$).

We show, first, that the worlds compatible with common knowledge remain the same with this modification. That is, $\{x \colon \mathbf{a}\, Q^* x\} = \{x \colon \mathbf{a}\, Q^{\#*} x\}$. Since the $Q^\#$s are extensions of the Qs, it is obvious that if $\mathbf{a}\, Q^* x$, then $\mathbf{a}\, Q^{\#*} x$. For the other direction, suppose, for reductio, that $\mathbf{a}\, Q^{\#*} x$ but not $\mathbf{a}\, Q^* x$. Then, by the definition of Q^*, there must be a sequence of worlds starting with $\mathbf{a}$ and ending with x such that, for any pair of successive worlds y and z in the sequence, there is a player i such that $y\, Q_i^\#\, z$, and there must be at least one such pair for which not $y\, Q_j\, z$ for any $j \in N$. Suppose y and z are the last pair in this sequence that meets the condition that not $y\,Q_j\,z$ for any j, so that $z\,Q^*\,x$. By the way the extension of the Qs is defined, if $y\,Q_i^{\#}\,z$ and not $y\,Q_i\,z$, then $\mathbf{a}\,Q^*\,z$. But since $z\,Q^*\,x$, it follows that $\mathbf{a}Q^*x$, contrary to what was supposed.

Second, we show that for all players i, worlds w, and strategies s for i, if s is perfectly rational for i in w in the original model, then it will be perfectly rational in the modified model. First, note that for any strategy s for i, $eu_{i,x}^{\#}(s) = (1/1 + \varepsilon) \times eu_{i,x}(s) + (\varepsilon/1 + \varepsilon) \times eu_{i,x}(s/E_i^1)$. Now suppose that $s \in r_{i,w}^{+}$. That is, suppose that s is perfectly rational for i in w in the original model, and let s' be any other strategy for i. By the definition of perfect rationality, one of the following three conditions must obtain: (1) $eu_{i,w}(s) > eu_{i,w}(s')$; (2) $eu_{i,w}(s) = eu_{i,w}(s')$, but $eu_{i,w}(s/E_i^1) > eu_{i,w}(s'/E_i^1)$; or (3) $eu_{i,w}(s) = eu_{i,w}(s')$, and also $eu_{i,w}(s/E_i^1) = eu_{i,w}(s'/E_i^1)$, but $eu_{i,w}(s/E_i^k) > eu_{i,w}(s'/E_i^k)$ for the first k (if any) for which they are not equal. In the first case, because ε is small enough to ensure that all positive differences in expected utilities are preserved, it will flow that $eu_{i,w}^{\#}(s) > eu_{i,w}^{\#}(s')$. In the second case, also $eu_{i,w}^{\#}(s) > eu_{i,w}^{\#}(s')$. In the third case, $eu_{i,w}^{\#}(s) = eu_{i,w}^{\#}(s')$ but, by the tie-breaking rule, s will still be as good as s' in the new model, since the relevant conditional expected utilities are unaffected by the modification. So s is perfectly rational in the modified model.

Third, note that the result of this modification is to change all worlds in which a first-degree error is made into worlds in which no error is made, thereby changing worlds in which a k-degree error is made into world in which only a $(k - 1)$-degree error is made. If k is the maximum degree error made by any player in any world compatible with common knowledge, then k iterations of this modification will result in a model in which no errors are made in any possible world compatible with common knowledge. That is, $\{x \in W: \mathbf{a}\,Q^{\#*}\,x\} \subseteq \{x \in W: x\,R_i^{\#}\,x \text{ for all } i\}$. So our modified model satisfies the more restrictive condition: the property of common knowledge (and so common belief) that all are perfectly rational is preserved, and the property of common knowledge that there is no error is assured by the modification.

Notes

Acknowledgment— I would like to thank Pierpaolo Battigalli, Giacomo Bonanno, Yannis Delmas, Drew Fudenberg, Philippe Mongin, Hyun Song Shin, Brian Skyrms, and an anonymous referee for helpful comments on several earlier versions of this essay.

The essay grew out of a talk at the Castiglioncello conference in 1992, and a version of it was also the basis of a talk at the 1993 summer workshop of the Stanford Institute of Theoretical Economics. I thank the participants at both occasions.

This version of the paper is a slight revision of the one that was published in *Economics and Philosophy*. The main addition is an appendix in which proofs of some theorems stated in the text are given. There are also some minor clarifications and corrections, and some additional notes and references.

1. Ernest Adams (1970) first pointed to the contrast illustrated by this pair of conditionals. The particular example is Jonathan Bennett's.

2. The relation between causal and evidential reasoning is the central concern in the development of causal decision theory. See Gibbard and Harper (1981), Skyrms (1982), and Lewis (1980).

3. That is, for all players i $(x)(\exists y)x R_i y$, $(x)(y)(z)((x R_i y \& y R_i z) \rightarrow x R_i z)$, and $(x)(y)(z)((x R_i y \& x R_i z) \rightarrow y R_i z)$.

4. It has been suggested that there is a substantive, and implausible, assumption built into the way that degrees of belief are modeled: Namely, that in any two worlds in which a player has the same *full* beliefs he also has the same *partial* beliefs. But this assumption is a tautological consequence of the introspection assumption, which implies that a player fully believes that he himself has the partial beliefs that he in fact has. It does follow from the introspection assumptions that player j cannot be uncertain about player i's partial beliefs while being certain about all of i's full beliefs. But that is just because the totality of i's full beliefs include his beliefs about his own partial beliefs, and, by the introspection assumption, i's beliefs about his own partial beliefs are complete and correct. Nothing, however, prevents there being a model in which there are different worlds in which player i has full beliefs about objective facts that are exactly the same, even though the degrees of belief about such facts are different. This situation will be modeled by disjoint but isomorphic sets of possible worlds. In such a case, another player j might be certain about player i's full beliefs about everything except i's own partial beliefs, while being uncertain about i's partial beliefs.

5. More precisely, for any given model $M = \langle W, \mathbf{a}, \langle S_i, R_i, P_i \rangle_{i \in N} \rangle$, not necessarily meeting the closure condition, define a new model M' as follows: $W' = W \times C$; $\mathbf{a}' = \langle \mathbf{a}, S(\mathbf{a}) \rangle$; for all $w \in W$ and $c \in C$, $S'(\langle w, c \rangle) = c$; for all $x, y \in W$ and $c, d \in C$, $\langle x, c \rangle R_i'\langle y, d \rangle$ iff the following three conditions are met: (i) $x R_i y$, (ii) $c_i = d_i$, and (iii) for all $j \neq i$, $S_j(y) = d_j$; $P_i'(\langle x, c \rangle) = P_i(x)$. This model will be finite if the original one was, and will satisfy the closure condition.

6. In these and other definitions, a variable for a strategy or profile, enclosed in brackets, denotes the proposition (event) that the strategy or profile is realized. So, for example, if $e \in C_{-i}$ (if e is a strategy profile for players other than player i) then $[e] = \{x \in W: S_j(x) = e_j$ for all $j \neq i\}$.

7. This model theoretic definition of rationalizability coincides with the standard concept defined by Bernheim (1984) and Pearce (1984) only in two-person games. In the general case, it coincides with the weaker concept, correlated rationalizability. Model theoretic conditions appropriate for the stronger definition would require that players' beliefs about each other satisfy a constraint that (in games with more than two players) goes beyond coherence: Specifically, it is required that no player can believe that any information about another player's strategy choices would be evidentially relevant to the choices of a different player. I think this constraint could be motivated, in general, only if one confused causal with evidential reasoning. The structure of the game ensures that players' strategy choices are made independently: If player one had chosen differently, it could not have influenced the choice of player two. But this assumption of causal independence has no consequences about the evidential relevance of information about player one's choice for the beliefs that a third party might rationally have about player two. (Brian Skyrms (1992, 147–48) makes this point.)

8. This characterization theorem is proved in Stalnaker (1994).

9. The earliest formulation, so far as I know, of what has come to be called the AGM belief revision theory was given by William Harper (1975). For a general survey of the belief revision theory, see Gärdenfors (1988). Other important papers include Alchourón and Makinson (1982), Alchourón, Gärdenfors, and Makinson (1985), Grove (1988), Makinson (1985) and Spohn (1987).

10. There is this difference between the conditional belief state $B_{i,x}(\phi)$ and the posterior belief state that would actually result if the agent were in fact to learn that ϕ: if he were to learn that ϕ, he would believe that he *then* believed that ϕ, whereas, in our static models, there is no representation of what the agent comes to believe in the different possible worlds at some later time. But the potential posterior belief states and the conditional belief states as defined do not differ with respect to any information represented in the model. In particular, the conditional and posterior belief states do not differ with respect to the agent's beliefs about his *prior* beliefs.

11. The work done by Q is to rank the worlds incompatible with prior beliefs; it does not distinguish between worlds compatible with prior beliefs—they are ranked together at the top of the ordering determined by Q. So Q encodes the information about what the prior beliefs are; that is why R becomes redundant. A model with both Q and R relations would specify the prior belief sets in two ways. Condition (q3) is the requirement that the two specifications yield the same results.

Here is a simple abstract example, just to illustrate the structure: Suppose there are just three possible worlds, x, y, and z, that are subjectively indistinguishable in those worlds to player i. Suppose $\{x\}$ is the set of worlds compatible with i's beliefs in x, y, and z, which is to say that the R relation is the set $\{\langle x, x\rangle, \langle y, x\rangle, \langle z, x\rangle\}$. Suppose further that y has priority over z, which is to say if i were to learn the proposition $\{y, z\}$, his posterior or conditional belief state would be $\{y\}$. In other words, the Q relation is the set $\{\langle x, x\rangle, \langle y, x\rangle, \langle z, x\rangle, \langle y, y\rangle, \langle z, y\rangle, \langle z, z\rangle\}$.

12. I do not want to suggest that this is the only way of combining the AGM belief revision structure with probabilities. For a very different kind of theory, see Mongin (1994). In this construction, probabilities are nonadditive and are used to represent the belief revision structure, rather than to supplement it as in the models I have defined. I do not think the central result in this paper (that the same belief revision structure that I am using is in a sense equivalent to a nonadditive, and so non-Bayesian, probability conception of prior belief) conflicts with, or presents a problem for, the way I have defined extended probability functions: the probability numbers just mean different things in the two constructions.

13. See Blume, Brandenburger, and Dekel (1991a, 1991b) and Brandeburger (1992), where an equivalent notion of rationality is defined.

14. For example, Fudenberg and Tirole (1992, 441) make the following remark about the relation between game theory and decision theory: "Games and decisions differ in one key respect: Probability-0 events are both exogenous and irrelevant in decision problems, whereas what *would* happen if a player played differently in a game is both important and endogenously determined." To the extent that this is true, it seems to me an accident of the way the contrasting theories are formulated, and to have no basis in any difference in the phenomena that the theories are about.

15. The proof of this theorem is sketched in the appendix. The argument is a variation of the proof of the characterization theorem for simple (correlated) rationalizability given in Stalnaker (1994). See Dekel and Fudenberg (1990) for justification of the same solution concept in terms of different conditions that involve perturbations of the payoffs.

I originally thought that the set of strategies picked out by this concept of perfect rationalizability coincided, in the case of two-person games, with perfect rationalizability as defined in Bernheim (1984), but Pierpaolo Battigalli pointed out to me that Bernheim's concept is stronger.

16. Most notably, Robert Aumann's important and influential result on the impossibility of agreeing to disagree and subsequent variations on it all depend on the partition

structure, which requires the identification of knowledge with belief. See Aumann (1976) and Bacharach (1985). The initial result is striking, but perhaps slightly less striking when one recognizes that the assumption that there is no disagreement is implicitly a premise of the argument.

17. If one were to add to the models we have defined the assumption that the R relation is reflexive and so (given the other assumptions) is an equivalence relation, the result would be that the three relations, R_i, Q_i, and $\approx_i$, would all collapse into one. There would be no room for belief revision, since it would be assumed that no one had a belief that could be revised. Intuitively, the assumption would be that it is a necessary truth that all players are Cartesian skeptics: they have no probability-one beliefs about anything except necessary truths and facts about their own states of mind. This assumption is not compatible with belief that another player is rational, unless it is assumed that it is a necessary truth that the player is rational.

18. There is an error in the definition of strong rationalizability given in an earlier paper, Stalnaker (1994). The requirement that all full beliefs actually be correct was left out of the definition: a strategy profile was said to be strongly rationalizable if there was common belief that there was no error, and common belief that all were rational. As G. Bonanno and K. Nehring pointed out to me, the characterization theorem stated in that paper is not correct with the weaker definition.

Bonanno suggests that the weaker notion that assumes common belief in no error, without excluding actual error, has independent interest. The wider class of models picked out by this notion characterizes the same set of strategies as the stronger definition, but a larger set of strategy *profiles*, since it allows strongly rationalizable strategies to be freely combined.

19. The algorithm, which eliminates iteratively profiles rather than strategies, is given in Stalnaker (1994), and it is also proved there that the set of strategies picked out by this algorithm is characterized by the class of models meeting the model theoretic condition. (Though as noted above, the proof works only when the model theoretic definition given in that paper is corrected.)

20. The modal logic for the knowledge operators in a language that was intepreted relative to this semantic structure would be S4.3. This is the logic characterized by the class of Kripke models in which the accessibility relation is transitive, reflexive, and weakly connected (if $x\,Q_i\,y$ and $x\,Q_i\,z$, then either $y\,Q_i\,z$ or $z\,Q_i\,y$). The logic of common knowledge would be S4.

21. Although in this paper we have considered only static games, it is a straightforward matter to enrich the models by adding a temporal dimension to the possible worlds, assuming that players have belief states and perform actions at different times, actually revising their beliefs in the course of the playing of the game in accordance with a belief revision policy of the kind we have supposed. Questions about the relationship between the normal and extensive forms of games, and about the relations between different extensive form games with the same normal form can be made precise in the model theory, and answered.

22. This same result was proved (independently) by Harborne Stuart; see Stuart (1997). Stuart presented this result at the 1993 SITE summer workshop. To use Stuart's terminology, a model in which it is everywhere believed that there is no error is an m.a.c. belief system (for "mutual absolute continuous").

23. In Stalnaker (1994) I claimed to have proved that for all perfect information games, all and only Nash equilibrium strategy profiles are strongly rationalizable, but the proof is incorrect, and the theorem is false. (Pierpaolo Battigalli pointed this out to me, with a counterexample.) This theorem can be proved only for a restricted class of

perfect information games: those for which every subgame has a unique Nash equilibrium outcome.

References

Adams E. 1970. "Subjunctive and indicative conditionals," *Foundations of Language*, 6:89–94.

Alchourón, C. and D. Makinson. 1982. "The logic of theory change: contraction functions and their associated revision functions," *Theoria*, 48:14–37.

Alchourón, C., P. Gärdenfors, and D. Makinson. 1985. "On the logic of theory change: partial meet functions for contraction and revision," *Journal of Symbolic Logic*, 50:510–30.

Aumann, R. 1976. "Agreeing to disagree," *Annals of Statistics*, 4:1236–39.

Bacharach, M. 1985. "Some extensions of a claim of Aumann in an axiomatic model of knowledge," *Journal of Economic Theory*, 37: 167–90.

Bernheim, B. 1984. "Rationalizable strategic behavior," *Econometrica*, 52:1007–28.

Blume, L., A. Brandenburger, and E. Dekel. 1991. "Lexicographic probabilities and choice under uncertainty," *Econometrica*, 59:61–79.

Blume, L., A. Brandenburger, and E. Dekel. 1991. "Lexicographic probabilities and equilibrium refinements," *Econometrica*, 59:81–98.

Brandenburger, Adam. 1992. "Lexicographic probabilities and iterated admissibility," in P. Dasgupta, et al. (eds.) *Economic Analysis of Markets and Games*. Cambridge, MA: MIT Press.

Dekel, E. and D. Fudenberg. 1990. "Rational behavior with payoff uncertainty," *Journal of Economic Theory*, 52:243–67.

Fudenberg, D. and J. Tirole. 1992. *Game Theory*. Cambridge, MA: MIT Press.

Gärdenfors, P. 1988. *Knowledge in Flux: Modeling the Dynamics of Epistemic States*. Cambridge, MA: MIT Press.

Gibbard, A. and W. Harper. 1981. "Counterfactuals and two kinds of expected utility," in C. Hooker, et al. (eds.) *Foundations and Applications of Decision Theory*, Western Ontario Series in the Philosophy of Science, *13*. Dordrecht-Holland: D. Reidel.

Grove, A. 1988. "Two modelings for theory change," *Journal of Philosophical Logic*, *17*:157–70.

Harper, W. 1975. "Rational belief change, popper functions and counterfactuals," *Synthese*, *30*:221–62.

Lewis, D. 1980. "Causal decision theory," *Australasian Journal of Philosophy*, 59:5–30.

Makinson, D. 1985. "How to give it up: a survey of some formal aspects of the logic of theory change," *Synthese*, 62:347–63.

Mongin, P. 1994. "The logic of belief change and nonadditive probability," in D. Prawitz and D. Westerstahl (eds.) *Logic and Philosophy of Science in Uppsala*. Dordrecht: Kluwer.

Pappas, G. and M. Swain (eds.) 1978. *Essays on Knowledge and Justification*. Ithaca, NY: Cornell University Press.

Pearce, G. 1984. "Rationalizable strategic behavior and the problem of perfection," *Econometrica*, 52:1029–50.

Pettit, P. and R. Sugden. 1989. "The backward induction paradox," *Journal of Philosophy*, 86:169–82.

Skyrms, B. 1982. "Causal decision theory," *Journal of Philosophy*, 79:695–711.

Skyrms, B. 1992. *The Dynamics of Rational Deliberation*. Cambridge, MA: Harvard University Press.

Spohn, W. 1987. "Ordinal conditional functions: a dynamic theory of epistemic states," in W. Harper and B. Skyrms (eds.) *Causation in Decision, Belief Change and Statistics*. Dordrecht: Reidel, 2:105–34.

Stalnaker, R. 1994. "On the evaluation of solution concepts," *Theory and Decision*, 37:49–73.

Stuart, H. 1997. "Common belief of rationality in the finitely repeated prisoner's dilemma," *Games and Economic Behavior*, 19:133–43.

CHAPTER 2

Consequentialism, Non-Archimedean Probabilities, and Lexicographic Expected Utility

Peter J. Hammond

> ma la natura la dà sempre scema
> similemente operando all'artista
> c'ha l'abito dell'arte e man che trema
> Dante, *La Divina Commedia*, Vol. III: *Paradiso* (Canto XIII, 76–78)

1. Introduction

1.1. Consequentialism in Single-Person Decision Theory

The consequentialist approach to single-person decision theory, with uncertainty described by specified objective probabilities, was previously described in Hammond (1988a, 1988b). In fact, the latter paper also deals with states of nature and subjective probabilities. Here non-Archimedean subjective probabilities will not be considered at all, but left for later work.

This consequentialist approach is based on three axioms. Of these, the first requires behavior to be well defined for an (almost) unrestricted domain of finite decision trees with (a) decision nodes where the agent makes a move, (b) chance nodes at which random moves occur with specified positive probabilities, and (c) terminal nodes which result in a single consequence within a specified domain of relevant consequences. It follows that behavior in any such tree results in a set of probability distributions over consequences. The second axiom requires behavior to be dynamically consistent in continuation subtrees, in the sense that behavior at any decision node is the same in a subtree as in a full tree. The third is the "consequentialist choice" axiom, requiring that the set of possible random consequences of behavior in any decision tree of the domain be explicable as the choice of desirable random consequences from the set of random consequences that the tree makes feasible.

The earlier work then showed how these three consequentialist axioms imply the existence of a preference ordering (i.e., a complete and transitive weak preference relation) defined on the space of random consequences. Moreover, this ordering must satisfy Samuelson's (1952) independence axiom. In this way, two of the most important and even controversial axioms of standard decision theory become implications of apparently weaker and possibly more appealing axioms of the consequentialist reformulation. Thereafter, an extra condition of continuity of behavior with respect to changing probabilities leads to the preference ordering having an expected utility representation.

1.2. Consequentialism in Game Theory

This essay is the second in a series whose purpose is to extend the scope of this consequentialist approach from single-person decision trees to multiperson extensive games. In fact, a decision tree is nothing more than a one-person "consequentialist extensive game" of perfect and complete information. The difference from the usual notion of a game in extensive form comes about because no payoffs are specified. Instead, terminal nodes are assumed to result in pure consequences within the specified domain of consequences. Then the existence of a payoff function defined on this domain of consequences is not assumed, but becomes an important implication of consequentialism.

The main obstacle to this extension of consequentialism comes about because the earlier single-person theory excludes zero probability chance moves—it is in this sense that the domain of allowable decision trees is *almost* rather than fully unrestricted. Such a restriction is excusable in single-person decision theory where there are no good reasons for retaining zero probability events. In multiperson game theory, however, testing to see whether a particular profile of strategies for each player constitutes an equilibrium involves seeing what happens when any player deviates and then all the other players react according to their presumed equilibrium strategies. Yet these reactions are behavior in the face of events which are supposed to have probability zero, since that is supposed to be the probability of any player deviating from equilibrium. So one is faced with the need to update probabilities in a Bayesian manner even though a zero probability event has occurred. For this reason, the zero probability restriction makes it difficult to apply consequentialist decision theory to multiperson games in a way that yields subgame perfect or other kinds of refined equilibria. The task of this work is to remove this burdensome restriction.

Not surprisingly, the zero probability problem has already led several game theorists to extend the space of ordinary probabilities in various ways. In particular, Selten (1975) and Myerson (1978) considered "trembles." Kreps and Wilson (1982), and then Blume, Brandenburger and Dekel (1991a, 1991b) considered lexicographic hierarchies of probabilities. Myerson (1986) considered complete conditional probability systems. Finally, McLennan (1989a, 1989b) considered logarithmic likelihood ratio functions whose values can be infinite. Hammond (1994) shows that all of these different extensions, when suitably formulated, are in fact equivalent to each other, and also to a particular space of "conditional rational probability functions."

In decision trees, it is usual to specify independent probabilities at each separate chance node. After all, in principle any causes of dependence can and should be modeled within the structure of the tree itself. Then, however, it is particularly important to be sure that the entire joint distribution of all chance moves is determined uniquely from the marginal probability distributions over the chance moves at each separate chance node of the decision tree. In the case of ordinary probabilities, this is trivial because joint probabilities are found by simply multiplying appropriate marginal probabilities. Yet Hammond (1994) also shows how the equivalent sets of extended probabilities mentioned in the previous paragraph all fail this crucial test. That is, many different joint extended probability distributions over nature's possible strategies in the decision tree can arise from the same collection of independent marginal probability distributions over nature's moves at different chance nodes. This is because such extended probabilities lack the structure of an algebraic field in which the operation of multiplication is well defined.

1.3. Consequentialism with Non-Archimedean Probabilities

It seems necessary to work with a richer space of extended probabilities, for which multiplication and other algebraic field operations are well defined. There should also be an ordering relation rich enough to give meaning to the statements that probabilities are nonnegative or positive and that they are larger or smaller. Now, within an ordered algebraic field such as the real line $\mathcal{R}$, the *Archimedean axiom* states that, for any positive number r, no matter how small, there is an integer n for which $nr > 1$. Overcoming the zero probability problem seems to require some kind of *non-Archimedean* ordered field with some positive elements so small that this axiom is violated. So any such field must have at least one positive "infinitesimal" element ε with the property that $n\varepsilon < 1$ for every positive integer n, even though ε is positive. Of course any such positive infinitesimal must be smaller than any positive real number; in particular, it cannot be a real number itself.

Section 2 below therefore begins by briefly reviewing the definition and key properties of non-Archimedean ordered fields. Particular attention is paid to the elementary field $\mathcal{R}(\varepsilon)$ whose use was recommended in Hammond (1994). All its members are rational functions of a single indeterminate infinitesimal denoted by ε. For any finite support in an appropriate sample space, Section 2 proceeds to consider a corresponding set of elementary non-Archimedean probabilities. In the case when the field is $\mathcal{R}(\varepsilon)$, such probabilities are called "rational probability functions" (or RPFs).

It then becomes natural to consider in Section 3 decision trees having RPFs or other non-Archimedean instead of ordinary positive probabilities attached to each chance move in the tree. Behavior in such trees gives rise to *non-Archimedean consequences*—i.e., RPFs or more general non-Archimedean conditional probability distributions over the domain of relevant consequences.

Within the corresponding domain of finite *non-Archimedean consequentialist decision trees* the previous consequentialist axioms can be applied almost without change. Most implications are also the same as in Hammond (1988a, 1988b), since virtually all the arguments in those two papers apply to probabilities taking values in a general ordered field, and not just to those taking values in the Archimedean ordered field $\mathscr{R}$. In particular, the three "consequentialist" assumptions mentioned in Section 1.1 imply the existence of a revealed preference ordering. And this ordering must satisfy Samuelson's (1952) independence axiom.

The set of preference orderings that satisfy the independence axiom on the space of relevant non-Archimedean random consequences is actually very large. Many such orderings, however, pay no attention to the interpretation of ε as an infinitesimal. In addition, recall that the only motivation which has been offered for non-Archimedean probabilities is to resolve the zero probability problem mentioned in Section 1.2. Now, were zero probabilities to be allowed, the problem they would create is that the usual decision criteria generate behavior sets that are too large. Accordingly, Section 4 proposes an additional and rather natural refinement axiom. This requires that in any decision tree whose chance moves have non-Archimedean probabilities differing only infinitesimally from those in an ordinary decision tree with real probabilities, behavior with non-Archimedean probabilities should refine that with ordinary probabilities. It is then shown how this refinement axiom implies that the strict preference relation over non-Archimedean random consequences must refine the corresponding relation over ordinary random consequences. And, in the special case of RPFs, there must be a unique extension which can be regarded as a lexicographic hierarchy of preference orderings over ordinary random consequences.

Another part of the theory where the non-Archimedean field structure makes some difference is in the continuity condition set out in Section 5 as a necessary and sufficient condition for expected utility maximization. Within a general non-Archimedean field, the construction used by Herstein and Milnor (1953) and others to determine the real values of a von Neumann–Morgenstern utility function is invalid, since it relies upon a continuity or "Archimedean" axiom. Nevertheless, the theory presented here is meant to extend the earlier standard theory of expected utility and subjective probability, so it seems reasonable to retain this Archimedean axiom for the subspace of decision trees with real-valued positive probabilities. In combination with the earlier axioms concerning behavior in decision trees, this *restricted continuity* axiom implies that, when probabilities are described by RPFs, all the preference orderings making up the lexicographic hierarchy described in Section 4 can be represented by the expected value of the same von Neumann–Morgenstern utility function. A particular feature of the new lexicographic expected utility criterion is that it generalizes the standard criterion presented by Blume, Brandenburger and Dekel (1991a, 1991b). For example, it allows and even requires expected utility hierarchies of differing lengths to be compared.

Now, the expectation of any real-valued utility function with respect to some non-Archimedean probability distribution is itself a member of the non-Archimedean ordered field introduced in Section 2. As Section 6 shows, the new lexicographic expected utility criterion is equivalent to maximizing non-Archimedean expected utility with respect to the ordering of the field $\mathscr{R}(\varepsilon)$ in which RPFs take their values.

Finally, Section 7 gathers together all the consequentialist axioms and their implications that have been set out in previous sections. They imply the existence of a unique class of cardinally equivalent von Neumann–Morgenstern utility functions such that consequentialist behavior must be "non-Archimedean" Bayesian rational in the sense that it maximizes the lexicographic expected utility preference criterion set out in Section 4. Moreover, any behavior which is non-Archimedean Bayesian rational in this sense will satisfy the consequentialist axioms. This is the main theorem of the essay.

2. Non-Archimedean Probabilities

2.1. General Non-Archimedean Ordered Fields

An *ordered field* $\langle \mathbb{F}, +, \cdot, 0, 1, > \rangle$ is a set $\mathbb{F}$ together with (i) the two algebraic operations $+$ (addition) and $\cdot$ (multiplication); (ii) the two corresponding identity elements 0 and 1; (iii) the binary relation $>$ which is a total order of $\mathbb{F}$ satisfying $1 > 0$. The set $\mathbb{F}$ must be closed under its two algebraic operations. The usual properties of real-number arithmetic also have to be satisfied—i.e., addition and multiplication both have to be commutative and associative, the distributive law must be satisfied, and every element of $x \in \mathbb{F}$ must have both an additive inverse $-x$ and a multiplicative inverse $1/x$, except that $1/0$ is undefined. The order must be such that $y > z \iff y - z > 0$, while the set of positive elements in $\mathbb{F}$ must be closed under both addition and multiplication. Both the real line and the rationals are important and obvious examples of ordered fields. The set $\mathscr{Q}(\sqrt{2})$ of real numbers expressible in the form $a + b\sqrt{2}$ for some pair of rationals $a, b \in \mathscr{Q}$ is a somewhat less familiar example.

Any ordered field $\mathbb{F}$ has positive integer elements $n = 1, 2, \ldots$ which can be found by forming the sums $n = 1 + 1 + \cdots + 1$ of n copies of the element $1 \in \mathbb{F}$. Then $\mathbb{F}$ is said to be "Archimedean" if, given any $x > 0$ in $\mathbb{F}$, there exists such a positive integer n for which $nx > 1$. So any non-Archimedean ordered field must have at least one *positive infinitesimal* ε with the property that $n\varepsilon \leq 1$ for all positive integers n.

The introduction claimed that the set of real-valued probabilities needs extending for a fully satisfactory decision theory. In future, therefore, $\mathbb{F}$ will always be a non-Archimedean ordered field that extends the real line $\mathscr{R}$. Now, for any positive $r \in \mathscr{R}$, there exists an ordinary positive integer n satisfying $1/n < r \in \mathbb{F}$. Any positive infinitesimal $\varepsilon \in \mathbb{F}$ must therefore satisfy $\varepsilon \leq 1/n < r$, and so must be smaller than any positive real number.

For any $x \in \mathbb{F}$, let $|x|$ denote x if $x \geq 0$ and $-x$ if $x < 0$. Say that any $x \in \mathbb{F}$ is *infinitesimal* if $|x| < r$ for all (small) real $r > 0$, and that x is *finite* if $|x| < r$ for some (large enough) real r. Any $x \in \mathbb{F}$ is said to be *infinite* if and only if it is not finite. Any nonzero $x \in \mathbb{F}$ is therefore infinitesimal if and only if $1/x$ is infinite.

Next, given any finite $x \in \mathbb{F}$, the two sets $\{r \in \mathcal{R} \mid r > x\}$ and $\{r \in \mathcal{R} \mid r \leq x\}$ partition the real line $\mathcal{R}$, and so form a Dedekind cut. The usual properties of the real line then ensure that there is a unique ${}^0x \in \mathcal{R}$, called the *real part* of x, defined by

$$ {}^0x := \inf\{r \in \mathcal{R} \mid r > x\} = \sup\{r \in \mathcal{R} \mid r \leq x\} $$

For any real $r > 0$, note that $x - r < {}^0x < x + r$. Define ${}^\varepsilon x := x - {}^0x$. Then $|{}^\varepsilon x| < r$ for all real $r > 0$, so ${}^\varepsilon x$ is infinitesimal. Since $x = {}^0x + {}^\varepsilon x$, it is natural to call ${}^\varepsilon x$ the *infinitesimal part* of x.

2.2. An Elementary Non-Archimedean Ordered Field

Since decision and game theory would seem to require some non-Archimedean ordered field $\mathbb{F}$ containing $\mathcal{R}$ as a subfield, it is natural to explore the simplest such field. This must contain at least one positive infinitesimal ε. So no candidate for the field $\mathbb{F}$ can possibly be simpler than the one that results from appending ε to $\mathcal{R}$, and then closing the resulting set $\mathcal{R} \cup \{\varepsilon\}$ under the operations of addition, subtraction, multiplication, and division except by zero. The result of this closure is a field denoted by $\mathcal{R}(\varepsilon)$ that has been discussed by Robinson (1973, pp. 88–89) in particular. Its members are all the "rational" functions which can be expressed as ratios

$$ f(\varepsilon) = \frac{A(\varepsilon)}{B(\varepsilon)} = \frac{a_0 + a_1\varepsilon + a_2\varepsilon^2 + \cdots + a_n\varepsilon^n}{b_0 + b_1\varepsilon + b_2\varepsilon^2 + \cdots + b_m\varepsilon^m} = \frac{\sum_{i=0}^{n} a_i\varepsilon^i}{\sum_{i=0}^{m} b_i\varepsilon^i} \tag{1} $$

of two polynomial functions $A(\varepsilon)$, $B(\varepsilon)$ of the indeterminate ε with real coefficients; moreover, not all the coefficients of the denominator $B(\varepsilon)$ can be zero.

Now, one can simplify (1) by successively (i) eliminating any leading zeros $a_0 = a_1 = \cdots = a_{k-1} = b_0 = b_1 = \cdots = b_{j-1} = 0$; (ii) dividing both numerator and denominator by the leading nonzero coefficient b_j of the denominator; (iii) canceling any positive powers of ε that are common to all terms of both numerator and denominator and relabeling the coefficients a_i, b_i accordingly. The result is that any $f(\varepsilon) \in \mathcal{R}(\varepsilon)$ given by (1) gets put into its *normalized form*

$$ f(\varepsilon) = \frac{\sum_{i=k}^{n} a_i\varepsilon^i}{\varepsilon^j + \sum_{i=j+1}^{m} b_i\varepsilon^i} \tag{2} $$

for some integers $j, k, m, n \geq 0$ such that $j = 0$ or $k = 0$ (or both). Moreover, $a_k \neq 0$ unless $f(\varepsilon) = 0$. Note too that each real number $r \in \mathcal{R}$ can be simply expressed in the form (2) by writing $r = r/1 \in \mathscr{R}(\varepsilon)$, with $j, k, m, n = 0$ and $a_0 = r$.

It remains to be shown that $\mathscr{R}(\varepsilon)$ really is a non-Archimedean ordered field. The binary relation $>$ will be defined so that $y > z \iff y - z > 0$ where, for any $x = f(\varepsilon) \in \mathscr{R}(\varepsilon)$ in its normalized form (2), one has $f(\varepsilon) > 0$ if and only if $a_k > 0$. Recalling that ε is intended to be an infinitesimal, this condition is entirely natural because it is equivalent to having $f(r)$, the corresponding real-valued rational function of the real variable r, be positive for all small positive r. For later reference, note that $>$ is effectively a lexicographic relation. For if $f(\varepsilon)$ is given by (1), then $f(\varepsilon) > 0$ if and only if $a_k/b_j > 0$, where a_k and b_j are the first nonzero coefficients of the numerator and denominator, respectively.

From the above definition, it is easy to check that $>$ is asymmetric and transitive, while either $f(\varepsilon) > 0$ or $f(\varepsilon) < 0$ unless $f(\varepsilon) = 0$. So $>$ is indeed a total order. And it is easy and routine to check that the corresponding set of positive elements is closed under addition and multiplication. Finally, $\mathscr{R}(\varepsilon)$ is non-Archimedean because $1 > 0$ and so the order $>$ defined above satisfies $1 - n\varepsilon > 0$ for every positive integer n.

Let $f(0) \in \mathscr{R}$ denote the value at $r = 0$ of the corresponding polynomial function $f(r)$ of the real variable r. Then it is easy to see that any $f(\varepsilon) \in \mathscr{R}(\varepsilon)$ given by (2) is infinitesimal if and only if $k > j = 0$, so that $f(0) = 0$. And any such $f(\varepsilon)$ is infinite if and only if $j > k = 0$, so that $f(0)$ is undefined. Finally, whenever $f(\varepsilon) \in \mathscr{R}(\varepsilon)$ is finite, $f(0)$ is equal to its real part $^0 f(\varepsilon)$.

Choosing a more appropriate algebraic field in which probabilities can be defined is an important first step. For the purposes of this paper and some later work in decision and game theory, the field $\mathscr{R}(\varepsilon)$ appears to be rich enough. However, some further extensions of $\mathscr{R}(\varepsilon)$ are eventually going to be necessary so as to accommodate countably additive non-Archimedean probability measures, continuous strategy spaces, and so on—for example, the set $\mathscr{R}^\infty(\varepsilon)$ mentioned in Hammond (1994, p. 48), whose members are ratios of power series $\sum_{k=0}^\infty a_k \varepsilon^k$ with real coefficients $a_0, a_1, a_2, \dots$. Accordingly, much of the discussion actually works with a general non-Archimedean ordered field $\mathbb{F}$ that extends $\mathscr{R}(\varepsilon)$. This field could be as rich as the whole nonstandard real line $^*\mathscr{R}$ of "hyperreals," or it could be one of many possible subfields of $^*\mathscr{R}$, including $\mathscr{R}^\infty(\varepsilon)$.

2.3. A Minimal Positive Cone

Probabilities are always nonnegative. Avoiding the zero probability problem requires them all to be positive. In fact, when requiring a probability to have some positive non-Archimedean value $p \in \mathbb{F}$, a more restrictive condition than $p > 0$ will be used. Probabilities will actually be given values in some convex *non-Archimedean positive cone* $\mathbb{P}$—that is, in a set $\mathbb{P} \subset \mathbb{F}_+ := \{ x \in \mathbb{F} \mid x > 0 \}$ containing all the positive reals and at least one infinitesimal, such that $\mathbb{P}$ is closed under addition, multiplication and division. Of course, such a cone cannot be closed under subtraction, so it is natural to have $\mathbb{P}$ as a minimal set in $\mathbb{F}$ with these properties. After all, this whole line of research is about having a space of probabilities that is no larger than absolutely necessary. The members of such a minimal $\mathbb{P}$ will be described as *strongly positive*.

When $\mathbb{F} = \mathscr{R}(\varepsilon)$, let $\mathscr{P}(\varepsilon)$ denote the set of all $f(\varepsilon) \in \mathscr{R}(\varepsilon)$ given by (1) whose real coefficients a_i ($i = 0$ to I) and b_j ($j = 0$ to J) are all nonnegative, while $f(\varepsilon) \neq 0$. Equivalently, the numerator and denominator of $f(\varepsilon)$ must each contain at least one positive real coefficient, and no negative coefficient. Obviously $\mathscr{P}(\varepsilon)$ is the smallest set containing both the positive part of the real line and ε that is also closed under addition, multiplication, and division. The set $\mathscr{P}(\varepsilon)$ is therefore a convex non-Archimedean positive cone, implying that one can take $\mathbb{P} = \mathscr{P}(\varepsilon)$.

2.4. Non-Archimedean Probabilities

Let Ω be a nonempty sample space. Note carefully that Ω is not required to be finite. Let F be any nonempty finite subset of Ω. A $\mathbb{P}$-*probability on* (or *with support*) F is a mapping $p(\cdot) : 2^{\Omega} \to \mathbb{P} \cup \{0\}$ which is defined on the domain 2^{Ω} of all subsets of Ω, and satisfies the three axioms:

  (i) $p(E) \in \mathbb{P}$ whenever $E \cap F \neq \emptyset$;
 (ii) $p(E) = 1$ whenever $F \subset E \subset \Omega$;
 (iii) $p(E \cup E') = p(E) + p(E')$ whenever $E, E' \subset \Omega$ are   such   that $E \cap E' = \emptyset$.

From axioms (ii) and (iii) it follows that, whenever $E \cap F = \emptyset$, then

$$1 = p(E \cup F) = p(E) + p(F) = p(E) + 1$$

and so $p(E) = 0$. Actually, apart from (i), these are the usual axioms of probability theory, but with $p(E)$ taking values in $\mathbb{P} \cup \{0\}$ instead of $\mathscr{R}_+$. However, axiom (i) strengthens the usual condition that $p(E) \geq 0$ for all $E \subset F$. To justify this strengthening, recall that the only reason for introducing extended and non-Archimedean probabilities has been the need to overcome the zero probability problem in decision and game theory. Note too that $p(E)$ is allowed to be an arbitrarily small strongly positive infinitesimal in $\mathbb{P}$.

Let $\Delta^0(F; \mathbb{P})$ denote the set of all such $\mathbb{P}$-probabilities with support F. This set is obviously an extension of the set $\Delta^0(F)$ of ordinary probability distributions with support F. Let $\Delta(\Omega; \mathbb{P})$ denote the set of all $\mathbb{P}$-probabilities that belong to $\Delta^0(F; \mathbb{P})$, for some finite $F \subset \Omega$. Thus all the members of $\Delta^0(F; \mathbb{P})$ definitely have F as their support, whereas each member of $\Delta(\Omega; \mathbb{P})$ has a support which can be any finite subset of Ω.

As usual with finitely supported probability distributions, any $p(\cdot) \in \Delta^0(F; \mathbb{P})$ is completely determined by its values $p(\{\omega\})$ on the singleton subsets $\{\omega\}$ ($\omega \in F$). With the customary slight abuse of notation, write these values as $p(\omega)$ ($\omega \in F$), all of which must be strongly positive. Moreover, it must be true that $p(\omega) = {}^0p(\omega) + \eta(\omega)$, where the real part ${}^0p(\cdot)$ is an ordinary probability distribution in $\Delta(F)$, while each $\eta(\omega)$ is infinitesimal in $\mathbb{F}$, and also

$\sum_{\omega \in F} \eta(\omega) = 0$. For any $\omega \in F$ it is necessary to have $^0p(\omega) > 0$ or $\eta(\omega) \in \mathbb{P}$ (or both).

In the special case when $\mathbb{P} = \mathscr{P}(\varepsilon)$, such non-Archimedean probabilities will be called *rational probability functions* (or RPFs). Let $\Delta^0(F; \varepsilon)$ denote the set of all such RPFs with support F. And let $\Delta(\Omega; \varepsilon)$ denote the set of all RPFs that belong to $\Delta^0(F; \varepsilon)$, for some finite $F \subset \Omega$.

Members of $\Delta^0(F; \varepsilon)$ have probabilities given, for all $\omega \in F$, by rational functions

$$p(\omega; \varepsilon) = \frac{A(\omega; \varepsilon)}{B(\omega; \varepsilon)} = \frac{a_0(\omega) + a_1(\omega)\,\varepsilon + a_2(\omega)\,\varepsilon^2 + \cdots + a_{I(\omega)}(\omega)\varepsilon^{I(\omega)}}{b_0(\omega) + b_1(\omega)\,\varepsilon + b_2(\omega)\,\varepsilon^2 + \cdots + b_{J(\omega)}(\omega)\varepsilon^{J(\omega)}}$$

$$= \frac{\sum_{i=0}^{I(\omega)} a_i(\omega)\,\varepsilon^i}{\sum_{j=0}^{J(\omega)} b_j(\omega)\,\varepsilon^j}$$

of the form (1). Here the coefficients $a_i(\omega)$ ($i = 0$ to $I(\omega)$) and $b_j(\omega)$ ($j = 0$ to $J(\omega)$) are all nonnegative real numbers and, for any $\omega \in F$, neither all the $a_i(\omega)$ nor all the $b_j(\omega)$ are zero. Now, the finite collection $B(\omega; \varepsilon)$ ($\omega \in F$) of polynomials has a positive lowest common denominator, which will be written as $L(\varepsilon) := \sum_{h=0}^{H} l_h \varepsilon^h$, where each $l_h \geq 0$. For all $\omega \in F$ one has

$$p(\omega; \varepsilon) = \frac{L(\omega; \varepsilon)}{L(\varepsilon)} = \frac{\sum_{h=0}^{H} l_h(\omega)\,\varepsilon^h}{\sum_{h=0}^{H} l_h \varepsilon^h}, \qquad \text{where } L(\omega; \varepsilon) := \frac{A(\omega; \varepsilon)\,L(\varepsilon)}{B(\omega; \varepsilon)} \qquad (3)$$

Moreover, $l_h(\omega) \geq 0$ for all $\omega \in \Omega$ and for $h = 0, 1, 2, \ldots, H$. After repeating the operations used to obtain the normalized form (2) of a general rational function (1)—i.e., eliminating any leading zeros, canceling redundant powers of ε, and dividing by the leading coefficient of the denominator—one obtains the *normalized form*

$$p(\omega; \varepsilon) = \frac{p_0(\omega) + \sum_{h=1}^{H} l_h(\omega)\,\varepsilon^h}{1 + \sum_{h=1}^{H} l_h \varepsilon^h} \qquad (4)$$

Here $\sum_{\omega \in F} p_0(\omega) = 1$ and $\sum_{\omega \in F} l_h(\omega) = l_h$ for $h = 1$ to H. Moreover, $p_0(\omega)$ must be equal to the real part $^0p(\omega; \varepsilon)$ of $p(\omega; \varepsilon)$, for all $\omega \in F$. In particular, $p_0(\cdot)$ is an ordinary probability distribution in $\Delta(F)$.

An alternative form of (4) will be used in Section 4. This comes from dropping any terms for which $l_h = 0$, while letting K denote the remaining set of those integers h with $l_h > 0$. Then (4) becomes

$$p(\omega; \varepsilon) = \frac{\sum_{k \in K} l_k\, p_k(\omega)\,\varepsilon^k}{\sum_{k \in K} l_k\, \varepsilon^k} \qquad (5)$$

where $p_k(\omega) := l_k(\omega)/l_k$ for $k \in K$ and all $\omega \in F$. Then $0 \in K$, $l_0 = 1$, and $p_k(\cdot) \in \Delta(F)$ for all $k \in K$.

Finally, note that (5) can be regarded as specifying probabilities

$$p^*(k, \omega; \varepsilon) := \frac{l_k \, p_k(\omega) \, \varepsilon^k}{\sum_{j \in K} l_j \, \varepsilon^j}$$

as functions of ε on the extended sample space $\mathcal{N} \times \Omega$, where $\mathcal{N}$ denotes the set of nonnegative integers, to be interpreted as various orders in a lexicographic hierarchy (cf. Blume et al., 1991a, 1991b). This is equivalent to compounding the ordinary conditional distributions $p^*(\omega|k) := p_k(\omega)$ (all $\omega \in F$ and $k \in K$) with the particular RPF $l(\cdot; \varepsilon) \in \Delta(\mathcal{N}; \varepsilon)$ given by

$$l(k; \varepsilon) := p^*(\{k\} \times \Omega; \varepsilon) = \frac{l_k \, \varepsilon^k}{\sum_{j \in K} l_j \, \varepsilon^j} \quad \text{(all } k \in K)$$

2.5. Independence

Suppose that the finite nonempty sample space Ω is the n-fold Cartesian product $\prod_{s=1}^{n} \Omega^s$. Suppose that, for $s = 1$ to n, there are $\mathbb{P}$-probability distributions $p^s(\cdot) \in \Delta^0(F^s; \mathbb{P})$ with respective finite supports $F^s \subset \Omega^s$. Then these n distributions are said to be *independent* if their joint distribution has support $F = \prod_{s=1}^{n} F^s$ and is described by the unique $\mathbb{P}$-probability distribution $p(\cdot) \in \Delta(F; \mathbb{P})$ that satisfies

$$p\left(\prod_{s=1}^{n} E^s \right) = \prod_{s=1}^{n} p^s(E^s) \quad \text{whenever } E^s \subset F^s \ (s = 1, 2, \dots, n)$$

This corresponds to the strongest of the three definitions of independence in Blume et al. (1991a) and in Hammond (1994). And it is the only one of the three allowing the joint distribution to be inferred uniquely from the independent marginal distributions.

2.6. Non-Archimedean Conditional Probabilities

Suppose that $p(\cdot) \in \Delta^0(F; \mathbb{P})$ is any $\mathbb{P}$-probability distribution on the finite subset $F \subset \Omega$. Then the non-Archimedean conditional probability

$$P(E|E') := p(E)/p(E') \in \mathbb{P} \tag{6}$$

is certainly well defined whenever $\emptyset \neq E \subset E' \subset F$. The zero probability problem has therefore been resolved.

Consider the case when $\mathbb{P} = \mathscr{P}(\varepsilon)$ and $p(\cdot; \varepsilon) \in \Delta^0(F; \varepsilon)$ is any RPF on the finite subset $F \subset \Omega$. Then the non-Archimedean conditional probability (6) takes the form

$$P(E|E'; \varepsilon) := p(E; \varepsilon)/p(E'; \varepsilon) \in \mathscr{P}(\varepsilon) \tag{7}$$

where $p(E; \varepsilon)$ and $p(E'; \varepsilon)$ are rational functions in $\mathscr{P}(\varepsilon)$, and so therefore is $P(E|E'; \varepsilon)$. Since ε is an infinitesimal, it is tempting in this case to consider the ordinary conditional probabilities that are defined by the limit

$$P(E|E') := \lim_{r \to 0+} P(E|E'; r), \tag{8}$$

of the positive real-valued rational function $P(E|E'; r)$ as r tends to zero through ordinary positive real values. The conditional probabilities $P(E|E')$ $(\emptyset \neq E \subset E' \subset F)$ then form a *complete conditional probability system* (or CCPS) on F, of the kind studied by Rényi (1955, 1970), Lindley (1965), and Myerson (1986), among others. Each such CCPS is obviously represented by an equivalence class of RPFs, where any two RPFs $p(\cdot; \varepsilon)$, $q(\cdot; \varepsilon) \in \Delta^0(F; \varepsilon)$ are to be regarded as equivalent if and only if

$$\lim_{r \to 0+} p(E; r)/p(E'; r) = \lim_{r \to 0+} q(E; r)/q(E'; r) \quad \text{whenever} \quad \emptyset \neq E \subset E' \subset F \tag{9}$$

Moreover, as pointed out in Hammond (1994), each such equivalence class of RPFs can be represented by a single *conditional rational probability function* satisfying the property that

$$p(\omega; \varepsilon) = \frac{p_{k(\omega)}(\omega)\, \varepsilon^{k(\omega)}}{\sum_{k=0}^{K} \varepsilon^k} \tag{10}$$

for all $\omega \in F$, where $p_k \in \Delta^0(F_k)$ are ordinary probability distributions whose supports

$$F_k = \{\, \omega \in F \,|\, p_k(\omega) > 0 \,\} = \{\, \omega \in F \,|\, k(\omega) = k \,\} \quad (k = 0 \text{ to } K)$$

form a partition of F. However, considering only such CCPSs loses a lot of valuable relevant information. For, as discussed in Section 1.2, the joint distribution of several independent random variables is only uniquely determined from the marginal distributions when non-Archimedean probabilities are represented by RPFs in general form, with values in an algebraic field.

3. Non-Archimedean Consequentialist Behavior

3.1. Non-Archimedean Consequentialist Decision Trees

Let Y be a given domain of consequences that could conceivably occur. As remarked in Section 1.1, consequentialism in single-person decision theory considers dynamically consistent behavior β in an almost unrestricted domain $\mathscr{T}(Y)$ of consequentialist finite decision trees. These are decision trees in the sense of Raiffa (1968), except that payoffs are not specified. Instead, any terminal node x in any tree $T \in \mathcal{T}(Y)$ has an associated consequence $y = \gamma(x)$ within the consequence domain Y.

This work will consider instead the set $\mathcal{T}(Y; \mathbb{P})$ of $\mathbb{P}$-*consequentialist* finite decision trees. Each member of $\mathcal{T}(Y; \mathbb{P})$ is a collection

$$T = \langle N, N^*, N^0, X, N_{+1}(\cdot), n_0, \pi(\cdot|\cdot), \gamma(\cdot) \rangle \qquad (11)$$

whose eight component parts are described and interpreted as follows:

(i) N is a nonempty finite set of *nodes* of the tree T, which is partitioned into the three disjoint sets N^*, N^0, and X having properties (ii)–(vii) below;

(ii) N^* is the (possibly empty) set of *decision nodes*;

(iii) N^0 is the (possibly empty) set of *chance nodes*;

(iv) X is the nonempty set of *terminal nodes*;

(v) $N_{+1} : N \twoheadrightarrow N$ is the *immediate successor* correspondence, which, so that T really is indeed a tree, must satisfy:
(a) $\forall n \in N : n \notin N_{+1}(n)$;
(b) $\forall n \in N : N_{+1}(n) = \emptyset \iff n \in X$;
(c) $\forall n, n' \in N : N_{+1}(n) \cap N_{+1}(n') \neq \emptyset \iff n = n'$;
and must also generate an acyclic binary *successor* relation $\succ$ on N, defined by the property that $n' \succ n$ if and only if there exists a chain $n_1, n_2, \ldots, n_k$ in N such that $n_1 = n$, $n_k = n'$, and $n_{j+1} \in N_{+1}(n_j)$ for $j = 1$ to $k - 1$;

(vi) n_0 is the unique *initial node* in N satisfying $\forall n \in N : n_0 \notin N_{+1}(n)$;

(vii) at each chance node $n \in N^0$, there is a non-Archimedean conditional probability distribution $\pi(\cdot|n) \in \Delta^0(N_{+1}(n); \mathbb{P})$ over the set $N_{+1}(n)$ (whose members are to be interpreted as the possible chance moves from n to each succeeding node $n' \in N_{+1}(n)$);

(viii) $\gamma : X \to Y$ is the *consequence mapping*, indicating the consequence $\gamma(x)$ of reaching each terminal node x.

Most of this definition is identical to that in Hammond (1988a, 1988b). Natural nodes and sets of possible states of the world are not considered, since consideration of subjective probabilities has been left for later work. Otherwise, only the concept of $\mathbb{P}$-probability in part (vii) and the consequence mapping in part (viii) are different. The latter has been changed so that each terminal node x gives rise to just one sure consequence $\gamma(x) \in Y$, rather than to a probability distribution over Y. The change is just to make clear how all uncertainty is eventually resolved within a decision tree. The proof of the Refinement Lemma in Section 4.1 contains an example illustrating this definition.

Where it is desirable to emphasize dependence on T, I shall write $N(T)$, $N^*(T)$, etc.

3.2. Dynamically Consistent Behavior

As in the earlier work described in Section 1.1, it will now be assumed that *behavior* is formally described by a correspondence β with a domain consisting of all pairs (T, n) satisfying $T \in \mathscr{T}(Y; \mathbb{P})$ and $n \in N^*(T)$. Its value is a *behavior set* $\beta(T, n)$, which is a nonempty subset of the appropriate set $N_{+1}(T, n)$ of all decisions that are feasible at the decision node n of the tree T in the domain $\mathscr{T}(Y; \mathbb{P})$ of non-Archimedean consequentialist decision trees.

Now, given any decision tree $T \in \mathscr{T}(Y; \mathbb{P})$ and any fixed node $\bar{n}$ of T, there is a "subtree" of T or a *continuation from* $\bar{n}$ with

$$T(\bar{n}) := \bar{T} = \langle \bar{N}, \bar{N}^*, \bar{N}^0, \bar{X}, \bar{N}_{+1}(\cdot), \bar{n}_0, \bar{\pi}(\cdot|\cdot), \bar{\gamma}(\cdot) \rangle \tag{12}$$

To define $T(\bar{n})$ explicitly, first let $N(n) := \{ n' \in N \mid n' \succ n \text{ or } n' = n \}$ denote the set of nodes in N which either succeed or coincide with n. Then $T(\bar{n})$ is the decision tree with the initial node $\bar{n}_0 := \bar{n}$, the set of nodes $\bar{N} := N(\bar{n})$, and with all of the other sets, correspondences, and functions $\bar{N}^*, \bar{N}^0, \bar{X}, \bar{N}_{+1}(\cdot), \bar{\pi}(\cdot|\cdot), \bar{\gamma}(\cdot)$ of (12) given by appropriate restrictions of $N^*, N^0, X, N_{+1}(\cdot), \pi(\cdot|\cdot), \gamma(\cdot)$ to the smaller set of nodes $\bar{N}$. From this definition it is obvious that $T(\bar{n})$ meets all the criteria set out in Section 3.1 above, and so is itself a non-Archimedean consequentialist decision tree in $\mathscr{T}(Y; \mathbb{P})$.

Suppose that n is any decision node of a tree $T \in \mathscr{T}(Y; \mathbb{P})$ with the set of nodes N. When the agent comes to make a decision at node n, the remaining decision problem is really sufficiently described by the tree $T(n)$. Behavior at node n must therefore be described by $\beta(T(n), n)$ as well as by $\beta(T, n)$. Thus it will also be assumed that behavior is *dynamically consistent* in the sense that $\beta(T, n) = \beta(T(n), n)$ at all decision nodes n of every tree $T \in \mathscr{T}(Y; \mathbb{P})$. This consistency condition is entirely natural since, as discussed in Hammond (1988a, 1988b), it is satisfied even by a naive agent who neglects changing tastes altogether. Of course, a naive agent's actual behavior usually departs from planned behavior. Also, except in very special cases, naive behavior violates consequentialism, as defined below (cf. Hammond, 1976).

From now on only consistent behavior will be considered and will be called simply *behavior*.

3.3. Non-Archimedean Consequences of Behavior

Finally, it will be presumed that the domain of consequences has been specified broadly enough to capture everything that is relevant for the agent's behavior. Then "consequentialism" means that in all decision trees in the domain, including the "continuation subtrees" of any tree, the agent's behavior gives rise to a nonempty set of possible "chosen" random consequences which depends only upon the feasible set of random consequences. Before this can be formalized, it is obviously necessary to see first what the feasible set and choice set are in any tree $T \in \mathscr{T}(Y; \mathbb{P})$.

Let $\Delta(Y; \mathbb{P})$ denote the set of all $\mathbb{P}$-probabilities when the sample space is taken to be the consequence domain Y. It turns out that, in any tree $T \in \mathcal{T}(Y; \mathbb{P})$, any kind of feasible behavior must yield a random consequence belonging to some nonempty *feasible set* $F(T) \subset \Delta(Y; \mathbb{P})$. Moreover, behavior β must yield a random consequence belonging to some nonempty *(revealed) choice set* $\Phi_\beta(T) \subset F(T)$. This is best demonstrated by using backward recursion to construct, in successively larger and larger subtrees $T(n)$ with earlier and earlier initial nodes n in $N(T)$, the corresponding pairs of subsets $F(T, n)$ and $\Phi_\beta(T, n)$ of $\Delta(Y; \mathbb{P})$. Moreover, backward induction can be used to show that

$$\emptyset \neq \Phi_\beta(T, n) \subset F(T, n) \subset \Delta(Y; \mathbb{P})$$

at every node $n \in N(T)$. Finally, of course, one works back to the initial node n_0 at which $F(T) = F(T, n_0)$ and $\Phi_\beta(T) = \Phi_\beta(T, n_0)$, so that

$$\emptyset \neq \Phi_\beta(T) \subset F(T) \subset \Delta(Y; \mathbb{P})$$

The backward recursion and backward induction start at the terminal nodes $x \in X$ where only a single consequence $\gamma(x)$ is possible. Then

$$\emptyset \neq F(T, x) = \Phi_\beta(T, x) = \{\delta_{\gamma(x)}(\cdot)\} \subset \Delta(Y; \mathbb{P}) \tag{13}$$

where $\delta_{\gamma(x)}(\cdot)$ denotes the unique degenerate $\mathbb{P}$-probability distribution in $\Delta^0(\{\gamma(x)\}; \mathbb{P})$ with $\delta_{\gamma(x)}(\{\gamma(x)\}) = 1$. At previous nodes $n \in N \setminus X$, both $F(T, n)$ and $\Phi_\beta(T, n)$ are calculated from the values of $F(T, n')$ and $\Phi_\beta(T, n')$ at all nodes $n' \in N_{+1}(n)$ that immediately succeed n. There are two different cases—cf. Hammond (1988b, section 4).

Case 1. At any decision node $n \in N^*$ one has

$$\begin{aligned} \emptyset \neq \Phi_\beta(T, n) &:= \bigcup_{n' \in \beta(T, n)} \Phi_\beta(T, n') \subset F(T, n) \\ &:= \bigcup_{n' \in N_{+1}(n)} F(T, n') \subset \Delta(Y; \mathbb{P}) \end{aligned} \tag{14}$$

Case 2. At any chance node $n \in N^0$ one has

$$\begin{aligned} \emptyset \neq \Phi_\beta(T, n) &:= \sum_{n' \in N_{+1}(n)} \pi(n'|n) \Phi_\beta(T, n') \\ &\subset F(T, n) := \sum_{n' \in N_{+1}(n)} \pi(n'|n) F(T, n') \subset \Delta(Y; \mathbb{P}) \end{aligned} \tag{15}$$

These constructions (14) and (15) evidently work just as well in the set $\Delta(Y; \mathbb{P})$ as they did before in $\Delta(Y)$. The proof of the Refinement Lemma in Section 4.1 provides a simple example of how they work in practice.

3.4. Non-Archimedean Consequentialist Behavior

The *non-Archimedean consequentialist choice axiom* requires behavior β to reveal a unique *non-Archimedean consequence choice function* C_β with the property that

$$\Phi_\beta(T) = C_\beta(F(T)) \tag{16}$$

in all the trees $T \in \mathscr{T}(Y; \mathbb{P})$. In particular, the structure of the decision tree must be irrelevant to consequentialist behavior, as long as the feasible set $F(T)$ of possible distributions stays the same.

3.5. Ordinality and Independence

The three consequentialist axioms require that the behavior sets $\beta(T, n)$: (i) are nonempty subsets of $N_{+1}(n)$ defined at every decision node n of every tree $T \in \mathscr{T}(Y; \mathbb{P})$; (ii) satisfy the consistency condition $\beta(T(n), n') = \beta(T, n')$ at all decision nodes n' of any subtree $T(n)$ of a tree $T \in \mathscr{T}(Y; \mathbb{P})$; (iii) satisfy the consequentialist choice axiom (16).

The arguments of Hammond (1988b, sections 5 and 6) can now be applied virtually without change, and so will not be repeated here. They show first that consequentialist behavior β reveals, not only a consequence choice function C_β but also a corresponding *consequence preference ordering* R—i.e., a complete transitive binary relation—on the set $\Delta(Y; \mathbb{P})$ of $\mathbb{P}$-probabilities. Thus, for every $T \in \mathscr{T}(Y; \mathbb{P})$, one has

$$\Phi_\beta(T) = \{\lambda \in F(T) \mid \mu \in F(T) \Rightarrow \lambda\, R\, \mu\}$$

Second, on the space $\Delta(Y)$ of ordinary probability distributions, which is of course a subset of $\Delta(Y; \mathbb{P})$, it was shown that the *independence condition* is another implication of consequentialism. For all ordinary probability distributions $\lambda, \mu, \nu \in \Delta(Y)$ and all real numbers α with $0 < \alpha < 1$, independence requires that

$$\lambda\, R\, \mu \iff [\alpha\lambda + (1-\alpha)\nu]\, R\, [\alpha\mu + (1-\alpha)\nu] \tag{17}$$

Exactly the same arguments now imply the *non-Archimedean independence condition* on $\Delta(Y; \mathbb{P})$. For all $\lambda, \mu, \nu \in \Delta(Y; \mathbb{P})$ this requires that

$$\lambda\, R\, \mu \iff \frac{\alpha\lambda + \theta\nu}{\alpha + \theta}\; R\; \frac{\alpha\mu + \theta\nu}{\alpha + \theta} \tag{18}$$

whenever $\alpha, \theta \in \mathbb{P}$, so that $\alpha(\alpha + \theta)^{-1}$ and $\theta(\alpha + \theta)^{-1}$ can be regarded as $\mathbb{P}$-probabilities over a pair of disjoint states.

In Hammond (1988b, section 8) it is also shown that any preference ordering R over the set $\Delta(Y)$ satisfying the independence condition (17) generates consequentialist and dynamically consistent behavior on the "almost unrestricted domain" of all finite consequentialist decision trees having strictly positive ordinary probabilities at all chance nodes. It is important to consider only trees in this almost unrestricted domain because, if a completely unrestricted domain of finite consequentialist decision trees were allowed instead, then the implication would be that all random consequences in each space $\Delta(Y)$ must be indifferent. Here, a corresponding result is true, but on the less restricted domain $\mathcal{T}(Y; \mathbb{P})$ of finite consequentialist decision trees having strongly positive non-Archimedean probabilities at all chance nodes. For any preference ordering R over the set $\Delta(Y; \mathbb{P})$ satisfying the new independence condition (18) will generate consequentialist and dynamically consistent behavior on this domain. The proof is exactly the same as before.

4. Lexicographic Refinements

4.1. A Refinement Axiom

There are many different preference orderings R on $\Delta(Y; \mathbb{P})$ satisfying independence (18). Some of these are implausible, however. For consider the case when $\mathbb{P} = \mathscr{P}(\varepsilon)$. Let $v : Y \to \mathscr{R}$ be any von Neumann–Morgenstern utility function defined on the set Y of all possible sure consequences. Then, for each positive real number r, there is a corresponding ordering R_r with the property that

$$p \; R_r \; q \iff \sum_{y \in Y} [p(y; r) - q(y; r)] \, v(y) \geq 0 \tag{19}$$

whenever $p, q \in \Delta(Y; \varepsilon)$, where $p(y; r)$ and $q(y; r)$ denote the real numbers obtained by regarding p and q as functions of the real variable r instead of the infinitesimal ε. The preferences defined by (19) obviously satisfy independence (18), as well as the restricted continuity condition to be considered later. Yet such orderings pay no attention to the intended interpretation of ε as an infinitesimal. A further assumption is needed.

As explained in Hammond (1994), the reason for introducing probabilities with values in a general non-Archimedean cone $\mathbb{P}$ is to refine consequentialist behavior in trees having zero probabilities at some chance nodes, while leaving unaffected such behavior in trees having positive probabilities at all chance nodes. Now, given any non-Archimedean tree $T \in \mathcal{T}(Y; \mathbb{P})$ as in Section 3.1, let $^0T \in \mathcal{T}(Y)$ be the corresponding ordinary tree obtained when every non-Archimedean probability $\pi(n'|n) \in \mathbb{P}$ ($n \in N^0$, $n' \in N_{+1}(n)$) in T is replaced by its corresponding real part $^0\pi(n'|n) \in \mathscr{R}$. Also, to ensure that $^0\pi(n'|n) > 0$ throughout ^0T, remove the entire subtree $^0T(n')$ from ^0T whenever $^0\pi(n'|n) = 0$ for some node $n' \in N_{+1}(n)$ immediately succeeding the chance node $n \in N^0$.

The *refinement axiom* then requires that, at any decision node $n \in N^*(^0T) \subset N^*(T)$, one must have $\beta(T, n) \subset \beta(^0T, n)$. In particular, if $n \in N^*(^0T)$ is such that $\beta(^0T, n) = \{n'\}$ for some unique $n' \in N_{+1}(n)$, then it must be true that $\beta(T, n) = \{n'\}$ as well. Actually, it will be enough to assume this weaker condition in what follows. The main implication of this refinement axiom is the following lemma, whose conclusion could almost have been stated as an alternative to the axiom.

Refinement Lemma

In combination with the consequentialist axioms of Section 3.5, the refinement axiom implies that, whenever $p, q \in \Delta(Y; \mathbb{P})$ and $^0p\ P\ ^0q$, then $p\ P\ q$.

Proof. First, let

$$Y_p := \{y \in Y \mid p(y) > 0\} \quad \text{and} \quad Y_q := \{y \in Y \mid q(y) > 0\}$$

denote the finite supports of the two distributions $p, q \in \Delta(Y; \mathbb{P})$. Then consider the particular finite decision tree $T \in \mathscr{T}(Y; \mathbb{P})$ with initial node n_0, which is the only decision node, while the other nodes satisfy

$$N_{+1}(n_0) = N^0 = \{n_p, n_q\} \quad \text{and} \quad X = X_p \cup X_q$$

where

and
$$\begin{aligned}
PX_p &:= N_{+1}(n_p) = \{x_p(y) \mid y \in Y_p\} \\
X_q &:= N_{+1}(n_q) = \{x_q(y) \mid y \in Y_q\}
\end{aligned}$$

Suppose too that the probabilities and consequences in T are given by

$$\begin{aligned}
\pi(x_p(y)|n_p) &= p(y) & \text{and} \quad \gamma(x_p(y)) &= y \text{ (all } y \in Y_p) \\
\pi(x_q(y)|n_q) &= q(y) & \text{and} \quad \gamma(x_q(y)) &= y \text{ (all } y \in Y_q)
\end{aligned}$$

Then the backward recursion construction of Section 3.3 shows that

$$\Phi_\beta(T, x_p(y)) = F(T, x_p(y)) = \{\delta_y\} \text{ (all } y \in Y_p)$$

and

$$\Phi_\beta(T, x_q(y)) = F(T, x_q(y)) = \{\delta_y\} \text{ (all } y \in Y_q)$$

at the terminal nodes, while

$$\Phi_\beta(T, n_p) = F(T, n_p) = \sum_{x \in X_p} \pi(x|n_p) F(T, x) = \sum_{y \in Y_p} p(y) \{\delta_y\} = \{p\}$$

$$\Phi_\beta(T, n_q) = F(T, n_q) = \sum_{x \in X_q} \pi(x|n_q) F(T, x) = \sum_{y \in Y_q} q(y) \{\delta_y\} = \{q\}$$

at the chance nodes. So finally the feasible set is

$$F(T) = F(T, n_0) = F(T, n_p) \cup F(T, n_q) = \{p\} \cup \{q\} = \{p, q\} \subset \Delta(Y; \mathbb{P})$$

Also the revealed choice set of consequences is $\Phi_\beta(T) = \Phi_\beta(T, n_0)$, where

$$p \in \Phi_\beta(T, n_0) \iff n_p \in \beta(T, n_0) \quad \text{and} \quad q \in \Phi_\beta(T, n_0) \iff n_q \in \beta(T, n_0)$$

Now ^0T differs from T only in replacing the probabilities $p(y)$ and $q(y)$ by their respective real parts $^0p(y)$, $^0q(y)$, while also excluding altogether any terminal nodes $x_p(y)$ or $x_q(y)$ for which $^0p(y) = 0$ or $^0q(y) = 0$, as appropriate. So a similar construction in ^0T shows that $F(^0T) = \{^0p, ^0q\} \subset \Delta(Y)$. Then the hypothesis $^0p \ P \ ^0q$ implies $\Phi_\beta(^0T) = \{^0p\}$. This obviously requires $\beta(^0T, n_0) = \{n_p\}$. But then the refinement axiom, even in its weak form, implies $\beta(T, n_0) = \{n_p\}$. Therefore $\Phi_\beta(T) = \{p\}$, implying that $p \ P \ q$. ∎

This lemma already gives the beginnings of a lexicographic preference criterion. It is incomplete, however, because in the case when $^0p \ I \ ^0q$ nothing yet has been said about what higher criterion determines whether or not $p \ P \ q$.

4.2. Lexicographic Preferences

This section will consider RPFs with values in $\mathscr{P}(\varepsilon)$ and show that there must be a complete lexicographic preference criterion in this special case. To this end, let

$$p(y; \varepsilon) = \frac{\sum_{i \in I} P_i \, p_i(y) \, \varepsilon^i}{\sum_{i \in I} P_i \, \varepsilon^i} \quad \text{and} \quad q(y; \varepsilon) = \frac{\sum_{j \in J} Q_j \, q_j(y) \, \varepsilon^j}{\sum_{j \in J} Q_j \, \varepsilon^j} \tag{20}$$

be any two RPFs $p, q \in \Delta(Y; \varepsilon)$ that have been expressed in the form (5). In particular, it must be true that $0 \in I \cap J$ and $P_0 = Q_0 = 1$, while $P_i > 0$, $p_i(\cdot) \in \Delta(Y)$ (all $i \in I$) and $Q_j > 0$, $q_j(\cdot) \in \Delta(Y)$ (all $j \in J$). Now these two RPFs can be given the common denominator

$$\sum_{k \in K} R_k \, \varepsilon^k := \sum_{i \in I} P_i \, \varepsilon^i \times \sum_{j \in J} Q_j \, \varepsilon^j$$

where $K := I + J$ (as the sum of the two sets of integers) and $R_k := \sum_{(i,j) \in H_k} P_i \, Q_j$ with $H_k := \{(i, j) \in I \times J \mid i + j = k\}$ (all $k \in K$). These definitions, together with the previously specified properties of I, J, and P_i ($i \in I$), Q_j ($j \in J$), also imply that $0 \in K$, while $R_0 = 1$ and $R_k > 0$ ($k \in K$). Then one has

$$p(y; \varepsilon) = \frac{\sum_{i \in I} P_i p_i(y) \varepsilon^i \times \sum_{j \in J} Q_j \varepsilon^j}{\sum_{k \in K} R_k \varepsilon^k} = \frac{\sum_{k \in K} \sum_{(i,j) \in H_k} P_i p_i(y) Q_j \varepsilon^k}{\sum_{k \in K} R_k \varepsilon^k} \qquad (21)$$

Now define $p_k^*(\cdot)$, $q_k^*(\cdot) \in \Delta(Y)$ (all $k \in K$) so that

$$p_k^*(y) := \sum_{(i,j) \in H_k} \frac{P_i Q_j}{R_k} p_i(y) \quad \text{and} \quad q_k^*(y) := \sum_{(i,j) \in H_k} \frac{P_i Q_j}{R_k} q_j(y) \qquad (22)$$

With this definition, (21) implies that

$$p(y; \varepsilon) = \frac{\sum_{k \in K} R_k p_k^*(y) \varepsilon^k}{\sum_{k \in K} R_k \varepsilon^k} \quad \text{and similarly} \quad q(y; \varepsilon) = \frac{\sum_{k \in K} R_k q_k^*(y) \varepsilon^k}{\sum_{k \in K} R_k \varepsilon^k}$$

So, after dropping the function arguments from the notation, one has

$$p = \frac{\sum_{k \in K} R_k p_k^* \varepsilon^k}{\sum_{k \in K} R_k \varepsilon^k} \quad \text{and} \quad q = \frac{\sum_{k \in K} R_k q_k^* \varepsilon^k}{\sum_{k \in K} R_k \varepsilon^k} \qquad (23)$$

Next, for any integer $m \in K$, define the following three subsets of K:

$$K_{<m} := \{ k \in K \mid k < m \} \qquad K_{>m} := \{ k \in K \mid k > m \}$$
$$K_{\geq m} := \{ k \in K \mid k \geq m \}$$

Furthermore, define

$$R^m(\varepsilon) := \sum_{k \in K_{\geq m}} R_k \varepsilon^k \qquad p^m := \frac{\sum_{k \in K_{\geq m}} R_k p_k^* \varepsilon^k}{R^m(\varepsilon)} \qquad q^m := \frac{\sum_{k \in K_{\geq m}} R_k q_k^* \varepsilon^k}{R^m(\varepsilon)}$$

$$(24)$$

Then one can rewrite (23) as

$$p = \frac{\sum_{k \in K_{<m}} R_k p_k^* \varepsilon^k + R^m(\varepsilon) p^m}{\sum_{k \in K_{<m}} R_k \varepsilon^k + R^m(\varepsilon)} \qquad q = \frac{\sum_{k \in K_{<m}} R_k q_k^* \varepsilon^k + R^m(\varepsilon) q^m}{\sum_{k \in K_{<m}} R_k \varepsilon^k + R^m(\varepsilon)}$$

In case $p_k^* I q_k^*$ for $k \in K_{<m}$, it follows from repeated application of the independence condition (18) that $p P q \iff p^m P q^m$.

Now, dividing by $R_m \varepsilon^m$ all the terms of both numerator and denominator in the definitions of p^m, q^m in (24) gives

$$p^m = \frac{p^*_m + \sum_{k \in K_{>m}} R_k \, p^*_k \, \varepsilon^{k-m} / R_m}{1 + \sum_{k \in K_{>m}} R_k \, \varepsilon^{k-m} / R_m}$$

and

$$q^m = \frac{q^*_m + \sum_{k \in K_{>m}} R_k \, q^*_k \, \varepsilon^{k-m} / R_m}{1 + \sum_{k \in K_{>m}} R_k \, \varepsilon^{k-m} / R_m}$$

The real parts of these probability distributions are therefore $^0 p^m = p^*_m$ and $^0 q^m = q^*_m$. Combining the above results with the refinement lemma then shows that, in case $p^*_k \, I \, q^*_k$ for all $k \in K_{<m}$, one has

$$p^*_m P q^*_m \iff {}^0 p^m P {}^0 q^m \implies p^m P q^m \iff p \, P \, q$$

and so $p^*_m \, P \, q^*_m \implies p \, P \, q$. Finally, in case $p^*_k I q^*_k$ for all $k \in K$, repeated application of the independence condition (18) shows that $p \, I \, q$. So it has been proved that:

Theorem
Suppose that the consequentialist axioms of Section 3.5 and the refinement axiom of Section 4.1 are all satisfied. Then, for all pairs of RPFs $p, q \in \Delta(Y; \varepsilon)$ given by (20), one has

$$p \, P \, q \iff \langle p^*_k \rangle_{k \in K} \, P_L \, \langle q^*_k \rangle_{k \in K}$$

where $\langle p^*_k \rangle_{k \in K}, \langle q^*_k \rangle_{k \in K} \in \Delta^K(Y)$ are the lexicographic hierarchies of probability distributions whose members are given by (22), and where P_L is the lexicographic preference criterion defined by

$$\langle p^*_k \rangle_{k \in K} \, P_L \, \langle q^*_k \rangle_{k \in K} \iff \exists m \in K : p^*_k \, I \, q^*_k \text{ (all } k \in K_{<m}) \, \& \, p^*_m \, P \, q^*_m$$

5. Continuity and von Neumann–Morgenstern Utility

5.1. Continuous Preferences

In Section 3.5 it was claimed that consequentialist behavior in trees $T \in \mathcal{T}(Y; \mathbb{P})$ must maximize a preference ordering R on $\Delta(Y; \mathbb{P})$ satisfying the non-Archimedean independence axiom (18). Because (18) implies the ordinary independence condition (17), two of Jensen's (1967) three axioms which imply expected utility maximization are satisfied. But discontinuous lexicographic preferences are still possible, even in trees with strictly positive ordinary probabilities at chance nodes. In single-person decision theory, the motivation for avoiding such discontinuities is not entirely clear, beyond analytical convenience and a feeling that continuity is anyway rather natural. In the case of n-person game theory, however, continuity of behavior as common expectations vary is crucial for the existence of equilibrium in general games.

To derive expected utility maximization, an axiom of continuity as probabilities vary—or what some have called an "Archimedean" axiom—will be added. The following was included as Jensen's (1967) third and last axiom, modifying Herstein and Milnor's (1953) simplification of the original von Neumann and Morgenstern (1944) formulation:

Restricted Continuity Axiom
If $\lambda, \mu, \nu \in \Delta(Y)$ *with* $\lambda P \mu$ *and* $\mu P \nu$, *then there exist real numbers* α *and* θ *with* $0 < \alpha < \theta < 1$ *such that*

$$[(1 - \alpha)\lambda + \alpha \nu] P \mu \quad \text{and} \quad \mu P [(1 - \theta)\lambda + \theta \nu]$$

As Jensen (1967) shows, this assumption, together with the fact that R is a preference ordering on $\Delta(Y)$ satisfying the independence axiom (17), implies the existence of a real-valued von Neumann–Morgenstern utility function (NMUF) v on Y such that

$$\lambda R \mu \iff \mathbb{E}_\lambda v \geq \mathbb{E}_\mu v \tag{25}$$

for all $\lambda, \mu \in \Delta(Y)$, where

$$\mathbb{E}_\lambda v := \sum_{y \in Y} \lambda(y) v(y) \tag{26}$$

denotes the expected value of v with respect to λ, and $\mathbb{E}_\mu v$ is defined similarly.

The two NMUFs v, $\tilde{v}$ on Y are said to be *cardinally equivalent* if there exist real numbers $\rho > 0$ and α such that $\tilde{v}(y) \equiv \alpha + \rho v(y)$ on Y. Then, as is well known, there is a unique cardinal equivalence class of NMUFs whose expected values all represent the ordering R on $\Delta(Y)$.

5.2. Continuous Behavior

Rather than assume directly continuity of preferences on the domain of ordinary probabilities $\Delta(Y)$, however, it is in the spirit of consequentialist decision theory to postulate continuity of behavior instead, whether or not that behavior is in fact consequentialist. Accordingly, let T be any ordinary decision tree in $\mathcal{T}(Y)$, with strictly positive real probabilities at all its chance nodes. Let n^* be any decision node of T, and n^0 any chance node of the subtree $T(n^*) \in \mathcal{T}(Y)$ whose initial node is n^*. Consider now a family of ordinary decision trees $T^\pi \in \mathcal{T}(Y)$ in which only the probability distribution $\pi = \pi(\cdot|n^0) \in \Delta(N_{+1}(n^0))$ at the chance node n^0 varies. To ensure that $\pi(n) > 0$ for all $n \in N_{+1}(n^0)$, and so that $T^\pi \in \mathcal{T}(Y)$, remove from T the entire subtree $T(n)$ following any node $n \in N_{+1}(n^0)$ with $\pi(n) = 0$. All the other features of the decision trees T^π should be entirely independent of the probabilities π.

Now, the behavior set $\beta(T^{\pi}, n^*)$ at the fixed decision node $n^* \in N^*$ is well defined and varies with π. Accordingly, one obtains a correspondence $\pi \longmapsto \beta(T^{\pi}, n^*)$ whose graph is

$$G_{\beta}(T, n^*, n^0) := \{ (\pi, n) \in \Delta(N_{+1}(n^0)) \times N_{+1}(n^*) \mid n \in \beta(T^{\pi}, n^*) \}$$

Since $\Delta(N_{+1}(n^0))$ is compact while $N_{+1}(n^*)$ is a finite set, this correspondence will have a compact graph, and so be upper hemicontinuous, provided that its graph is a closed set. So behavior β is said to be *continuous* provided that $G_{\beta}(T, n^*, n^0)$ is indeed closed, for every decision tree $T \in \mathcal{T}(Y)$, decision node $n \in N^*(T)$, and chance node $n^0 \in N^0(T(n^*))$. Formally, this is weaker than the stronger condition which requires β to be jointly continuous as *all* probabilities vary in each decision tree. In combination with the other axioms, however, the weaker continuity condition used here is actually equivalent to joint continuity.

The proof given in Hammond (1988b, section 9) shows how such continuous behavior implies the restricted continuity axiom stated in Section 5.1. Then there must indeed exist a unique cardinal equivalence class of von Neumann–Morgenstern utility functions whose expected values are maximized by the random consequences of behavior in the restricted trees of $\mathcal{T}(Y)$.

6. Non-Archimedean Expected Utility

6.1. Representing Lexicographic Preferences

Suppose that non-Archimedean probabilities are RPFs taking values in the positive cone $\mathcal{P}(\varepsilon)$. Suppose that the restricted continuity axiom of Section 5.1 is satisfied by consequentialist behavior in the domain $\mathcal{T}(Y; \varepsilon) := \mathcal{T}(Y; \mathcal{P}(\varepsilon))$ of all finite decision trees with such RPFs attached to their chance nodes. Then the restriction of the ordering R to $\Delta(Y)$ is represented by the expected value of an NMUF $v : Y \to \mathcal{R}$, as in (25).

Define the ordinary real-valued expected utility function $U : \Delta(Y) \to \mathcal{R}$ so that

$$U(\lambda) := \mathbb{E}_{\lambda} v = \sum_{y \in Y} \lambda(y) v(y) \tag{27}$$

for all $\lambda \in \Delta(Y)$. This definition can now be extended from ordinary probability distributions to RPFs in an obvious way. The result will be the *non-Archimedean expected utility function* $U(\cdot; \varepsilon) : \Delta(Y; \varepsilon) \to \mathcal{R}(\varepsilon)$ which is defined so that, given any

$$p = p(y; \varepsilon) = \frac{\sum_{i \in I} P_i \, p_i(y) \, \varepsilon^i}{\sum_{i \in I} P_i \, \varepsilon^i} \in \Delta(Y; \varepsilon)$$

one has

$$U(p; \varepsilon) := \mathbb{E}_p \, v = \sum_{y \in Y} p(y; \varepsilon) \, v(y) = \frac{\sum_{i \in I} P_i \sum_{y \in Y} p_i(y) \, v(y) \, \varepsilon^i}{\sum_{i \in I} P_i \, \varepsilon^i}$$

$$= \frac{\sum_{i \in I} P_i \, U(p_i) \, \varepsilon^i}{\sum_{i \in I} P_i \, \varepsilon^i} \tag{28}$$

Suppose that the refinement axiom of Section 4.1 is imposed in addition. Section 4.2 characterized the resulting lexicographic preferences. Now these preferences can be interpreted as maximizing expected utility with respect to the total ordering on the space $\mathscr{R}(\varepsilon)$. To see this, let $p, q \in \Delta(Y; \varepsilon)$ be any pair of rational probability functions of ε taking the form (20). They can be given a common denominator and put in the form

$$p = \frac{\sum_{k \in K} R_k \, p_k^* \, \varepsilon^k}{\sum_{k \in K} R_k \, \varepsilon^k} \qquad \text{and} \qquad q = \frac{\sum_{k \in K} R_k \, q_k^* \, \varepsilon^k}{\sum_{k \in K} R_k \, \varepsilon^k}$$

as in (23) of Section 4.2, with the ordinary probability distributions $p_k^*(\cdot), q_k^*(\cdot) \in \Delta(Y)$ given by (22), and with $R_k > 0$ (all $k \in K$). So $U(p; \varepsilon) > U(q; \varepsilon)$ in $\mathscr{R}(\varepsilon)$ if and only if

$$\frac{\sum_{k \in K} R_k \, U(p_k^*) \, \varepsilon^k}{\sum_{k \in K} R_k \, \varepsilon^k} - \frac{\sum_{k \in K} R_k \, U(q_k^*) \, \varepsilon^k}{\sum_{k \in K} R_k \, \varepsilon^k}$$

$$= \frac{\sum_{k \in K} R_k \, [U(p_k^*) - U(q_k^*)] \, \varepsilon^k}{\sum_{k \in K} R_k \, \varepsilon^k} > 0 \text{ in } \mathscr{R}(\varepsilon)$$

or if and only if

$$\sum_{k \in K} R_k \, [U(p_k^*) - U(q_k^*)] \, \varepsilon^k > 0 \text{ in } \mathscr{R}(\varepsilon) \tag{29}$$

But (29) is true if and only if the following lexicographic criterion is satisfied: There must exist an integer $m \in K$ for which $U(p_k^*) = U(q_k^*)$ whenever $k \in K$ with $k < m$, while $U(p_m^*) > U(q_m^*)$. However, for all $k \in K$ one has $U(p_k^*) > U(q_k^*) \iff p_k^* \, P \, q_k^*$. Also, the theorem stated at the end of Section 4.2 shows that

$$p \, P \, q \iff \exists m \in K : p_k^* \, I \, q_k^* \, (k < m) \, \& \, p_m^* \, P \, q_m^*$$

Finally, therefore, this chain of equivalences shows that $U(p; \varepsilon) > U(q; \varepsilon)$ in $\mathscr{R}(\varepsilon)$ if and only if $p \, P \, q$. This is true for all pairs $p, q \in \Delta(Y; \varepsilon)$. So the preference ordering R is perfectly represented by the non-Archimedean expected utility function $U(\cdot; \varepsilon)$, provided that the (lexicographic) total ordering in $\mathscr{R}(\varepsilon)$ is applied to each pair of non-Archimedean $\mathscr{R}(\varepsilon)$-valued expected utilities.

6.2. Why Refinement is Needed

Lemma

Suppose that $f(\varepsilon), g(\varepsilon) \in \mathscr{P}(\varepsilon)$ with $f(\varepsilon) > g(\varepsilon)$. Suppose too that $p, q \in \Delta(Y; \varepsilon)$ with $p\, P\, q$. Then, given any other $h(\varepsilon) \in \mathscr{P}(\varepsilon)$ and the two members $p_f, p_g \in \Delta(Y; \varepsilon)$ defined by

$$p_f := \frac{f(\varepsilon) p + h(\varepsilon) q}{f(\varepsilon) + h(\varepsilon)} \quad \text{and} \quad p_g := \frac{g(\varepsilon) p + h(\varepsilon) q}{g(\varepsilon) + h(\varepsilon)}$$

it must be true that $p_f\, P\, p_g$.

Proof. For the non-Archimedean expected utility function $U(\cdot; \varepsilon)$ which represents R on $\Delta(Y; \varepsilon)$, one has

$$U(p_f) - U(p_g) = \frac{f(\varepsilon)\, U(p; \varepsilon) + h(\varepsilon)\, U(q; \varepsilon)}{f(\varepsilon) + h(\varepsilon)} - \frac{g(\varepsilon)\, U(p; \varepsilon) + h(\varepsilon)\, U(q; \varepsilon)}{g(\varepsilon) + h(\varepsilon)}$$

$$= \frac{[f(\varepsilon) - g(\varepsilon)]\, h(\varepsilon)}{[f(\varepsilon) + h(\varepsilon)]\, [g(\varepsilon) + h(\varepsilon)]}\, [U(p; \varepsilon) - U(q; \varepsilon)] > 0$$

when $f(\varepsilon) > g(\varepsilon)$ and $p\, P\, q$, because then $f(\varepsilon) - g(\varepsilon)$, $f(\varepsilon)$, $g(\varepsilon)$, $h(\varepsilon)$, and $U(p; \varepsilon) - U(q; \varepsilon)$ are all positive elements of $\mathscr{R}(\varepsilon)$. ■

This lemma is important because it shows the need to distinguish the two members $f(\varepsilon), g(\varepsilon) \in \mathscr{P}(\varepsilon)$ whenever $f(\varepsilon) \neq g(\varepsilon)$. For if these two were not distinguished, the corresponding two members $p_f, p_g \in \Delta(Y; \varepsilon)$ would have to be regarded as identical, and so indifferent according to the conditional relation I. But then, since the order $\geq$ on $\mathscr{R}(\varepsilon)$ is total, one of the pair $f(\varepsilon), g(\varepsilon)$ is greater than the other—say, $f(\varepsilon) > g(\varepsilon)$. Finally, the lemma would imply that $p\, I\, q$ for all $p, q \in \Delta(Y; \varepsilon)$, so that all random consequences would have to be indifferent. For this reason, nontrivial consequentialist decision theory requires all the different members of $\mathscr{P}(\varepsilon)$ to be distinguished.

7. Main Theorem

Suppose probabilities take strongly positive values in the particular non-Archimedean field $\mathscr{R}(\varepsilon)$. For this particular case, the five assumptions introduced in previous sections are:

(A1) **Unrestricted domain**: There is a nonempty behavior set $\beta(T, n)$ $\subset N_{+1}(n)$ at every decision node n of every tree T in the domain $\mathscr{T}(Y; \varepsilon)$ of finite decision trees having (strongly positive) $\mathscr{P}(\varepsilon)$-valued probabilities at all chance nodes and consequences in Y at all terminal nodes.

(A2) **Dynamic consistency**: Whenever $T \in \mathscr{T}(Y; \varepsilon)$ and n' is a decision node of the subtree $T(n)$, then $\beta(T(n), n') = \beta(T, n')$.

(A3) **Consequentialist choice**: There is a revealed consequence choice function C_β such that the set $\Phi_\beta(T)$ of possible random consequences of behavior β in any tree $T \in \mathcal{T}(Y; \varepsilon)$ satisfies $\Phi_\beta(T) = C_\beta(F(T))$, where $F(T)$ is the set of random consequences which are feasible in T.

(A4) **Refinement**: Given any tree $T \in \mathcal{T}(Y; \varepsilon)$, let $^0T \in \mathcal{T}(Y)$ be the tree which is derived from T by replacing the $\mathcal{P}(\varepsilon)$-valued probabilities $\pi(n'|n; \varepsilon)$ $(n' \in N_{+1}(n))$ at each chance node n of T by their corresponding real parts $^0\pi(n'|n)$, followed by omitting any nodes which can only be reached with probability zero according to the probabilities $^0\pi$. Then one should have $\beta(T, n) \subset \beta(^0T, n)$ at every decision node n of ^0T.

(A5) **Restricted continuity**: For every ordinary decision tree $T \in \mathcal{T}(Y)$, decision node n^* in T, and chance node n^0 in the subtree $T(n^*)$ with initial node n^*, the correspondence $\pi \longmapsto \beta(T^\pi, n^*)$ from real-valued probabilities $\pi \in \Delta(N_{+1}(n^0))$ to behavior at n^* in the tree $T^\pi \in \mathcal{T}(Y)$ with probabilities π at n^0 has a closed graph.

Now:

Main Theorem

(1a) *Any behavior satisfying the first four axioms (A1)–(A4) above reveals a (complete and transitive) preference ordering R defined on $\Delta(Y; \varepsilon)$ with the properties that:*

   (i) *There is a restricted preference ordering ^0R on the space $\Delta(Y)$ which, whenever $\lambda, \mu, \nu \in \Delta(Y)$ and $0 < \alpha < 1$, satisfies the independence condition*

$$[\alpha \lambda + (1 - \alpha) \nu] \;^0R\; [\alpha \mu + (1 - \alpha) \nu] \Longleftrightarrow \lambda \;^0R\; \mu$$

   (ii) *Suppose that*

$$p = \frac{\sum_{k \in K} R_k p_k^* \varepsilon^k}{\sum_{k \in K} R_k \varepsilon^k} \quad and \quad q = \frac{\sum_{k \in K} R_k q_k^* \varepsilon^k}{\sum_{k \in K} R_k \varepsilon^k}$$

   are any two RPFs in $\Delta(Y; \varepsilon)$ that have been given a common denominator, while $R_k > 0$ and $p_k^*, q_k^* \in \Delta(Y)$ for all $k \in K$, where K is a nonempty set of nonnegative integers. Then one has $p \, P \, q$ if and only if the lexicographic criterion

$$\exists m \in K : p_k^* \;^0I\; q_k^* \; (k < m \;\&\; k \in K) \quad and \quad p_m^* \;^0P\; q_m^*$$

   is satisfied.

(1b) *Conversely, if R is any ordering defined on $\Delta(Y; \varepsilon)$ that is derived by applying the lexicographic criterion in part (ii) of (1a) to an ordering ^0R on $\Delta(Y)$ satisfying the independence condition in part (i) of (1a),*

then behavior that maximizes R in each decision tree of $\mathcal{T}(Y; \varepsilon)$ will
satisfy (A1)–(A4).

(2a) Behavior will satisfy all five axioms (A1)–(A5) above only if, in
addition, there is a unique cardinal equivalent class of NMUFs
$v: Y \to \mathcal{R}$ for which

$$\lambda \, {}^0 R \, \mu \iff \sum_{y \in Y} [\lambda(y) - \mu(y)] \, v(y) \geq 0 \qquad \text{whenever } \lambda, \mu \in \Delta(Y)$$

in which case the ordering R on $\Delta(Y; \varepsilon)$ is the unique ordering induced
by applying the (lexicographic) total order $\geq$ in $\mathcal{R}(\varepsilon)$ to values $U(p; \varepsilon)$
of the non-Archimedean expected utility function that is defined for all
$p \in \Delta(Y; \varepsilon)$ by

$$U(p; \varepsilon) := \sum_{y \in Y} p(y; \varepsilon) \, v(y)$$

(2b) Conversely, maximizing the non-Archimedean expected value of any
such NMUF in the (lexicographic) order of $\mathcal{R}(\varepsilon)$ will generate behavior satisfying (A1)–(A5).

Proof. First, (1a) is proved by combining the arguments of Hammond
(1988a, 1988b)—see also Section 3.5 above—with the theorem of Section
4.2. Conversely, (1b) is proved by a dynamic programming argument like
that in Hammond (1988b, section 8); the refinement axiom (A4) is then
obviously satisfied because of the lexicographic criterion in part (ii) of
(1a).

For (2a), Section 5 explained why (A5) would imply the existence of a
unique cardinal equivalence class of NMUFs, and then Section 6.1
showed that behavior would maximize non-Archimedean expected utility
in the (lexicographic) total order $\geq$ of $\mathcal{R}(\varepsilon)$. Conversely, the single hypothesis of (2b) obviously implies all the hypotheses of (1b), so (A1)–(A4) will
be satisfied. Furthermore, behavior in ordinary decision trees with random
consequences in $\Delta(Y)$ will maximize ordinary expected utility and so
satisfy the restricted continuity axiom (A5).   ■

An important corollary of this Main Theorem is that all attempts to treat as
equivalent any pair of non-Archimedean probability distributions having different values in $\mathcal{P}(\varepsilon)$ are doomed to fail. For, when combined with the five
axioms set out above, any such attempt leads to the unacceptable conclusion
that all non-Archimedean random consequences are indifferent—see Section
6.2.

Acknowledgments—During the academic year 1986–87, some initial work for this and
related papers was generously supported by the Guggenheim Foundation and by
C.O.R.E. at the Université Catholique de Louvain. Much of a preliminary draft entitled
"Consequentialism, Extended Probabilities, and Lexicographic Expected Utility" was

written during a fruitful visit, arranged by Joe Stiglitz, to the Department of Economics at Princeton University in the spring semester of 1987. Later, in spring 1988 I received support from the Deutsche Forschungsgemeinschaft through Sonderforschungsbereich 303 while visiting the University of Bonn as a guest of Dieter Bös.

The work reported here and in related papers owes its origins to particularly useful interaction with Adam Brandenburger and Eddie Dekel. C.O.R.E. also provided the opportunity for many helpful discussions with Jean-François Mertens. Earlier versions were incorporated in presentations to the conference on "Sequential Equilibria and Structural Stability" at Luminy, January 1987, to Reinhard Selten's workshop on "Game Theory in the Behavioral Sciences" at the Zentrum für Interdisziplinäre Forschung at the University of Bielefeld in April 1988, and to the mathematical economics seminars at Princeton, Stanford, Harvard, and Bonn Universities, as well as the University of California at San Diego. Other improvements and encouragement have resulted from helpful comments by several seminar participants, Bill Zame, Reinhard Selten, Barry Nalebuff, Avinash Dixit, Andrew Caplin, and Pierpaolo Battigalli in particular. My thanks to all of these individuals and institutions.

References

Blume, L., A. Brandenburger, and E. Dekel (1991a), "Lexicographic Probabilities and Choice Under Uncertainty," *Econometrica*, **59**: 61–79.

Blume, L., A. Brandenburger, and E. Dekel (1991b), "Lexicographic Probabilities and Equilibrium Refinements," *Econometrica*, **59**: 81–98.

Hammond, P.J. (1976), "Changing Tastes and Coherent Dynamic Choice," *Review of Economic Studies*, **43**: 159–73.

Hammond, P.J. (1988a), "Consequentialism and the Independence Axiom," in *Risk, Decision, and Rationality: Proceedings of the 3rd International Conference on the Foundations and Applications of Utility, Risk, and Decision Theories*, edited by B. Munier (Dordrecht: D. Reidel), pp. 503–16.

Hammond, P.J. (1988b), "Consequentialist Foundations for Expected Utility," *Theory and Decision*, **25**: 25–78.

Hammond, P.J. (1994), "Elementary Non-Archimedean Representations of Probability for Decision Theory and Games," in *Patrick Suppes: Scientific Philosopher, Vol. I: Probability and Probabilistic Causality*, edited by P. Humphreys (Dordrecht: Kluwer Academic Publishers), ch. 2, pp. 25–59.

Herstein, I.N. and J. Milnor (1953), "An Axiomatic Approach to Measurable Utility," *Econometrica*, **21**: 291–97.

Jensen, N.E. (1967), "An Introduction to Bernoullian Utility Theory, I: Utility Functions," *Swedish Journal of Economics*, **69**: 163–83.

Kreps, D. and R. Wilson (1982), "Sequential Equilibrium," *Econometrica*, **50**: 863–94.

Lindley, D.V. (1965), *Introduction to Probability and Statistics from a Bayesian Viewpoint, Part 1: Probability* (Cambridge: Cambridge University Press).

McLennan, A. (1989a), "The Space of Conditional Systems is a Ball," *International Journal of Game Theory*, **18**: 125–39.

McLennan, A. (1989b), "Consistent Conditional Systems in Noncooperative Game Theory," *International Journal of Game Theory*, **18**: 141–74.

Myerson, R. (1978), "Refinements of the Nash Equilibrium Concept," *International Journal of Game Theory*, **7**: 73–80.

Myerson, R. (1986), "Multistage Games with Communication," *Econometrica*, **54**: 323–58.

Raiffa, H. (1968), *Decision Analysis: Introductory Lectures on Choices under Uncertainty* (Reading, Mass.: Addison-Wesley).

Rényi, A. (1955), "On a New Axiomatic Theory of Probability," *Acta Mathematica Academiae Scientiarum Hungaricae*, **6**: 285–335.

Rényi, A. (1970), *Probability Theory* (New York: Elsevier).

Robinson, A. (1973), "Function Theory on Some Nonarchimedean Fields," *American Mathematical Monthly: Papers in the Foundations of Mathematics*, **80**: S87–S109.

Samuelson, P.A. (1952), "Probability, Utility, and the Independence Axiom," *Econometrica*, **20**: 670–78.

Selten, R. (1975), "Re-examination of the Perfectness Concept for Equilibrium Points of Extensive Games," *International Journal of Game Theory*, **4**: 25–55.

von Neumann, J. and O. Morgenstern (1944, 1953), *Theory of Games and Economic Behavior* (3d edn.) (Princeton: Princeton University Press).

CHAPTER 3

Solutions Based on Ratifiability and Sure Thing Reasoning

William Harper

Two-person extensive form games provide a context in which an explication of the von Neumann–Morgenstern indirect argument for restricting solutions to Nash equilibria can support refinements of the Nash solution concept. The causal information provided by the tree structure of the extensive form can be used to show that some Nash equilibrium strategies will not pass the test provided by the demand that choice of that strategy be ratifiable under the assumptions for applying the indirect argument to it. This provides for a more subtle form of forward induction than that discussed in Kohlberg and Mertens (1986). It also generates set valued solutions in some extensive form games they used to discuss set valued solutions generated by their concept of stability.

In normal form contexts the application of the basic test must be followed up by further tests if a refinement is to be provided for.[1] One natural idea is to follow it up by an application of Savage's sure thing principle to rule out weakly dominated strategies.[2] This normal form refinement gives the solution for each of the games that was used to show that the basic test provided an interesting refinement in the extensive form.[3]

Van Damme's money burning game provides a vivid example where simple forward induction in the extensive form gives a surprising result that is backed up by sure thing reasoning in the normal form. The extensive form of the indirect test also backs up this result. Finally, Stalnaker's models provide an excellent framework in which to explore the assumptions used in the test and the solutions arrived at when the test is successful.

1. The Indirect Test in Extensive Form Games

Consider yourself a player in a two-person noncooperative game. You make the classical game theoretic assumptions that the rationality of the players, the game tree, and the utilities of each player for each possible outcome are common knowledge. Provisionally at least, you assume that the game has a solution that rational players will end up commonly knowing they will do their parts to realize. You have not yet, however, figured out what the solution to the game is. Under these assumptions the following test can be applied to rule out candidate strategies that are not eligible to count as part of the solution.[4] To apply the test to a strategy X, assume provisionally that X is your part of the solution. Given the rest of the assumptions, this assumption about X supports the belief that the other player will make some best reply to X. Strategy X will fail the test if, given this belief, you would expect that you would be better off doing something else instead of X.

Let us use the simple forward induction game in Figure 3.1 to introduce the application of the indirect test to extensive form games.[5] You are player 1. On the assumption that you will end up playing BC as your part of the solution, you will expect that player 2 will play e and your expected utility for playing BC will be 3. On the assumption that you are going to play BC, you would be better off playing A instead. We have $U_{BC}(BC) = 3$ but $U_{BC}(A) = 4$, where $U_{BC}(BC)$ is the utility of BC on the assumption that you are going to end up playing it and $U_{BC}(A)$ is the utility on the assumption that you will end up playing BC that you would expect if you were to play A instead.

Under the assumptions of the indirect test, choice of strategy BC is unratifiable. Choice of an act X is unratifiable just in case the assumption that you are going to end up doing it supports the expectation that you would be better off doing something else instead. Choice of X is ratifiable just in case $U_X(X) \geq U_X(X')$ for all alternatives X'. Ratifiability is a condition on individual rational choice.[6]

We have seen how BC fails the test. The best reply to BD is f, so that $U_{BD}(BD) = 10$, which is as high as player 1's expected utility of any act. BD passes the test. Indeed, it is the only strategy (mixed or pure; Harper 1991, 284)

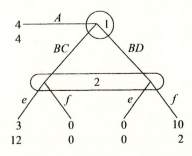

Figure 3.1

of player 1 that meets player 2's information set that does pass the test. To see that *A* fails the test, note that, if you were to play *BD* instead of *A*, player 2 would know that you had not played *A*. Whatever you may have assumed player 2 would plan, given that *A* was your part of the solution, your assessment of what player 2 would do if you were to do *BD* instead depends on what you would expect player 2 to reason about you were player 2 to actually reach the information set that your choice would put her in. As *BD* is the only choice of yours that both passes the test and reaches player 2's information set, you can expect that player 2 would believe that you had played *BD* if she were to be put in the information set. You would therefore expect that player 2 would play *f*, her best response to *BD*, if you were to put her in the information set. Thus, choice of *A* does not pass the test, since $U_A(A) = 4$ but $U_A(BD) = 10$.[7]

Consider the game in Figure 3.2.[8] In this game *M* is the only strategy of player 1 that meets player 2's first information set and also passes the indirect test (Harper 1991, 288–90), as was the case with *BD* in the simple forward induction game. This leads to the outcome where *M* and *r* are played and illustrates the subtlety of the forward induction reasoning that can be supported by the indirect test in extensive form games.[9] It also allows player 2's specification of what he would do in the zero sum subgame if his choice of *r* turned out to be made in the other branch leading to his information set to be any mixture $yl'(l - y)r'$, where *y* is between 1/8 and 7/8 so that player 1 would not be enticed away from *M* if he were to figure out that player 2 was committed to playing the *y* mixture if the subgame were reached.

The simpler game shown in Figure 3.3 also illustrates such a set valued solution. In addition, unlike either of the previous games, what will count as the solution does not reach player 2's information set at all.[10] For player 2 the

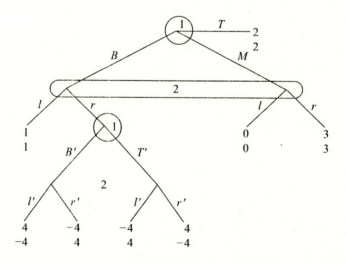

Figure 3.2

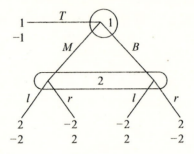

Figure 3.3

set of strategies that pass the test are exactly those mixed strategies $(pl, (1 - p)r)$ where $1/4 \leq p \leq 3/4$. For player 1, any strategy other than T will fail the test.

What about T itself? An assumption of the test is that player 2 has figured out that player 1 is committed to playing T as 1's part of the solution that all rational players are committed to do their parts in. When player 1 evaluates what she would expect if she were to play an alternative X instead of T she knows that player 2 would know that T had not been played. For T to pass the test, for each alternative X, her playing X instead of T must be compatible with her assigning probability between $1/4$ and $3/4$ to player 2's doing l.

2. The Test with Sure Thing Reasoning in Normal Form Games

Consider the game shown in Figure 3.4, which has the same normal form as the one we have been considering. In this game tree player 2's choices are causally independent of player 1's, so that to see that T passes the test it is sufficient to note T would be best against at least some best reply to it. Player 1 does not have to evaluate what player 2 would do if player 2 were to actually find out that player 1 had not played T in order to evaluate what to expect if she were to play some alternative X instead.[12]

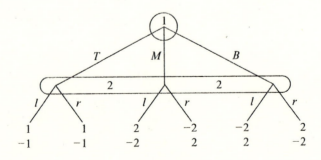

Figure 3.4

The normal form for these games is

	l	r
T	(1, −1)	(1, −1)
M	(2, −2)	(−2, 2)
B	(−2, 2)	(2, −2)

The normal or strategic form masks any information about causal dependencies that is built into an extensive form game. When the indirect test is applied to the normal form of a game, the player's choices are treated as if they were causally independent, as would be the case in the second version of the extensive form game.

When the independence built into the normal form applies, all Nash strategies (strategies which are part of any Nash equilibrium) pass the test (Harper 1991, 275). In this game the normal form application leads to a set of strategies that can realize the provisional assumption made by the test. This counts as a solution because every pairing of T with any one of the strategies in the set is an equilibrium. Knowledge that the other player would do their part would give neither player grounds to shift from their part.

Consider the normal form for the simple forward induction game:

	e	f
A	(4, 4)	(4, 4)
BC	(3, 12)	(0, 0)
BD	(0, 0)	(10, 2)

If we apply the indirect argument to this normal form game, the only strategy that fails the test is row-chooser's strategy BC, which is not part of any equilibrium.

In the normal form the result of applying the indirect test to this game does not result in an exchangeable set of equilibria, so it cannot be regarded as having succeeded in finding a solution. The result of eliminating BC does, however, make column-chooser's strategy e weakly dominated, so that Savage's sure thing principle can be applied to rule it out.[13] The result of following up the indirect argument with such an application of sure thing reasoning will, therefore, be that the solution is the single equilibrium pair (BD, f), just as it was in the extensive form game using the indirect test alone.[14]

Here is the normal form for the more complex game in which the solution was in player 2's information set:

	l	r, r′	r, l′
T	(2, 2)	(2, 2)	(2, 2)
M	(0, 0)	(3, 3)	(3, 3)
BB′	(1, 1)	(−4, 4)	(4, −4)
BT′	(1, 1)	(4, −4)	(−4, 4)

The first-stage application of the indirect argument rules out BB′ and BT′ for row-chooser and any mixture $yrl'((1 − y)rr')$ for column chooser where the probability y of rl' is either lower than 1/8 or higher than 7/8. Once the B strategies have been ruled out for row-chooser, sure thing reasoning applies to limit column-chooser to the admissible rl', rr' mixtures.[15] This yields the set of pairs (M, yl') where $1/8 \leq y \leq 7/8$.[16] All these pairs are interchangeable equilibria. Neither player would have grounds to depart from their part if they found out the other player was playing one of that player's specified strategies.

In all these games the normal form application of the test, followed up by sure thing reasoning to eliminate weakly dominated strategies if necessary, yields the same solution that was generated in the extensive form application, even when the extensive form application appealed to causal dependencies that were not represented in the normal form.[17]

3. Burning Money

Van Damme (1989) has presented some games in which allowing one of the players the option of publicly burning some money before making her move in a symmetric battle of the sexes game presents that player with a signaling opportunity that uniquely picks out that player's desired equilibrium even when that player does not burn the money. The mere existence of the asymmetric opportunity is enough to make simple forward induction pick out that as the salient equilibrium. Van Damme showed that this forward induction reasoning is backed up by sure thing reasoning in that the same result is obtained by eliminating weakly dominated strategies. He also showed that Kohlberg and Mertens' stable paths lead to it. The indirect test in the extensive form provides an additional argument to this result.

The tree for a version of this game is depicted in Figure 3.5.[18] Consider the indirect test for BR, the option of signaling and then playing weak.

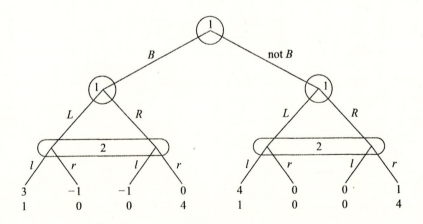

Figure 3.5

$U_{BR}(BR) = 0$, since, on the assumption that BR is player 1's part of the solution, player 2 will make a best reply which is to play r. $U_{BR}(BL) = -1$, so if BR is to be unratifiable it must lose to some not B option.[19] Any such option would give player 2 information that some not B option had been played instead of BR.[20] Any belief of player 1 that assigned positive probability to player 2's playing r at the information set for not B would make not-B,R beat B, R and any assignment of positive probability to l at that same information set would make not-B,L beat it. BR is therefore not ratifiable on the assumption that it is player 1's part of the solution, since doing not-B,R or doing not-B,L instead of BR would take player 2 to the same information set and player 1 must assign positive probability to either l or r on the assumption that player 2 reaches that information set.[21]

Any mixed strategy that meets the B information set and assigns positive probability to BR will fail to pass the test.[22] The results so far leave BL as the only strategy that meets the B information set that could pass the test.[23] Now look at not-B,R. On the assumption that it realizes player 1's part of the solution, player 2 will make her best reply r, so $U_{\text{not-}B,R}(\text{not-}B,R) = 1$. When player 1 considers what would result if she were to play BL instead she can use the result that BL is the only strategy meeting the B information set that could pass the test to infer that player 2 would play l if he were to be put at that information set. This makes $U_{\text{not-}B,R}(BL) = 3$ and shows that not-B,R fails the test. None of the mixed strategies that assigns positive probability to not-B,R will pass.[24] Strategy not-B,L does pass the test, since $U_{\text{not-}B,L}(\text{not-}B,L) = 4$, which is as high as any outcome can be. Now that it has been established that not-B,L is the only not-B strategy that passes the test, we can show that BL fails since, even on the assumption that BL is player 1's part of the solution, player 1 would be better off choosing not-B,L instead.

It does not seem out of line that when players share the knowledge that they are in such an asymmetric version of the game, the player who is known to be the only one with the opportunity to signal her commitment to her favored equilibrium should not have to actually burn the money in order to make clear the strategic advantage both players already know she has.

It may be surprising that an act that intuitively would be available to either player (but would be commonly regarded as irrelevant) in a real situation that we would be inclined to model as a symmetric battle of the sexes game could have such consequences. For such surprise to undercut the reasonableness of forward induction or removal of weakly dominated strategies, it would need to turn out that irrational recommendations to burn were forthcoming in more symmetric versions of the game where the opportunities to burn would correspond to acts that would be available in such situations.[25] I doubt that such examples can be found. Rather, the lesson to be drawn seems to be that setting up a game to represent a real strategic situation is more subtly dependent on the details of the situation than may have been thought.[26]

4. Stalnaker Models

Stalnaker (this volume) has provided interesting models in which the knowledge and beliefs of the agents are explicitly represented. These models are designed to represent a particular play of a game by agents who already know what they are going to do, who know their own beliefs—which are assumed to be coherent—and who know the options available and the utilities of outcomes for all the players. In order to represent all the options that the game specifies are open to the players, the models do not build in the assumption that the players' choices are rational. Particular assumptions about rationality can be investigated by looking at the Stalnaker models in which the play of the game in the actual world is by agents who satisfy those assumptions.

The Stalnaker framework can be applied to the indirect test of a player's choice of a strategy by checking whether any model where that choice is made is compatible with the assumptions of the test. The highest ranked assumption is that it is common knowledge that players actually maximize expected utility. The two provisional assumptions are that it is common knowledge that the game has a solution that the players will end up commonly knowing they will do their parts to realize and the, even more provisional, assumption that strategy X, the one under test, realizes its player's part of this solution.

In the normal form application of the indirect test to the simple forward induction game, the reasoning sketched above shows that there is no Stalnaker model where strategy BC passes the test. Strategies A and BD, however, both pass the test to use Stalnaker models to recover the reasoning sketched above, either the models have to be extended to take into account the causal information built into an extensive form game (that is suppressed in its normal form representation) or some way of representing the follow-up of the indirect test by sure thing reasoning must be provided.

Both can be done. Here are the sort of assumptions that would provide for the sure thing follow-up. After the most highly ranked assumption, and before the provisional assumptions, rank the additional assumption that it is common knowledge that agents do not play weakly dominated strategies. This is not by itself enough. We need to specify what the beliefs will be after applying the indirect argument. The first step after the indirect argument is to allow only those models where the beliefs of each agent about the other allow exactly the alternatives left open by the indirect test. The outcome of this step will eliminate models where the chosen strategies are weakly dominated relative to these alternatives. Go on to the models where the beliefs of each agent about the other correspond to the outcome of the preceding step. Continue in such stages until no further eliminations result.[27]

The outcome of these tests in the relevent normal form representations will leave exactly the models where the actual strategies are those specified in the solutions discussed above. In these games, common belief can be substituted for common knowledge in the assumptions that are ranked to control how the agents would revise their beliefs under various suppositions. The work is done by the provisional assumptions and by the ranking that makes common knowledge of rationality more secure than those assumptions.[28]

5. What Counts as a Solution?

In what sense is a solution reached by successful application of the indirect test a solution? Stalnaker's models can help analyze this question. We have said that an application is successful in reaching a solution when the strategies left form an interchangeable set of Nash equilibria. Comparison with the the battle of the sexes game where the indirect test does not reach such a solution can help make clear what is provided when such a solution is reached.

In the symmetric battle of the sexes game used to illustrate what would be provided by adding opportunities to burn money, the indirect test allows L,R and the mixed strategy $(\frac{1}{5}L, \frac{4}{5}R)$ for player 1 and l,r and the mixed strategy $(\frac{4}{5}l, \frac{1}{5}r)$ for player 2. Assume the outcome is common belief that each player will play one of these strategies that pass the test. This does not provide for common belief that the player's choices will be ratifiable. For any of the choices left open to either player there are worlds compatible with common belief in which that player would be better off choosing some other alternative instead.[29]

By contrast, common belief that both players will choose their strategies from the same set of interchangeable equilibria supports common belief that their choices are ratifiable. Indeed, any Stalnaker model where such a solution is reached is one where both agents know that their choice is ratifiable on the defeasibility account of knowledge discussed by Stalnaker. According to this account, your belief that your choice was ratifiable can count as knowledge if you both are doing your parts in this solution, because no adding of factual information such as the actual choice of the other agent would undercut it.

Consider player 2 in the Kohlberg and Mertens figure 10 game. After the test you have found that (T, pl) where $1/4 \le p \le 3/4$ is the solution. T is a best reply to each mixture and each is a best reply to T. What is to count as factual information in a world where player 2 has decided to play some mixed strategy, say $p = 0.4$, in the solution set? As long as the factual information that can be added is restricted to the chance specified in one of the admissible mixtures, such information will not undercut common belief that the player's choices are mutually ratifiable. Under these assumptions, such a solution will yield common knowledge of mutual ratifiability of the choices.

What should you assume if you were now to go on and commit yourself to choice of l, which is also a best reply to T? You are not, as you were in the indirect test, assuming that you are doing l as your part of the solution; therefore, you are no longer under assumptions that make you expect that player 1 will have chosen a best reply. We cannot use best reply reasoning to criticize your choice. We can, however, point out that your commitment to choose l, rather than one of the admissible mixtures,[30] would undercut common knowledge that your and the other player's choices are mutually ratifiable.[31] It would also seem to undercut whatever reasonable grounds you may have had for assuming that you know that your own choice is ratifiable.

Notes

Acknowledgment—I am grateful to Robert Stalnaker for consultations which saved me from error and which guided me to understand more about symmetric opportunities to burn in the van Damme game.

1. When the test is applied to two-person normal form games, the causal independence between the players' choices of strategies built into the normal form has the effect that the set of strategies that pass the test are exactly the strategies that are part of some Nash equilibrium (Harper 1988, 35–37). In the normal form the application of the von Neumann–Morgenstern test is no refinement at all to the Nash solution concept.

2. This natural idea generates a normal form refinement (Harper 1991, 279–80) that not only provides for trembling hand perfection but that also yields the correct solution in the game Myerson (1978) used to motivate his proposal to strengthen perfection to the requirement that equilibria be proper if they are to be able to count as candidates for solutions.

3. The refinement also provides an argument against a proposal by Harsanyi and Selten (1988) for a solution concept based on a very strong form of backward induction. This argument was an application of the indirect test to an extensive form game that they introduced to meet a challenge from Kohlberg and Mertens—to provide two games with the same normal form but having different solutions, each of which is intuitively compelling. This challenge was directed to those who would defend Kreps and Wilson's (1982) suggestion that the extensive form information (not available in the normal form representation of a game) is vital to solutions for some games.

4. This is the test suggested by von Neumann and Morgenstern's (1994, 147–48) indirect argument. It was introduced in Harper (1988); it was defended as an appropriate version of the sort of hypothetical post hoc reasoning called for in von Neumann and Morgenstern's argument in Harper (1989); and it was applied to generate a refinement for extensive form games in Harper (1991).

5. This game results from collapsing player 1's two information sets in the Harsanyi and Selten subgame game (see figure 9.7, p. 281 in Harper (1991) and figure 10.9, p. 351 in Harsanyi and Selten (1988)), which they argued could be used to answer Kohlberg and Merten's challenge. The application of the test to this game was given in Harper (1991). The details of the application are repeated here as a convenient way to introduce what is involved in the test.

6. Ratifiability was introduced by Richard Jeffrey (1983). Causal decision theory provides for the following explication of the conditional expectations relevant for assessing ratifiability (Harper 1986).

$$U_X(X') = \sum_i P(X'\square \rightarrow b_i | X) u(X', b_i)$$

where the b_i are the relevant outcome-determining states, each $X'\square \rightarrow b_i$ is the subjunctive conditional "If I were do X' (instead of X) then b_i would be the case," and $u(X', b_i)$ is the utility of doing X' when b_i is the case. The information about causal dependence and independence of the one player's choices on the other's informs the evaluation of the conditional probabilities of these conditions (Harper 1991, 266–70).

Jeffrey's original formulation was based on the idea (Selten 1975) of leaving some small probability that a mistake will happen. See Shin (1991) for two versions of ratifiability based on this idea, and Shin (1992) for a version of ratifiability based on an interpretation of counterfactuals that builds in the independence assumptions appropriate to the normal form representation of a game. The extensive form can introduce causal dependencies that will violate these independence assumptions, as is the case in the present forward induction game.

7. The forward induction argument discussed by Kohlberg and Mertens also supports (BD, f) as the solution of this game. According to this argument, when player 2 is actually confronted with the information set she will know that player 1 has given up the payoff of utility 4 in order to choose an act that reaches the information set. Of the two pure acts that do reach it, only BD can have a payoff higher than 4 for player 1; therefore, player 1 can expect player 2 to realize that by putting her in the information set player 1 has signaled the choice of BD.

This solution for this game is also supported by sure thing reasoning, since player 1's act BC is dominated by A. The application of the indirect test was offered (Harper 1991, 283–85) as an additional argument to these two, which were both discussed and rejected by Harsanyi and Selten (1988, 350–53).

8. This game does not allow the simple sort of forward induction to apply, since both the B and the M branches offer opportunities for payoffs higher than the T branch where player 1 can guarantee herself an expectation of 2 by choosing to avoid the subgame.

9. This game is a version (where the first two information sets of player 1 have been identified) of the game in figure 6 of Kohlberg and Mertens (1986, 1016). They point out that bad equilibria where player 1 sticks with T satisfy very many of the refinements that had been suggested in the literature (p. 1016). I used this game to illustrate that the indirect test can successfully reach a solution without specifying the exact strategies that would be played off the equilibrium path (Harper 1991, 289).

10. This is a version of the game given in figure 10 of Kohlberg and Mertens (1986).

11. In this extensive form game T would pass if, for every alternative strategy X, $P(X\square \rightarrow 1|T)$ is between 1/4 and 3/4. Many such assignments of conditional belief to counterfactuals are compatible with the assumption that T will be played as player 1's part of the solution, even if the antecedent of the counterfactual would give player 2 information that T had not been played.

If player 1 were committed absolutely to the idea that the game has a solution binding on all rational players and that T is the unique choice that realizes her part in it, then she would assume that her choice of X would lead to a breakdown of common knowledge of rationality. For example, she might attribute to 2 the belief that her choice was a mistake, or attribute to 2 the belief that she (player 1) expects that player 2 is going to make a mistake that she can take advantage of by playing something other than T. This would make the ratifiability of her choice of T depend on her judgements about what to expect in such breakdowns of common knowledge of rationality.

The assumptions in the indirect test are ordered so that, in games where it can generate a solution, ratifiability of recommended choices need not depend on judgments about what to expect when common knowledge of rationality breaks down. Here is what this ranking will lead player 1 to expect were 2 to find out that she had not played T. Lowest ranked is the provisional assumption that T is 1's part of the solution. Giving this up, however, will not remove the difficulty when 2 has discovered that all the rest of

1's choices have actually failed the test. Now 1 can assume that 2 will have to give up the more highly ranked provisional assumption that the game has a solution that all rational players will do their parts to realize.

The even more highly ranked assumption of common knowledge that the players maximize expected utility can be maintained, so 1 will assume that 2 does so. This requires that 2 assign to 1 beliefs that would optimize some choice other than T. Only beliefs where 1 assigns at most 1/4 or at least 3/4 as 1's epitemic probability for 2's playing 1 can do this. This limits 1's optimal strategies to the two pure strategies M and B (and to mixtures of each of them with T).

Any of 2's strategies is rationalizable by some assignment or other distributing 2's beliefs over these rationalizable options of 1. This allows for cases where 1's epistemic probability for 2 playing 1 would remain between 1/4 and 3/4, for every alternative X that 1 might choose instead of T. The assumptions of the indirect argument are, therefore, compatible with strategy T counting as player 1's part of the solution.

12. In general, when the other player's choice among the b_i is causally independent of whether or not a given player chooses an alternative X instead of strategy A, we have that $P(X\square \rightarrow b_i|A) = P(b_i|A)$ (Harper 1991, 267).

13. Some advantages of Savage's sure thing principle as the basis for eliminating weakly dominated strategies are suggested in Harper (1991, 273–80). One important advantage is that it movitates removing all weakly dominated strategies for either player, before considering further stages of elimination. This avoids the objectionable order dependencies which arise when sequential elimination of weakly dominated strategies is taken one strategy at a time.

14. In this game the strategy BC, which failed the test, was also strongly dominated by A, so that removing dominated strategies in stages would have been sufficient to reach the correct solution.

15. In this game the application of the indirect test to rule out the B strategies cannot be replaced by sure thing reasoning since no strategies are strongly or weakly dominated until the B strategies have been eliminated.

16. The indirect argument was applied to the extensive form of this game in Harper (1991, 288–90). It is a game where the extensive form application of the indirect test clearly gives the same set valued solution as it gives in the normal form discussed below.

17. This also turns out to be the case in the extensive form game from Kreps and Wilson's figure 9 that was also discussed in Harper (1991).

18. Here is the simple forward induction argument. By burning, player 1 would have given up a sure expectation of at least 0; therefore, player 2 can expect that player 1 played L if player 2 reaches player 2's information set where player 1 has burned, since that is the only option that would offer player 1 a chance of doing better than 0. Player 2, therefore, would play 1 (the best reply to L), which will give player 1 a payoff of 3.

This result, in turn, supports the further forward induction that, since player 1 could have expected 3 by burning, he must expect more than 3 if she gives up the opportunity to burn. This leads player 2 to expect that player 1 has played L when player 2 is put in the information set where player 1 has not burned.

As one might expect from van Damme's result about eliminating weakly dominated strategies, the result of following up the normal form version of the indirect test by such elimination also supports the forward induction argument in this game.

Van Damme uses a (3,1) rather than a (4,1) version of the symmetric battle of the sexes game as is done here. He also gives what would count as the stable paths afforded by the opportunity to burn amounts of money corresponding to different utility losses.

19. Choosing *BL* instead of *BR* would leave player 2 in the same information set that he would be in under the assumption that BR was played as player 1's part of the solution. Player 2's choice between *l* and *r* at that information set is, therefore, causally independent of whether player 1 were to stick to her assumed commitment to play *BR* or were to play *Bl* instead. This gives $P(BL \square \to r|BR) = P(r|BR)$.

20. Here we have causal dependence, as the choice of say not-*B,L* (rather than *BR*) would put player 2 in a different information set.

21. Player 2's choice between *l* or *r* is independent of whether player 1 plays not-*B,R* or not-*B,L*, since either would put player 2 into the same information set. This independence requires that $P(\text{not-}B,R \square \to l|BR) = P(\text{not-}B,L \square \to l|BR)$ and that they both equal $P(l|\text{not-}B)$.

22. For mixed strategy $x_1(BL)$, $x_2(BR)$, $x_3(\text{not-}B,L)$, $x_4(\text{not-}B,R)$, let $y = x_2/x_1 + x_2$, the conditional probability of *BR* given that the *B* information set was reached. If $y > 1/5$, then *r* is best against the mixture *x* at the *B* information set so that, as was the case with *BR*, whatever player 1 assigns as her probability of *l* being played were player 2 to reach the not-*B* information set, the mixture will be beaten by the result of adding the probabilities x_1 and x_2 to either not-*B,L* or not-*B,R*.

23. Without specific information about what strategies that meet the not-*B* information set pass the test one cannot establish whether *BL* would fail, for it is only not-*B,L* that could beat it and it would do so only if not-*B,R* (and mixtures assigning sufficiently high probability to it) can be ruled out. The corresponding information that all but *Bl* are ruled out at the *B* information set did not depend on such specific results about the not-*B* set.

24. Consider a mixed strategy $x_1(BL)$, $x_2(BR)$, $x_3(\text{not-}B,L)$, $x_4(\text{not-}B,R)$ and, this time, let $y = x_3/x_3 + x_4$ the conditional probability of not-*B,L* given that the not-*B* information set was reached. Suppose $y > 4/5$. This makes *l* the best reply to the mixture in the not-*B* information set, so that not-*B,L* would beat it. When $y < 4/5$, *r* is best against it at the not-*B* information set, so *BL* would beat it. When $y = 4/5$, then *l* ties with *r* at the not-*B* information set. Let *p* be player 1's epistemic probability for 2's playing *l* given that the mixture met the not-*B* information set. If $p < 3/4$, player 1 would want to play *BL* instead of the mixture, but if $p > 1/5$, then not-*B,L* would beat the mixture.

25. An example is a situation where either player could transform the basic game by initiating an act that would count as a burn, but would know that the other player would then have the opportunity to burn too. Choosing to initiate a burn in such a situation would amount to making oneself the first to play in a sequential burn game where the other player got to move second. The normal form for such a sequential game has 8 strategies for the first player and 16 for the second. Iterated removal of weakly dominated strategies leads to the result that the second player's equilibrium will be reached and that the second player does not have to burn to reach it. This result also holds in the game that results when the second player is confronted with the first player having already burned.

Van Damme offers results for symmetric versions where the two players simultaneously have the opportunity to burn or not and both will know the outcome before they play the main battle of the sexes game. He points out that Kohlberg and Mertens's stability requires equilibria that give some positive probability to burning, but that elimination of weakly dominated strategies does not lead to this result. Elimination of weakly dominated strategies gives very little guidance. The indirect test followed by elimination gives slightly more, but does not lead to a solution. Stability gives quite a bit of guidance but also does not lead to a solution.

Robert Stalnaker led me to see that complex mixed strategies that offer some chance of burning (as do those recommended by stability) will pass the indirect test and do not seem at all irrational. He suggested the following: For player 1 play B in the burn game with probability x; then if the outcome of the simultaneous opportunity to burn is B; not-b where player 1 burns and player 2 does not, player 1 plays L (strong); if the outcome is not-B; b where player 1 does not burn and player 2 does, player 1 plays R (weak); for both burn and for both do not burn, player 1 plays her maximin mixed strategy for the basic game (1/5 strong and 4/5 weak). If player 2 plays the equivalent strategy, then setting the probability of burning at 1/17 will make the payoff for each independent of whether the other player burns or not and the two strategies will be an equilibrium. This mixed strategy offers a higher expected utility (0.9294) at this equilibrium than the simple maximin strategy does in the basic game (0.8).

26. More positively, some real situations may be illuminated by identifying what can count as opportunities to burn before proceeding to what can be modeled as a battle of the sexes game. Stalnaker (in conversation) has suggested that this might illuminate some of the maneuvering that can go on before a negotiation.

27. This use of the belief sets in Stalnaker models has the nice effect of automatically removing at once all strategies that become weakly dominated at any stage.

28. Stalnaker has remarked (see this volume) that in order to validate forward induction and iterated weak dominance, *in general*, an implausibly strong assumption of robust common belief in rationality is required. In the games discussed here, the applications of the indirect test and weak dominance to rule out candidate strategies do not require any such implausibly strong assumption.

29. If, for example, player 1 plays the mixed strategy but player 2 plays l, then player 1 would have been better off playing T.

For a player using the indirect test to reason out what to do, this may undercut the provisional assumption that the game has such a solution unless that player has available some follow-up tests that would lead to a solution. A theorist, on the other hand, would be in a position to leave the question open until further investigation makes it clearer whether or not such follow-ups are plausible.

An approach like that of Harsanyi that aims for a method that will provide a solution for any game will exploit the symmetry here to argue for the mixed equilibrium. The weaker concept of rationalizability, which in this game allows all strategies, is what would result in a Stalnaker model where the provisional assumption that the game had a solution was given up. I think that unless the context allows for some way to make one of the equilibria salient, or makes available resources such as those assumed in bargaining, this game is one for which one should not demand that a theory provide a solution.

30. This depends on being able to make sense of the difference between committing yourself to l directly and assuming that you will end up playing l when you execute a mixed strategy having, say, a 0.4 chance of leading you to do l (it may therefore present a situation where an agent has a motive for choosing a mixed strategy). As long as the agents can be assumed to be provided with appropriate random devices with which to execute their mixed strategies, the differences can be made sense of in a straightforward way. The commitment that will matter for the analysis is that to which mixed strategy to execute, not, say, your commitment to choose l once the random device happens to have so instructed you.

31. Here is an argument that, in two-person games at least, a Stalnaker model where there is common knowledge (in the defeasibility sense) of mutual ratifiability is one where there is common commitment of the players to choose strategies that realize

their parts in the same exchangeable set of Nash equilibria, or is one where it is common knowledge that the choices will be correlated.

Assume that players of a game have common knowledge that their choices of strategies to commit themselves to are ratifiable. It is, therefore, common knowledge that whatever pair (s_1, s_2) they end up committing themselves to will be an equilibrium. To see this, suppose that there is a world consistent with their common knowledge where (s_1, s_2) is the pair they end up committing themselves to and that this pair is not an equilibrium. In that world there will be factual information (the strategy the other player is committed to) that would lead one of the players to know that he would have been better off if he had committed to something else instead. Given that it is common knowledge that what they will end up committing themselves to will be an equilibrium, it follows that either the candidate pairs all have interchangeable strategies (as in the Nash solution concept) or the choices of strategies are known to be correlated (as in Aumann's correlated equilibria).

References

Aumann, R. (1987) "Correlated equilibrium as an expression of Bayesian rationality," *Econometrica* 55, 1–18.
Bacharach, M. and Hurley, S., eds. (1991) *Foundations of Decision Theory*. Cambridge: Basil Blackwell.
Bicchieri, C. and Dalla Chiara, M.L., eds. (1992) *Knowledge, Belief and Strategic Interaction*. New York: Cambridge University Press.
Harper, W.L. (1986) "Mixed strategies and ratifiability in causal decision theory," *Erkenntnis* 24, 25–36.
Harper, W.L. (1988) "Causal decision theory and game theory," in Harper, W.L. and Skyrms, B., eds. *Causation in Decision, Belief Change, and Statistics*. Dordrecht: Kluwer.
Harper, W.L. (1989) "Decisions, games and equilibrium solutions," *PSA1988* 2, 344–62.
Harper, W.L. (1991) "Ratifiability and refinements (in two-person noncooperative games)," in Bacharach and Hurley (1991).
Harsanyi, J. and Selten, R. (1988) *A General Theory of Equilibrium Selection in Games*. Cambridge, MA.: MIT Press.
Jeffrey, R.C. (1983) *The Logic of Decision*, 2d ed. Chicago: University of Chicago Press.
Kohlberg, E. and Mertens, J.-F. (1986) "On the strategic stability of equilibria," *Econometrica* 54, 1003–37.
Kreps, D. and Wilson, R. (1982) "Sequential equilibria," *Econometrica* 50, 863–94.
Myerson, R. (1978) "Refinements of the Nash equilibrium concept," *International Journal of Game Theory* 7, 73–80.
Selten, R. (1975) "Reexamination of the perfectness concept of equilibrium in extensive games," *International Journal of Game Theory* 4, 25–55.
Shin, H.S. (1991) "Two notions of ratifiability and equilibrium in games," in Bacharach and Hurley (1991, 242–62).
Shin, H.S. (1992) "Counterfactuals and a theory of equilibrium in games," in Bicchieri and Dalla Chiara (1992).
van Damme, E. (1989) "Stable equilibria and forward induction," *Journal of Economic Theory* 48, 476–96.
von Neumann, J. and Morgenstern, O. (1944) *Theory of Games and Economic Behavior*. Princeton: Princeton University Press.

CHAPTER 4

Undercutting and the Ramsey Test for Conditionals

André Fuhrmann and Isaac Levi

1. The Ramsey Test

According to a suggestion made by F.P. Ramsey (1931), a conditional *if A then C* is accepted (or assertible) according to an agent X if and only if the consequent C follows from the 'minimal revision' of X's state of belief needed to accommodate the antecedent A. A belief state (or corpus, or theory) will here be represented by a set of sentences in some suitably regimented language closed under logical consequence. More succinctly the *Ramsey test* for conditionals (of the counterfactual variety) may be stated thus:

(RT) $\qquad\qquad\qquad A > C @ T \text{ iff } C \in T * A$

where T is a theory and $T * A$ is the revision of T by the antecedent sentence A. For our present purpose it does not matter how the notion of acceptance, denoted by @, is to be analyzed. We merely note that $\in$ is a tempting candidate—though in Levi (1988) it is argued that the temptation ought to be resisted. The *revision* of T by A, $T * A$, is the logical closure of $T \cup \{A\}$ (the *expansion* of T by A, also written $T + A$), if A is consistent with T; otherwise the revision results by first removing $\neg A$ from T and then expanding the result by A. It is understood that the removal of A from T (the *contraction* of T by A) should incur no gratuitous loss of information.

2. An Ambiguity

There is an ambiguity present in the presystematic use of conditionals. Consider the following claim:

(1) If coin *a* were tossed 1,000 times, it would land heads approximately 500 times.

According to the Ramsey test, (1) is acceptable (or assertible) according to an agent *X* if and only if "coin *a* lands heads approximately 500 times" is a consequence of *X*'s beliefs after they have been revised so as to contain "coin *a* is tossed 1,000 times."

It is easily seen that (1) is unacceptable by *X* in most cases by this criterion. Suppose that "coin *a* is not tossed 1,000 times" is not in *X*'s corpus *T*. Then the Ramsey test amounts to claiming that "coin *a* lands heads approximately 500 times" is a consequence of *T* and "coin *a* is tossed 1,000 times." If by 'consequence' we mean logical (or deductive) consequence as is customary, it is clear that the claim that coin *a* is unbiased and tossed 1,000 times does not logically imply that it lands heads approximately 500 times. The premises are consistent with coin *a* landing heads any number of times from 0 to 1,000. The Ramsey test, as usually construed, fails to warrant the assertibility of (1).

Assertibility is not regained in the belief-contravening case where *T* contains the claim that coin *a* is not tossed 1,000 times. In such cases we should first contract *T* by removing "coint *a* is not tossed 1,000 times" in a way which minimizes loss of informational value and then add "coin *a* is tossed 1,000 times." (1) remains unacceptable relative to *T*.

Nonetheless, presystematically, we are often prepared to assert or accept claims like (1). Indeed, students of nonmonotonic logic or of conditionals often use examples very much like the coin example, calling them cases of default reasoning. According to *T* we are told that birds fly. This does not mean that all birds fly but that most birds fly or that almost all birds fly. Given this background information in *T*, we are told that it is a legitimate 'default' principle of reasoning to infer that Tweety flies from the premise that Tweety is a bird. The premise is alleged to 'defeasibly imply' the conclusion. According to the translation manual furnished us by D. Makinson and P. Gärdenfors (1991), this should mean that "Tweety flies" is in the minimal revision of *T* by adding "Tweety is a bird." But then by the Ramsey test we have

(2) Tweety is a bird > Tweety flies.

Observe, however, that "Tweety flies" is not a deductive consequence of the corpus obtained by first removing from *T* "Tweety is not a bird" and then adding "Tweety is a bird."

Similarly, if *T* contains the information that nearly all Swedes are Protestants and nearly all Swedes of Italian descent are not Protestants, then the Ramsey test does *not* license "*x* is a Swede > *x* is a Protestant" nor does it license "*x* is a Swede of Italian descent > *x* is not a Protestant."

We do not think that the circumstance just noted reveals an inadequacy in the Ramsey test as a test for conditionals or in the views of those who find (1) and (2) acceptable. To the contrary, we think that there is an ambiguity in the way conditionals are to be understood. This ambiguity can be explicated by reference to two nonequivalent ways in which acceptability conditions may be specified for conditionals: (1) acceptability conditions may be given with the aid of the Ramsey test (RT), and (2) acceptability conditions may be given with the aid of the

Inductive Ramsey Test
$A >_i C$ @ T iff $C \in (T * A) + B$,
for a strongest B that is inductively justified by $T * A$.

The idea behind the inductive Ramsey test may be explained as follows: First perform a minimal revision of T by adding the antecedent A ("coint a is tossed 1,000 times") of the conditional $A >_i C$. The result is $T * A$. Relative to $T * A$ identify any B (consistent with $T * A$) that is not a deductive consequence of $T * A$ such that $(T * A) + B$ constitutes the set of all sentences the agent is inductively justified in adding to $T * A$ via some form of 'ampliative' or inductive inference (Levi 1980, 1991). B is a strongest sentence inductively justified by $T * A$ and $(T * A) + B$ is the *inductive expansion* of $T * A$. If the consequent C ("coin a is tossed approximately 500 times") is in the inductive expansion, the conditional under test is assertible.

The inductive Ramsey test does not rely on any special notion of acceptance or expansion. It does appeal to some characterization of the set $in(T)$ of inductively justified sentences relative to T such that (a) $In(T)$ contains T and is closed under logical consequence and (b) there is a sentence B such that $In(T) = T + B$. With this understood, we may put the inductive Ramsey test thus:

$$A >_i C \text{ @ } T \text{ iff } C \in In(T * A)$$

For the purpose of this discussion, we do not wish to rule out that there may be other kinds of conditionals that fit neither the plain nor the inductively extended Ramsey test.

If the inductive Ramsey test is employed to determine acceptability of conditionals, both (1) and (2) may turn out acceptable. To establish that this is so would require appeal to some account of inductive acceptance. That is not our concern in this discussion. Fortunately, we need not do so since the idea that one should expect coin a to land heads approximately 500 times in 1,000 tosses seems to be a commonly endorsed inductive rule of thumb as is the parallel case with birds and flying.

Thus, we can say that (1) is not Ramsey assertible but is inductively Ramsey assertible relative to T and similarly for (2). We can go further: the negation of (1) is Ramsey assertible while it fails to be inductively Ramsey assertible. Here the negation of (1) can be translated as "if coin a were tossed 1,000 times, it might not land heads approximately 500 times." In point of fact, not only is not-(1) Ramsey assertible but so is the following:

(1*) If coin *a* were tossed 1,000 times, it could land heads every time.

The examples we have cited where conditionals can be construed in two distinct ways are all examples where the background information in *T* is of either a quantitatively or qualitatively statistical character. It is either claimed that the percentage of individuals in some population *S* which are *P*s is some more or less precisely specified value or it is claimed that the chance or natural probability that an event of kind *P* will occur on a trial of kind *S* is some more or less precisely specified value. We are then given information—in the if-clause of the conditional—that an individual has been selected at random from the population *S* or that a trial of kind *S* has occurred. The then-clause claims that the individual is a *P* or that an event of kind *P* occurs.

Unless 100% of *S*s are *P*s, the Ramsey test will not sustain the conditional. However, one can identify principles of direct inference which license a credal probability assignment to *x* being a *P* relative to a theory or corpus $T * (x$ is $S)$ that contains the information that the percentage of *P*s among the *S*s is *r*. The credal probability will take the value *r* provided the agent's corpus $T * (x$ is $S)$ contains no information about *x* additional to the claim that *x* is an *S*. (This will be so also when, instead of precise information about the percentage, the agent has only indeterminate information, such as that almost all *S*s are *P*s.) These credal probabilities play an important role in determining whether it is legitimate for the inquirer to inductively expand $T * (x$ is $S)$ so that it contains "*x* is *P*."

How this happens is not our concern here. (See Levi (1967a, 1976b, 1980, 1986, 1991) for further discussion.) It is important, however, to keep in mind that the legitimacy of inductive expansion in such settings depends on the credal probability judgments derivable via direct inference from the statistical assumptions contained in $T * A$ and, in addition, on the information contained in the 'reference description' for *x* (often misleadingly described as the 'reference class' to which *x* belongs). Thus, the credal probability that coin *a* will land heads approximately 500 times is extremely close to 1 relative to $T * A$ (where *A* is "coin *a* is tossed 1,000 times"). The credal probabilities of frequencies deviating significantly from 500 are so small that even very cautious individuals may be prepared to take the risks of error entailed by rejecting them. The result of rejecting such frequencies is that the agent will end up in suspense between hypotheses about frequencies near 500 and, hence, will expand by adding the claim that coin *a* will land heads approximately 500 times. So (1) is assertible according to the inductive Ramsey test. But the Ramsey test does not allow for rejecting any of the 1,001 hypotheses about the frequency of heads in 1,000 tosses consistent with $T * A$ using the probability based inductive rule for rejecting highly improbable alternatives (or any other inductive rule).

There are, as is well known, many anti-inductivists who, following either Popper or Carnap, would deny the legitimacy of any sort of inductive expansion. The Carnapians would be prepared to assign credal probabilities but would, like the Popperians, disallow inductive expansion. Such authors should disallow the assertibility of conditionals like (1) altogether. To the extent, however, that presystematic judgment seems to acknowledge that such conditionals are assertible in some contexts while the Ramsey test seems inadequate to account for their assertibility, anti-inductivists should either offer an alternative to the inductivist account of assertibility sketchged here or explain why they are absolved from this undertaking.

We shall take for granted the importance of the ambiguity in the following discussion and the rough and ready adequacy of the account already offered of how the ambiguity is to be removed. Our focus wll be on some interesting formal differences between the properties of Ramsey conditionals of the type $A > B$ and inductive Ramsey conditionals of the type $A >_i B$ and their bearing on so-called nonmonotonic or defeasible inference.

3. Why Open Ramsey Conditionals Cannot Be Undercut

Ramsey conditionals are nonmonotonic in at least two ways. First, we may not arbitrarily augment the antecedent of a conditional, thereby weakening the conditional as a whole. We cannot proceed from the assumption that $A > C @ T$ to $A \wedge B > C @ T$ for arbitrarily chosen B. To give an example, the following pair of conditionals could be Ramsey assertible relative to the same corpus T:

(3) If you had come to the party, you would have met Grannie.
(4) If you had come to the party with Gramps, you might not have met Grannie.

Nonmonotonicity in this sense—i.e., failure of the inference known as 'weakening'—is just a presystematic fact about conditionals of the belief-contravening (or counterfactual) variety. Via the Ramsey test it also reflects a fact about the concept of revision at issue here: revision fails to be right-monotonic. That is to say, from $A \vdash B$, we may not infer $T * A \subseteq T * B$.

Second, Ramsey conditionals may be undercut. This is a stronger sense of nonmonotonicity than the failure of weakening. Not only may the conditional no longer hold after augmenting the if-clause. It may, moreover, result in the denial of the original then-clause. Thus, we may have $A > C @ T$ and, for some choices of B, $A \wedge B > \neg C @ T$. To give an example, (3) and

(5) If you had come to the party with Gramps, you would not have met Grannie.

could be jointly Ramsey assertible relative the same corpus T.

Sometimes weakening is harmless. We can even state a general principle of restricted weakening:

(RW)   if $A > C$ @ T and $A > \neg B$ @ T, then $A \wedge B > C$ @ T

(RW) corresponds to the schema $(A > C) \wedge \neg(A > \neg B) \vdash A \wedge B > C$ whose instances are usually theorems of conditional logics. The conversion of (RW), via the Ramsey test, into a condition on belief revision,

$$\text{if } \neg B \notin T * A \text{ then } T * C \subseteq T * A \wedge B$$

is an immediate consequence of the Gärdenfors postulates for belief revision (see, e.g., Alchourrón, Gärdenfors, and Makinson (1985) or Gärdenfors (1988)).

Similarly, some augmentations of antecedents avoid undercutting conditionals. A conditional $A > C$ will be called *open* with respect to a corpus T if A is consistent with T (i.e., $\neg A \notin T$). If both the unweakened and the weakened conditional are open, undercutting is prohibited. This is to say, when A and B are jointly compatible with T, $A > C$ cannot be undercut by B:

(NU)   if $A > C$ @ T and $\neg(A \wedge B) \notin T$, then $A \wedge B > \neg C$ @ T

Again, the Ramsey test may be used to turn (NU) ('no undercutting') into a condition on belief revision:

$$\text{if } C \in T * A \text{ and } \neg B \notin T + A, \text{ then } \neg C \notin T * A \wedge B$$

That Ramsey conditionals have this property follows from an uncontentious assumption about the concept of a revision operation.

We assume that $(\ ) * (\ )$ is an operation that maps theories to theories by adding some sentence A to T after removing enough sentences from T to render the result compatible with A. Thus $T * A$ is like the corresponding expansion $T + A$ except that the latter adds A to the corpus without first removing sentences incompatible with A. We should, therefore, require that $T * A$ cannot be stronger than $T + A$. That is to say,

(incl) $T * A \subseteq T + A$

To verify that Ramsey conditionals cannot be undercut by compatibles, suppose $A > C$ @ T and $\neg(A \wedge B) \notin T$. Then by the Ramsey test, $C \in T * A$ whence $C \in T + A$ by (incl). So $C \in (T + A) + B$ by the monotonicity of truth functional consequence. But $(T + A) + B = T + A \wedge B$ and if $C \in T + A \wedge B$, then $A \wedge B \supset C \in T$ by the deduction theorem for classical logic. Suppose further—for reductio—that B undercuts $A > C$ in T, that is, $A \wedge B > \neg C$ @ T. Then by the Ramsey test, $\neg C \in T * A \wedge B$. Hence, by (incl), $\neg C \in T + A \wedge B$ and so $A \wedge B \supset \neg C \in T$. Thus, $\neg(A \wedge B) \in T$, contradicting our assumption that A and B are compatible according to T.

Where Ramsey conditionals are at issue, we may also derive (NU) from (RW) together with (incl) and the consistency condition (cons) $T * A$ is consistent, unless $\neg A$ is a tautology

This is another elementary integrity constraint on revision operations. It requires that revisions achieve their purpose by consistently adding to a corpus—except when the sentence to be added is too badly chosen. To derive (NU) assume the antecedent and—for reductio—$(A \wedge B) > \neg C \ @ \ T$. Then, by the Ramsey test, $C \in T * A$ and $\neg C \in T * A \wedge B$. Moreover, since $\neg(A \wedge B) \notin T$, $T * A \wedge B$ is consistent whence $C \notin T * A \wedge B$ by (incl); hence, $A > B \ @ \ T$ by the Ramsey test. Applying (RW), we obtain $A \wedge B > C \ @ \ T$, that is, $C \in T * A \wedge B$ by the Ramsey test—contradiction!

Thus, for conditionals generated by the Ramsey test, the no-undercutting condition (NU) follows—under plausible assumptions—from the condition of restricted weakening (RW). Note that in the above argument we had to apply the Ramsey test in both directions. Thus, the argument fails when the inductive Ramsey test is at issue. In the next section, we argue that when the inductive Ramsey test is used as a condition of acceptability for conditionals, undercutting occurs even in the case of open conditionals in violation of (NU). Moreover, (RW) also fails.

4. Inductively Extended Ramsey Tests

Whether (1) or (1*) are belief-contravening (counterfactual) or open, the inductively extended Ramsey test determines whether the credal probability judgments grounded on the statistical assumptions contained in $T * A$ (where A is "coin a is tossed 1,000 times") justifies expanding $T * A$ by adding some B and forming the deductive closure and testing whether C ("coin a lands heads approximately 500 times") is in this expansion.

If $T * A$ contains information about the coin tosses other than that they are coin tosses, this could alter the credal probability that coin a lands heads approximately 500 times. The credal probability that coin a lands heads approximately 500 times is near 1 given that part of $T * A$ that provides the information that it is tossed 1,000 times. But the credal probability that coin a lands heads approximately 500 times given tht it is tossed 1,000 times by Morgenbesser may be quite different. Indeed, it could be near 0. $T * A$ might contain the claim that the chance of coin a landing heads on a toss is 0.5 (and tosses are independent and identically distributed) and also the claim that the chance of coin a landing heads on a toss by Morgenbesser is 0.01 (and tosses by Morgenbesser are independent and identically distributed). Since A asserts that a is tossed 1,000 times and leaves it open whether the tosses are by Morgenbesser, the credal probabilities for hypotheses as to the frequency of heads far removed from 500 are well below the threshold for rejection so that one might well be justified in adding to $T * A$ the claim C that the coin landed heads approximately 500 times.

On the other hand, if we consider $T * A \wedge A'$ where A' asserts that coin a is tossed each of the 1,000 times by Morgenbesser, the credal probability distribution over the hypotheses about frequency will assign probabilities below the threshold of rejection to hypotheses asserting the frequency to be far removed from 10. One might then be justified not only in affirming that if coin a were tosses a thousand times by Morgenbesser it might not land heads approximately 500 times but in asserting that if coin a were tossed a thousand times by Morgenbesser it would not land heads approximately 500 times.

Observe that these possibilities can obtain even in cases where $A \wedge A'$ is consistent with T so that the conditionals are all open. Hence (NU) fails.

Does (RW) apply when the inductively extended Ramsey test is used? For a negative answer we need to exhibit an example along the following pattern: A provides good enough evidence to inductively warrant conclusion C; B undercuts that evidence, while A is not sufficient to reject B.

Suppose we are told that 90% of Swedes are Protestants and so are 10% of Swedes born of Italian parents. A little calculation reveals that the percentage of Swedes who are born of Italian parents is greater than 0 but less than 11.1%. Relative to the result of consistently expanding T by adding the information that x was randomly selected from the Swedes, one is justified in asserting that x is a Protestant. Moreover, one might justifiably reject any conjecture that x's religion is other than Protestant on the grounds that its probability grounded on the available statistical information is too low. But if one also supposed that x is a Swede born of Italian parents, one might not be prepared to reject inductively the claim that x is a Protestant even though one would not accept it either. We have a case where $A >_i C @ T$ but not $A \wedge B >_i C @ T$. If (RW) obtained, we should also have $A >_i \neg B$. But on the information that x is randomly selected from the Swedes, the chance of x being born of Italian parents ranges from 0% to 11.1%. If we knew the chance to be near the upper end of the range, we would not reject the hypothesis that x is born of Italian parents. Since we cannot reject the claim that the chance is 11.1%, we still cannot reject the hypothesis: $A >_i \neg B$ is not acceptable according to the inductive Ramsey test. So (RW) is violated.

5. Conclusion

Two types of tests for the acceptability of conditionals have been proposed: the Ramsey test and the Inductive Ramsey test. As we have pointed out, whenever the initial corpus T contains statistical assumptions which can be used to license nondeductive or inductive inferences based on probability judgments, both types of test can be applied and will sometimes yield different verdicts. These statistical assumptions appear to play the role of default rules which license inferences in nonmonotonic (or defeasible) logics. Such assumptions can work the way they are supposed to only if some form of inductive expansion procedure is invoked.

We have seen that when inductive expansions are introduced into the Ramsey test, the resulting inductive Ramsey conditionals fail to exhibit some of the properties satisfied by plain Ramsey conditionals, notably (RW) and

(NU). Using the translation scheme of Makinson and Gärdenfors (1991), these properties may be recast as conditions on a (nonmonotonic) inference relation $\mathrel{\vrule height 1ex width 0.05em depth 0.3ex}\kern-0.15em\sim$:

(RWI) $A \mathrel{\mid\sim} C \,\&\, A \wedge B \mathrel{\not\mid\sim} C \Longrightarrow A \mathrel{\mid\sim} \neg B$

(NUI) $A \mathrel{\mid\sim} C \,\&\, A \wedge B \mathrel{\mid\sim} \neg C \Longrightarrow \mathrel{\mid\sim} A \supset \neg B$

We have argued that these conditions should be violated whenever the inference relation under consideration is based on default rules of overtly or covertly statistical character; that is, whenever inferences are licensed by some form of inductive expansion. Thus, satisfaction of (RWI) and (NUI) rules out certain interpretations of nonmonotonic inference.

Gärdenfors and Makinson (1993) have proposed an approach to generating nonmonotonic inference relations from belief revision operations which differs from the one presented in Makinson and Gärdenfors (1991) in that the revision operation is now assumed to operate on sets of 'expectations'. Implicit in their proposal is the following Ramsey test for 'expectation-based' conditions:

$$A >_e C \ @\ T \text{ iff } C \in In(T) * A$$

where $In(\ )$ is the inductive closure operation briefly introduced in Section 2. Thus, the main difference between the Ramsey tests for i-type and e-type conditionals is that for the former we consider the inductive closure of a revision of T while for the latter we consider a revision of the inductive closure of T. But Gärdenfors and Makinson seem to endorse both (RWI) and (NUI) for the nonmonotonic inference relation associated with expectation-based conditionals. As noted in the last paragraph, this rules out that the expectations in question have been generated by inductive procedures. It is then no longer clear what notion of expectation is presupposed. In our view, this interpretational problem points to deeper rooted problems with the approach followed in Gärdenfors and Makinson (1993). But a thorough treatment of these problems is beyond the scope of the present paper and will thus have to be left for another occasion.

(RWI) has been discussed in the literature on nonmonotonic logic under the name of rational monotony (see, e.g., Kraus, Lehmann and Magidor (1990) and Makinson (1994)). None of the major approaches to nonmonotonic inference, at least in their plain versions, satisfy rational monotony. Some of these approaches, such as *epsilon*-inference and preferential entailment can be naturally amended so as to obey rational monotony. The remarks we have made here indicate that for an important class of nonmonotonic inference relations one should abstain from such amendments.

The condition (NUI), though less prominent than rational monotony, is not unknown to students of nonmonotonic logics. Let $C(X) = \{A : X \mathrel{\mid\sim} A\}$ be the consequence operation associated with the inference relation $\mathrel{\mid\sim}$. Makinson

(1994) has observed that (NUI) follows the three salient conditions on non-monotonic reasoning: for any sets of sentences X and Y,

Distribution: $\qquad\qquad C(X) \cap C(Y) = C(Cn(X) \cap Cn(Y))$

Supraclassicality: $\qquad\qquad Cn(X) \subseteq C(X)$

Absorption: $\qquad\qquad Cn(C(X)) = C(X) = C(Cn(X))$

These conditions enjoy considerably more approval than rational monotony. Absorption and supraclassicality appear to be ubiquitous. Distribution is a powerful principle which most nonmonotonic logics do not satisfy in their raw versions though it holds in most upgraded versions. However, since upgrading to distribution yields (NUI), it ought to be resisted if the kind of nonmonotonicity rooted in appeals to total evidence and induction is to be kept in view. Neither rational monotony nor the no-undercutting condition can be recommended as general constraints on nonmonotonic inference.

Acknowledgments—We thank Peter Gärdenfors and David Makinson for helping us to improve earlier versions of this essay.

References

Alchourrón, C.E., P. Gärdenfors, and D. Makinson: 1985, "On the logic of theory change: Partial meet functions for contraction and revision," *Journal of Symbolic Logic*, 50, 510-30.

Gärdenfors, P.: 1988, *Knowledge in Flux*, Bradford–MIT, Cambridge, Mass.

Gärdenfors, P. and D. Makinson: 1993, "Nonmonotonic inferences based on expectations," *Artificial Intelligence*, 65, 197–246.

Kraus, S., D. Lehmann, and M. Magidor: 1990, "Nonmonotonic reasoning, preferential models and cumulative logics," *Artificial Intelligence*, 44, 167–207.

Levi, I.: 1967a, *Gambling with Truth*, A. Knopf, New York.

Levi, I.: 1967b, "Information and inference," *Synthese*, 17, 369–91.

Levi, I.: 1980, *The Enterprise of Knowledge*, MIT, Cambridge, Mass.

Levi, I.: 1986, *Hard Choices*, Cambridge University Press, Cambridge.

Levi, I.: 1988, "Iteration of conditionals and the Ramsey test," *Synthese*, 76, 49–81.

Levi, I.: 1991, *The Fixation of Belief and Its Undoing*, Cambridge University Press, Cambridge.

Makinson, D.: 1994, "General patterns of nonmonotonic reasoning," in *Handbook of Logic in Artificial Intelligence and Logic Programming*, Vol. 3: *Nonmonotonic Reasoning and Uncertain Reasoning* (ed. D. M. Gabbay, C. J. Hogger, and J. A. Robinson), Oxford University Press, Oxford, pp. 35–110.

Makinson, D. and P. Gärdenfors: 1991, "Relations between the logic of theory change and nonmonotonic logic," in *The Logic of Theory Change* (ed. by Fuhrmann/Morreau), *Lecutre Notes in Artificial Intelligence* 465, Springer, Heidelberg.

Ramsey, F.P.: 1931, "General propositions and causality," in his *Foundations of Mathematics and Other Logical Essays*, Routledge & Kegan Paul, London.

CHAPTER 5

Aumann's "No Agreement" Theorem Generalized

Matthias Hild, Richard Jeffrey, and Mathias Risse

In "Agreeing to Disagree," Robert Aumann (1976) proves that a group of agents who once agreed about the probability of some proposition for which their current probabilities are common knowledge must still agree, even if those probabilities reflect disparate observations. Perhaps one saw that a card was red and another saw that it was a heart, so that, as far as that goes, their common prior probability of 1/52 for its being the Queen of hearts would change in the one case to 1/26, and in the other to 1/13. But if those are indeed their current probabilities, it cannot be the case that both know them, and both know that both know them, and so on.

In Aumann's framework, new probabilistic states of mind can only arise by conditioning old ones on new knowledge. In such a framework, current probabilities must derive from what is in effect knowledge, that is, true full belief. But here we derive Aumann's result from common knowledge of a probability, however arrived at. We work with possible worlds in which the agents' probabilities and their evolution are matters of fact, represented within the model (i.e., as proposed by Samet (1990, 205)).

Independence of particular update rules is a central feature of the new framework. But of course we need some constraint on how agents update their probabilities. For this we use Goldstein's (1983) requirement that current expectations of future expectations equal current expectations. This is the workhorse for our proof of the Generalized "No Agreement" theorem.

Related projects proceed differently. Thus Samet generalizes the theorem for agents who condition on certainties that need not be true, provided only that all agents are certain of their certainties; and both Cave (1983) and Bacharach (1985) generalize it for agents whose common knowledge is not of probabilities but of decisions. But in each case the gain in generality remains within the confines of the conditioning framework, where new probabilities can only stem from new certainties.

1. Aumann's Theorem

Aumann's framework provides for a finite number of *agents*; call them $i = 1, \cdots, N$. These individuals are about to learn the answers to various multiple-choice questions—perhaps by making observations. The possible answers to agent i's question form a set $\mathcal{Q}_i$ of mutually exclusive, collectively exhaustive propositions. We think of propositions as subsets of a nonempty set Ω of *worlds*, representing all possibilities of interest for the problem at hand. Then $\mathcal{Q}_i$ is a *partition* of Ω: each world ω belongs to exactly one element of each $\mathcal{Q}_i$. We call that element '$\mathcal{Q}_i\omega$'.

Perhaps it is only certain propositions, certain subsets of Ω, that are of interest to the agents. Among them will be all propositions in any of the N partitions, and perhaps other propositions as well. We will suppose that they form a σ-field $\mathcal{A}$.

The propositions agents know after learning the answers to their questions are the members of $\mathcal{A}$ that those answers imply: In world ω agent i knows A if and only if $\mathcal{Q}_i\omega \subseteq A \in \mathcal{A}$. Then for each i, Def. K, below, defines a knowledge operator K_i which, applied to any set $A \in \mathcal{A}$, yields the set $K_i A \in \mathcal{A}$ of worlds in which i knows A.

(Def. K) $$K_i A = \{\omega \colon \mathcal{Q}_i\omega \subseteq A\}$$

For each natural number n, Def. MK then defines an operator M_n, "nth degree mutual knowledge": A is true, and everybody knows that, and everybody knows *that*, and so on—with n 'knows'. Finally, Def. CK defines *common knowledge*, κ, as mutual knowledge of all finite degrees:

(Def. MK) $$M_0 A = A$$

$$M_{n+1} A = \bigcap_{i=1}^{N} K_i M_n A$$

(Def. CK) $$\kappa A = \bigcap_{n=0}^{\infty} M_n A$$

The key to the proof of Aumann's theorem is the following lemma.

Lemma 1.1

Where something is common knowledge, everyone knows it is: If $\kappa A \neq \emptyset$ then κA is the union of some subset $\mathcal{D}_i$ of $\mathcal{Q}_i$.

Proof. If $\omega \in \kappa A$ then by Def. CK and Def. M, $\omega \in K_i M_n A$ for all agents i and degrees n of mutual knowledge. Therefore by Def. K, $\mathcal{2}_i\omega \subseteq M_n A$ for all n, and thus by Def. CK, $\mathcal{2}_i\omega \subseteq \kappa A$. ∎

The first hypothesis of Aumann's theorem 1.2, below, says that $\langle \Omega, \mathcal{A}, P \rangle$ is a probability space, that $\mathcal{A}$ includes each of the partitions $\mathcal{2}_1, \ldots, \mathcal{2}_N$ of Ω, and that each of those partitions is countable. In jargon: $\langle \langle \Omega, \mathcal{A}, P \rangle, \mathcal{2}_1, \ldots, \mathcal{2}_N \rangle$ is a *countable partition space*. $\mathcal{A}$ will then be closed under all of the operators K_i and M_n, and under κ.

P is the old probability measure that is common to all the agents. In Aumann's theorem we consider a hypothesis $H \in \mathcal{A}$ for which the various agents' probabilities are $q_1, \ldots, q_N$ after they condition P on the answers to their questions. The proposition $C \in \mathcal{A}$ identifies these probabilities:

(Def. C)
$$C = \bigcap_{i=1}^{N} \{\omega:\ P(H|\mathcal{2}_i\omega) = q_i\}$$

The second hypothesis says that the possibility of C's becoming common knowledge is not ruled out in advance: $P(\kappa C) \neq 0$.

Theorem 1.2 (Aumann's "No Agreement" Theorem)
If $\langle \langle \Omega, \mathcal{A}, P \rangle, \mathcal{2}_1, \ldots, \mathcal{2}_N \rangle$ *is a countable partition space, and* $P(\kappa C) > 0$, *then* $P(H|\kappa C) = q_1 = \cdots = q_N$.

Proof.

$$P(H|\kappa C) = \frac{P(H \cap \bigcup \mathcal{2}_i)}{\sum_{D \in \mathcal{2}_i} P(D)} = \frac{\sum_{D \in \mathcal{2}_i} P(H|D)P(D)}{\sum_{D \in \mathcal{2}_i} P(D)} = \frac{\sum_{D \in \mathcal{2}_i} q_i P(D)}{\sum_{D \in \mathcal{2}_i} P(D)} = q_i$$

The first equation is justified by Lemma 1.1; the second by the probability calculus; the third by Def. C; the fourth by independence of q_i from D. ∎

This remarkable result is limited by the assumption that agents update only by conditioning on authoritative answers to questions. Before removing that limitation, we pause to see why conditioning is not the only way to update.

2. Conditioning Generalized

In Aumann's framework, agents update their probabilities by conditioning on countable partitions of Ω. This will soon be replaced by a framework which is independent of how agents update. But first we point out an intermediate generalization of Aumann's updating scheme, in which (1) partitions are replaced by more general structures, and (2) conditioning is replaced by a more general operation.

2.1. Sufficient Subfields

The partitions $\mathcal{Q}_i$ are meant to represent the possible answers to questions that agents might obtain, for example, by making observations. But even in the simplest cases, where the most specific answers form a finite partition of Ω, observation may only identify the disjunction of two or more partition elements as true without identifying any one element as true. And in case the observation is made on the value of a continuous magnitude, where total precision is unattainable, the possible results will form no partition but a family of overlapping intervals.

In a generalization of Aumann's model covering such cases, partitions $\mathcal{Q}$ of Ω are replaced by sub-σ-fields $\mathcal{F}_i$ of $\mathcal{A}$, and the partition element $\mathcal{Q}_i\omega$ which answers agent i's question in world ω is replaced by the subset $\mathcal{F}_i\omega = \{A : \omega \in A \in \mathcal{F}_i\}$ of $\mathcal{A}$ consisting of the elements of $\mathcal{F}_i$ that are true in world ω. (Billingsley 1995, 57). In the special case where the subfield is atomic, there is an equivalent partition model in which the elements of the partition are the atoms of the subfield. Here the notion of sufficiency has a simple definition: *Sufficiency* of $\mathcal{Q}_i$ for a family of measures means that conditioning on any member of $\mathcal{Q}_i$ wipes out all differences between members of the family. Where the family is the pair $\{P, Q_i\}$, the definition comes to this:[1]

(Sufficiency) $\qquad\qquad Q_i(\cdot|A) = P(\cdot|A)$ for any $A \in \mathcal{Q}_i$

Problem. In world ω, how is agent i to update P to a suitable new probability measure Q_i, upon discovering which member of $\mathcal{Q}_i$ is true? The discovery is a matter of full belief in the true member of $\mathcal{Q}_i$:

(Certainty) $\qquad\qquad\qquad Q_i(\mathcal{Q}_i\omega) = 1$

This problem has no general solution.[2] But as is easily verified, it has the following solution if, and only if, Sufficiency is satisfied:

(Conditioning) $\qquad\qquad\qquad Q_i(\cdot) = P(\cdot|Q_i\omega)$

2.2. Uncertain Information

Whether or not partitions are replaced by subfields, we can drop the certainty condition to obtain a way of updating on uncertain information that is more broadly applicable than conditioning. Thus, in the case of a countable partition model, observation under less than ideal conditions may change i's probabilities for elements of $\mathcal{Q}_i$ from those given by the common prior measure P to new values, given by some measure Q_i for which $Q_i(\mathcal{Q}_i\omega) < 1$ for all ω. If Sufficiency is satisfied, this is updating by *Generalized Conditioning:*[3]

(Generalized Conditioning) $$Q_i(\cdot) = \sum_{A \in \mathcal{Q}_i} P(\cdot|A)Q_i(A)$$

Generalized conditioning is not a universally applicable method of updating. Rather, it is applicable if and only if the Sufficiency condition is met. Where Sufficiency fails, other special conditions may hold, in the presence of which other methods of updating may be applicable. It would be a hopeless task to try to form an inventory of all updating methods and their conditions of applicability. Instead, we now turn to a revised framework, in which we can track flows of probability without reference to whatever update rules they follow.

3. The Theorem Generalized

As before, $1, \ldots, N$ are the agents, Ω is a nonempty set of possible worlds, and $\mathcal{A}$ is a σ-field over Ω. And as before, each possible world specifies a complete history, past, present, and future; but now agents belong to worlds, and as time goes by, their probabilities concerning their own and other agents' probabilities evolve along with their probabilities concerning the rest of the world—for example, my probability for your probability for my probability for a Republican president in the year 2000.

The time index t takes values in some linearly ordered set T. Probability measures $pr_{i\omega t}$ represent ideally precise probabilistic states of mind of agents i in worlds ω at times t. The common prior P in Theorem 1.2 is such a measure; but in the present framework we need to spell out the commonality assumption, and in doing so we see that there might be different common priors in different worlds: perhaps the probability measures $pr_{i\omega t}$ are the same for all i, and so are $pr_{i\omega' t}$, but $pr_{i\omega t}(A) \neq pr_{i\omega' t}(A)$ for some A.

Now Def. B^t defines *Belief*—that is, certainty, full belief—as 100% probability, and Def. K^t replaces the old partition-based Def. K by a definition of knowledge simply as true full belief:

(Def. B^t) $B_i^t A = \{\omega: pr_{i\omega t}(A) = 1\}$

(Def. K^t) $K_i^t A = A \cap B_i^t A$

The old definitions of mutual and common knowledge are then adapted to the new definition of knowledge:

(Def. MK^t) $M_0^t A = A$

$$M_{n+1}^t A = \bigcap_{i=1}^{N} K_i^t M_n^t A$$

(Def. CK^t) $\kappa^t A = \bigcap_{n=0}^{\infty} M_n^t A$

In the generalized theorem, $t = 1$ and $t = 2$ are times at which agents have their old and new probabilities for some hypothesis $H \in \mathcal{A}$. In world ω those probabilities are $pr_{i\omega 1}(H)$ and $pr_{i\omega 2}(H)$—which we now write simply as $P_\omega(H)$ and $Q_\omega(H)$, respectively, with the subscript i understood, and with the work of the time subscripts 1 and 2 done by writing P and Q:

(Shorthand)
$$P_\omega = pr_{i\omega 1}$$
$$Q_\omega = pr_{i\omega 2}$$

Thus, with $t = 2$, Def. B' would be written

(Def. B^2)
$$B_i^2 A = \{\omega\colon Q_\omega(A) = 1\}$$

In the generalized theorem the proposition C^2 specifies $q_1, \ldots, q_N$ as the agents' new probabilities for H:

(Def. C^2)
$$C^2 = \bigcap_{i=1}^{N} \{\omega\colon Q_\omega(H) = q_i\}$$

The crucial hypothesis of the generalized theorem is Goldstein's (1983) principle (G) that *old probabilities = old expectations of new probabilities*. Here the integrand $Q(A)$ is a random variable, a P_ω-measurable function of ω which takes real values $Q_{\omega'}(A)$ as ω' ranges over Ω :

(G)
$$P_\omega(A) = \int_\Omega Q(A)\, dP_\omega$$

The second hypothesis says that whenever A is in $\mathcal{A}$, so are the N propositions saying—perhaps, falsely—that at time 2 the several agents are sure that A is true. This guarantees that $\mathcal{A}$ is closed under all the operations K_i^2, M_n^2, and κ^2.

To prove the theorem we use two lemmas. The first is the analog of the lemma (1.1) used to prove Aumann's theorem in Section 1.

(More Shorthand)
$$B = B_i^2, \qquad \kappa = \kappa^2, C = C^2$$

Lemma 3.1
While something is common knowledge, everyone is sure it is; for example, $\kappa C \subseteq B\kappa C$.

Proof. For the example, use Def. CK^2, MK^2, and K^2. ∎

Lemma 3.2
If (G) holds, then $\int_{\Omega - \kappa C} Q(\kappa C)\, dP_\omega = 0$.

Proof. $P_\omega(\kappa C) = \int_\Omega Q(\kappa C)\,dP_\omega = \int_{\kappa C} Q(\kappa C)\,dP_\omega + \int_{\Omega-\kappa C} Q(\kappa C)\,dP_\omega$ by (G). By Lemma 3.1 the first term of this sum $= \int_{\kappa C} 1\,dP_\omega = P_\omega(\kappa C)$, so the second term $= 0$.   ∎

Theorem 3.3 (Aumann's "No Agreement" Theorem Generalized)
Hypotheses: (G) holds, B maps $\mathscr{A}$ into itself, P_ω is the same for all i,
$P_\omega(\kappa C) > 0$. *Conclusion: $P_\omega(H|\kappa C) = q_1 = \cdots = q_N$.*

Proof.

$$P_\omega(H|\kappa C) = \frac{\int_\Omega Q(H \cap \kappa C)\,dP_\omega}{\int_\omega Q(\kappa C)\,dP_\omega} \quad \text{by (G)}$$

$$= \frac{\int_{\kappa C} Q(H \cap \kappa C)\,dP_\omega + \int_{\Omega-\kappa C} Q(H \cap \kappa C)\,dP_\omega}{\int_{\kappa C} Q(\kappa C)\,P(d\omega) + \int_{\Omega-\kappa C} Q(\kappa C)\,dP_\omega}$$

$$= \frac{\int_{\kappa C} Q(H \cap \kappa C)\,dP_\omega}{\int_{\kappa C} Q(\kappa C)\,dP_\omega}$$

by Lemma 3.2, since $Q(A \cap \kappa C) \le Q(\kappa C)$

$$= \frac{\int_{\kappa C} Q(H)\,dP_\omega}{\int_{\kappa C} 1\,dP_\omega} \quad \text{by Lemma 3.1}$$

$$= \frac{\int_{\kappa C} q_i\,dP_\omega}{\int_{\kappa C} dP_\omega} \quad \text{by Def. } C^2$$

$$= q_i, \text{ i.e., the same for all } i.$$

∎

4. Remarks

4.1. Solo Epistemology

Aumann's theorem 1.2 was the start of what he would later (1995) call *interactive epistemology*. Here we use the term *solo epistemology* for the special case in which the number N of agents is 1. In this case Theorem 3.3 assumes the form of Corollary 4.1 below, with C and κC assuming especially simple forms:

(Solo C) $C = \{\omega: Q_\omega(H) = q\}$

(Solo κC) $\kappa C = C \cap BC \cap BBC \cap \cdots$

Corollary 4.1
Hypotheses: (G) holds, B maps $\mathscr{A}$ into itself, $P_\omega(\kappa C) > 0$. Conclusion:
$P_\omega(H|C \cap BC \cap BBC \cap \cdots) = q.$

This says that in the presence of two more hypotheses, (G) implies a variant of van Fraassen's (1984) *reflection principle*:

(Reflection) $P_\omega(H|C) = q$

Goldstein (1983) and van Fraassen (1984) offer a scoring rule argument and a Dutch book argument for (G) and Reflection as diachronic coherence principles.

4.2. Tightness

The only properties of κC used in the proof of Theorem 3.3 are $\kappa C \subseteq C$ (to get from line 5 to line 6) and $\kappa C \subseteq B\kappa C$ (to get from line 4 to line 5). In fact κC fits this pair of properties tightly, in the following sense.

Corollary 4.2
κC is the largest $A \subseteq C$ for which $A \subseteq BA$.

Proof. By Def. CK^2, κC satisfies both conditions on A. And by induction, any A satisfying both conditions is included in κC. (Basis: $A \subseteq M_0^2 A$ by Def. M_0^2. Induction step: If $A \subseteq M_n^2 A$ then as the second condition holds for all $i = 1, \ldots, N$, $A \subseteq M_{n+1}^2 A$. Then $A \subseteq \kappa C$ by Def. CK^2.) ■

4.3. Belief and Knowledge

In Aumann's framework, true belief, that is, 100% new probability for a truth, is definable (Def. K), but mere belief is indefinable. In the new framework, belief is definable as in Def. B^t in Section 3, so that in the new framework Def. K^t defines knowledge as true belief.

The weakness of this notion of belief is indicated by the inventory (B0)–(B6) of conditions on mappings $M : \mathcal{A} \to \mathcal{A}$ that are satisfied ($\Uparrow$) and violated ($\Downarrow$) when M is belief, $M = B_i^t$, as in Def. B^t. But despite their apparent weakness, the four conditions it does satisfy suffice for the generalized "No Agreement" theorem.

$\Uparrow$(B0) $(MA_1 \cap MA_2 \cap \cdots) \subseteq M(A_1 \cap A_2 \cap \cdots)$.
          Distributivity

$\Uparrow$(B1)   If $A_1 \subseteq A_2$ then $MA_1 \subseteq MA_2$
          Deductive closure

$\Downarrow$(B2) $MA \subseteq A$
          Infallibility

$\Downarrow$(B3) $MA \subseteq MMA$
          Positive introspection

$\Downarrow$(B4) $\neg MA \subseteq M\neg MA$
          Negative introspection

$\Uparrow$(B5) $M\emptyset = \emptyset$
          Consistency

$\Uparrow$(B6) $M\Omega = \Omega$
          Necessity

4.4. Demurrals

Since Plato's *Theaetetus* it has been a philosophical commonplace that true belief need not be knowledge. Then (Def. K^t) in Section 3 is suspect as an analysis of knowledge, as philosophers understand the matter. Nor are the credentials of Def. B^t as an analysis of what is normally called belief any better, for we may truly be said to believe propositions for which our probabilities fall slightly short of 100%. Nor can precise probability measures be taken seriously as general models of human judgmental states. Interactive epistemology is best understood as a branch of a theory of judgmental probability in which the notions of all-or-none belief and knowledge, and of precise judgmental probabilities, appear for the most part as limiting cases.

Notes

1. In general, $\mathscr{F}_i$ is a sufficient subfield iff $Q_i(\cdot \| \mathscr{F}_i) = P(\cdot \| \mathscr{F}_i)$. See Billingsley (1995, 450).

2. In the playing card example at the beginning, certainty about the true member of the partition {*heart, diamond, club, spade*} brought with it certainty about the true member of the partition {*red, black*}, but conditioning on these certainties led to different probabilities (1/26, 1/13) for the card's being the Queen of hearts.

3. This follows from Sufficiency by the Law of Total Probability. For fully generalized conditioning, i.e., on a sub-σ-field $\mathscr{S}_i$, the definition would be $Q_i(\cdot) = \int_\Omega P(\cdot \| \mathscr{S}_i)\, dQ_i = E(P(\cdot \| \mathscr{S}_i))$, where E is the updated expectation operator. (Generalized Conditioning is sometimes called 'probability kinematics'.) For references and further information see Diaconis and Zabell (1982) or Jeffrey (1992).

References

Aumann, R.J. (1976), "Agreeing to Disagree," *Annals of Statistics* **4**, 1236–39.

Aumann, R.J. (1995), "Interactive Epistemology," Discussion Paper No. 67, Center for Rationality and Interactive Decision Theory, The Hebrew University of Jerusalem.

Bacharach, M. (1985), "Some Extensions of a Claim of Aumann in an Axiomatic Model of Knowledge," *Journal of Economic Theory* **37**, 167–90.

Billingsley, P. (1995), *Probability and Measure*, New York: John Wiley & Sons.

Cave, A.K. (1983), "Learning to Agree," *Economics Letters* **12**, 147–52.

Diaconis, P. and Zabell, S. (1982), "Updating Subjective Probabilities," *Journal of the American Statistical Association* **77**, 822–30.

Goldstein, M. (1983), "The Prevision of Prevision," *Journal of the American Statistical Association* **78**, 817–19.

Jeffrey, R.C. (1992), *Probability and the Art of Judgment*, Cambridge: Cambridge University Press.

Samet, D. (1990), "Ignoring Ignorance and Agreeing to Disagree," *Journal of Economic Theory* **52**, 190–207.

van Fraassen, B. (1984), "Belief and the Will," *Journal of Philosophy* **81**, 235–56.

CHAPTER 6

Rational Failures of the KK Principle

Timothy Williamson

It is tempting to suppose that rational thinkers satisfy the *KK principle* that if one knows something, then one knows that one knows it.[1] This essay investigates a variety of phenomena which cause the KK principle to fail. The failures are rational in the sense that they can be described within a framework on which thinkers know all the logical consequences of what they know. Of course, actual thinkers fail to draw all these consequences; the point of the idealization is that this failure of deductive closure is quite separate from, because not necessary for, the failure of the KK principle. A positive proposal will be made as to the logic of rational knowledge.

The technical framework for the discussion will be the standard possible-worlds semantics for modal logic, interpreted epistemically.[2] It is intended radically to idealize the epistemic capacities of actual thinkers, with the aim of showing that not even this radical idealization removes all objections to the KK principle. Section 1 briefly rehearses some elementary epistemic logic; those familiar with such material should go straight to Section 2.

1. Epistemic Logic

There is a set W of *worlds*, thought of as mutually exclusive and jointly exhaustive situations or outcomes (they need not specify features irrelevant to the purpose of the model). The *propositions* are the subsets of W; a proposition P is true in a world w if and only if $w \in P$. Thus negations are complements in W, conjunctions are intersections, and so on. For a thinker S in a world w, worlds are of two kinds. Some are *accessible* or epistemically possible; the others are inaccessible or epistemically impossible. Accessibility is a relation R between worlds; different thinkers may have different accessibility relations. S is treated as omniscient about what is true at each world from a world-neutral point of view; what S may not know is which world she is in. If the proposition P is false in some world accessible from w, it is false in a world that, for all S in w knows, is actual, so S in w does not know P. Conversely, if S in w does not know P, there must be a world accessible from w in which P is false, otherwise S would not be perfectly rational. Thus S in w knows P if and only if P is true in every world accessible from w. What S knows in each world is determined simply by the pair $\langle W, R \rangle$. Any pair $\langle W, R \rangle$, where W is a set and R is a binary relation on W, constitutes a *frame*. If several thinkers are in question, each has her own accessibility relation, so a frame $\langle W, \{R_i\}_{i \in I} \rangle$ is needed, where $\{R_i\}_{i \in I}$ is an indexed set of binary relations.

A class of frames $\langle W, R \rangle$ determines an epistemic logic. We start with the language of the propositional calculus, with propositional variables p, q, p', $q', \ldots$, negation ($\neg$) and conjunction ($\&$). Disjunction ($\vee$) and implication ($\rightarrow$) are defined in terms of $\neg$ and $\&$ in the usual way. We then add a knowledge operator **K** to the language. If the frames are of the form $\langle W, \{R_i\}_{i \in I} \rangle$ (I fixed), an indexed set of knowledge operators $\{\mathbf{K}_i\}_{i \in I}$ must be added; for simplicity, only one knowledge operator will be discussed. Any mapping [ ] of the propositional variables to propositions in a frame $\langle W, R \rangle$ determines a mapping of all formulas in the language to propositions in $\langle W, R \rangle$ by

$$[\neg A] = W - [A]$$
$$[A \ \& \ B] = [A] \cap [B]$$
$$[\mathbf{K}A] = \{w \in W : \forall x \in W \ w R x \Rightarrow x \in [A]\}.$$

A formula A is valid in $\langle W, R \rangle$ if and only if for every such mapping [ ], $[A] = W$, the proposition is true in every world. The epistemic logic L_C determined by a class C of frames is simply the set of formulas valid in every frame in C. L_C can easily be shown to have the following properties (writing $\vdash A$ for $A \in L_C$):

(US)	If $\vdash A$ and σ is a uniform substitution then $\vdash \sigma A$.
(Taut)	For any truth-functional tautology A, $\vdash A$.
(MP)	If $\vdash A$ and $\vdash A \rightarrow B$ then $\vdash B$.
(K)	$\vdash \mathbf{K}(p \rightarrow q) \rightarrow (\mathbf{K}p \rightarrow \mathbf{K}q)$.
(Nec)	If $\vdash A$ then $\vdash \mathbf{K}A$.

(US), (Taut), and (MP) are what one would expect of any classical logic. (K) and (Nec) say, in effect, that if a conclusion follows from a (perhaps empty) set of premises, and every premise is known, then the conclusion is known. An epistemic logic satisfying those five constraints is *normal*.

If C is the class of all frames, L_C is the weakest normal logic. More restricted classes of frames yield stronger logics. For example, if we require R to be reflexive, we gain

(T) $$\vdash \mathbf{K}p \rightarrow p$$

That is, one knows only what is true. All the frames considered in this paper are reflexive.

The transitivity of R corresponds to the KK principle, known in modal logic as the S4 or 4 axiom:

(4) $$\vdash \mathbf{K}p \rightarrow \mathbf{KK}p$$

To state the correspondence more exactly: (4) holds in L_C if and only if for every frame $\langle W, R \rangle$ in C, R is transitive. It may be helpful to rehearse the argument. Suppose that accessibility is transitive. If $\mathbf{K}p$ is true in a world w, then p is true in every world accessible from w, so by transitivity p is true in every world accessible from a world accessible from w, so $\mathbf{K}p$ is true in any world accessible from w, so $\mathbf{KK}p$ is true in w. Conversely, suppose that y is accessible from x and z from y, but z is not accessible from x. Assign to p the set of worlds accessible from x. Thus p is true in every world accessible from x, but not in z. Thus $\mathbf{K}p$ is true in x but not in y, so $\mathbf{KK}p$ is not true in x.

We can often use an idealized picture of knowledge to single out a class of frames, and explore the implications of the picture by identifying the epistemic logic determined by that class. To undermine the KK principle, we need non-transitive frames. However, we may begin with a picture of knowledge that singles out a class of transitive frames, for it helps to explain the appeal of the KK principle.

2. Appearance and Reality

The picture is that rational thinkers know everything about the way things appear to them, and nothing about anything else. For a given rational thinker S, there is a function a taking each possible world w to the way things appear to S in w, $a(w)$. S is omniscient about this function and about its value for the actual world. Thus if S is in w, a world x is epistemically possible just in case x is the same in appearance as w; x is accessible from w if and only if $a(x) = a(w)$. S knows a proposition if and only if it is true in every world with the same apearance as the world S is in. Thus accessibility is not just reflexive and transitive, but symmetric as well. We are therefore directed to look at frames $\langle W, R \rangle$ where R is an equivalence relation. The picture does not formally require any further constraints, for whenever R is an equivalence relation, a function like a can be defined.[3] The logic determined by these frames is S5, the weakest normal logic satisfying (T) and

(5) $$\vdash \neg \mathbf{K}p \rightarrow \mathbf{K}\neg \mathbf{K}p$$

The KK principle is derivable in S5. In effect, (5) says that if S does not know something, she knows that she does not know it.

There are many objections to (5), even as a principle about rational knowl-edge. One problem is that it does not allow for the fallibility of the sources of knowledge. If rational thinkers are not to be embarrassingly ignorant, their empirical knowledge will be drawn from sources that occasionally deliver false beliefs. On excellent evidence, S rationally believes the false proposition P. Since P is false, S does not know P. Now the evidence may be so good that S rationally believes that S knows P (surely rational thinkers often know that they know an empirical proposition, and are therefore willing to believe that they know such a proposition). Thus S fails to believe that she does not know P, so S fails to know that she does not know P.[4] (5) should be avoided. What this indicates about the picture of rational knowledge is that either rational knowledge can go beyond appearances or appearances can be false. Subtler objections to (5) use the idea that a rational thinker's ability to discriminate between appearances may vary from world to world. These objections need not be pressed, for the failure of the system S5, and in particular of axiom (5), in the logic of rational knowledge will follow in any case from the failure of rational knowledge to satisfy the KK principle. But the objections above, even if accepted, do not undermine the KK principle. For that a different picture of knowledge is needed. Four phenomena will be investigated: plural knowledge; time delays; limited discrimination; margins for error.[5]

3. Plural Knowledge

The KK principle is traditionally formulated for single subjects. However, we may begin by rehearsing its familiar failure for a plurality of subjects. Suppose that Peter and Paul each toss a coin. Each sees which way up his coin landed, and has no idea which way up the other's coin landed. Both men are rational and understand the structure of the situation. In fact, both coins landed heads. Neither Peter nor Paul is in a position to know that, of course, but each of them knows that at least one coin landed heads. However, Peter does not know that Paul knows that at least one coin landed heads; if Peter did know that, he could work out that Paul's coin landed heads, for he knows that if Paul knows that at least one coin landed heads then Paul's coin landed heads. Symmetrically, Paul does not know that Peter knows that at least one coin landed heads. Thus, although Peter and Paul know that at least one coin landed heads, Peter and Paul do not know that Peter and Paul know that at least one coin landed heads. As a plural subject, Peter and Pual fail the KK principle. They both know something, but they do not both know that they both know it; the knowledge they both have is not mutual or common between them. It is just such cases that the concept of common or mutual knowledge is designed to exclude. People have common knowledge of a proposition only if they all know it, they all know that they all know it, they all know that they all know that they all know it, and so on. If "they all know" satisfied the KK principle, this conjunction would collapse into its first conjunct.

For the sake of simplicity, Peter and Paul may each be assumed to satisfy the appearance/reality model of rational knowledge individually. There are just four worlds to consider, depending on the outcome of the two tosses. They form a set $W = \{hh, ht, th, tt\}$; for example, ht is the world in which Peter's coin lands heads and Paul's coin lands tails. To Peter, worlds have the same appearance if and only if his coin lands the same way in them. His accessibility relation R_1 is an equivalence relation, partitioning W according to the way his coin lands into the two equivalence classes $\{hh, ht\}$ and $\{th, tt\}$. The logic of "Peter knows" is S5; in particular, if Peter knows something, he knows that he knows it. Similarly, Paul's accessibility relation R_2 is an equivalence relation, partitioning W according to the way his coin lands into the two equivalence classes $\{hh, th\}$ and $\{ht, tt\}$. The logic of "Paul knows" is S5; in particular, if Paul knows something, he knows that he knows it.

In a world w, it is false that Peter and Paul know a proposition P if and only if either Peter fails to know P or Paul fails to know P, that is, if and only if, for some world x, either wR_1x or wR_2x, where P is false in x. Contrapositively, in w Peter and Paul know P if and only if P is true in every world x such that either $w R_1 x$ or $w R_2 x$. Thus Peter and Paul plurally have an accessibility relation R; it is the disjunction of R_1 and R_2. The notion of a frame can be applied to plural knowledge if it can be applied to singular knowledge. For example, $hh\,R\,hh$, $hh\,R\,ht$ and $hh\,R\,th$ but not $hh\,R\,tt$. Similarly, $ht\,R\,hh, ht\,R\,ht$ and $ht\,R\,tt$ but not $ht\,R\,th$. R is nontransitive, for $hhRht$ and $htRtt$ but not $hhRtt$; consequently, "Peter and Paul know" fails the KK principle. The underlying logical point is a simple one: the disjunction of two equivalence relations need not itself be an equivalence relation; in particular, it need not be transitive. Correspondingly, the conjunction of two operators each with an S5 logic need not itself have an S5 logic. The point generalizes to any number of rational thinkers. The accessibility relation for "each of them knows" is the disjunction of the accessibility relations for each of them. Even if each of the latter is an equivalence relation, the former need not be.[6]

What is the logic of plural knowledge, on the simplifying assumption that the logic of individual knowledge is S5? Equivalently, what follows about a relation given that it is the disjunction of a number of equivalence relations? The answer is rather complex, for combinatorial reasons, if we fix the number of individual thinkers, and so of equivalence relations. Let R be the disjunction of n equivalence relations $R_1, \ldots, R_n$. Then R has the following property:

$(*_n)$ If $wRx_1, \ldots, wRx_{n+1}$ then x_kRx_j for some $j, k (1 \leq j < k \leq n+1)$

For if $wR_{i(1)}x_1, wR_{i(2)}x_2, \ldots, wR_{i(n+1)}x_{n+1}$, where for $1 \leq j \leq n+1, 1 \leq i(j) \leq n$, then for some j and k, with $j < k$, $i(j) = i(k)$. Thus $wR_{i(j)}x_j$ and $wR_{i(j)}x_k$. By hypothesis, $R_{i(j)}$ is an equivalence relation, so $x_kR_{i(j)x_j}$, so x_kRx_j. $(*_n)$ induces the following constraint on the logic of joint knowledge for n thinkers:

$(**_n)$ $\qquad \vdash \mathbf{K}p_1 \vee \mathbf{K}(\mathbf{K}p_1 \to p_2) \vee \mathbf{K}(\mathbf{K}(p_1 \,\&\, p_2) \to p_3) \vee \cdots \vee$

$\qquad\qquad \mathbf{K}(\mathbf{K}(p_1 \,\&\, \cdots \,\&\, p_{n-1}) \to p_n \vee \mathbf{K}\neg\mathbf{K}(p_1 \,\&\, \cdots \,\&\, p_n)$

For if $(**_n)$ is false at a world w, there are worlds $x_1, \ldots, x_{n+1}$ such that $wRx_1, \ldots, wRx_{n+1}$, p_1 is false at x_1, $\mathbf{K}(p_1 \,\&\, \cdots \,\&\, p_{i-1})$ is true and p_i false at $x_i (1 < i \le n)$ and $\mathbf{K}(p_1 \,\&\, \cdots \,\&\, p_n)$ is true at x_{n+1}. Choose j and k as in $(*_n)$. Since $1 < k$, $\mathbf{K}(p_1 \,\&\, \cdots \,\&\, p_{k-1})$ is true at x_k; since $x_k R x_j$, $p_1 \,\&\, \cdots \,\&\, p_{k-1}$ is true at x_j; since $j < k$, p_j is therefore true at x_j; but $j < n + 1$, so this is contrary to hypothesis. Thus $(**_n)$ is valid in any class of frames satisfying $(*_n)$. For one thinker, $(**_n)$ is equivalent to the S5 axiom. For two, it says, for example: either (a) they both know that at least one coin landed heads or (b) they both know that if they both know that at least one coin landed heads then at least one coin landed tails or (c) they both know that it is false that they both know that at least one coin landed heads and at least one coin landed tails (in this example, (c) is true in every world). If $m \le n$, $(**_m)$ implies $(**_n)$ in every normal logic.

The strength of $(**_n)$ decreases strictly with n, for, given $n + 1$ or more persons, $(**_n)$ is false in Littlewood's "dirty face" story.[7] It is common knowledge that everyone can see every face but her own and that there is no communication. $\mathbf{K}$ is read as "persons $1, 2, \ldots, n + 1$ know," p_i as "either person i has a dirty face or someone else has a clean face." Suppose that in fact everyone has a dirty face. The first disjunct in $(**_n)$, $\mathbf{K}p_1$, is false because, for all person 1 knows, she has a clean face and everyone else has a dirty face, making p_1 false. The ith disjunct, $\mathbf{K}(\mathbf{K}(p_1 \,\&\, \cdots \,\&\, p_{i-1}) \to p_i)$, is false because, for all person i knows, she has a clean face and everyone else has a dirty face, making p_i false and $\mathbf{K}(p_1 \,\&\, \cdots \,\&\, p_{i-1})$ true, for everyone other than person i would know that someone other than persons $1, \ldots, i-1$—namely, person i—had a clean face, and person i would (and does) know that persons $1, \ldots, i-1$ have dirty faces. Similarly, the final disjunct, $\mathbf{K}\neg\mathbf{K}(p_1 \,\&\, \cdots \,\&\, p_n)$, is false because person $n + 1$ lacks the attributed knowledge. Thus $(**_n)$ is false in the envisaged situation. Thus if $m \neq n$, the logic of "S5-like thinkers $1, \ldots, m$ know that" differs from the logic of "S5-like thinkers $1, \ldots, n$ know that."

Matters are simpler if we ask for the logic of plural knowledge for a varying number of S5-like thinkers. Equivalently, what follows about a relation R given that it is the disjunction of some equivalence relations, but nothing about how many? Since any disjunction of reflexive relations is reflexive, and any disjunction of symmetric relations is symmetric, it follows that R is reflexive and symmetric. In fact, nothing more follows. We can show this by showing that if R is reflexive and symmetric, it is a disjunction of equivalence relations. Treat R as a set of ordered pairs. For each ordered pair $\langle x, y \rangle$, there is an equivalence relation R_{xy} containing just the ordered pairs $\langle x, y \rangle$, $\langle y, x \rangle$ and $\langle z, z \rangle$ for each z in the domain. R is simply the disjunction of all R_{xy} such that $\langle x, y \rangle \in R$.

The logic of plural knowledge for a varying number of S5-like thinkers is thus determined by the class of reflexive symmetric frames. The axiom corresponding to symmetry is known, for no very good reason, as the Brouwerian axiom:

(B) $\vdash \neg p \rightarrow \mathbf{K}\neg\mathbf{K}p$

(B) is valid in a frame $\langle W, R \rangle$ if and only if R is symmetric. On the present reading, (B) says that if a proposition is false then everyone knows that not everyone knows it. For each thinker S satisfies the axiom by hypothesis (it is a theorem of S5), and so knows that she does not know the proposition, and deduces that not everyone knows it. If (B) is wrong for plural rational knowledge, it is wrong for singular rational knowledge. The logic of plural knowledge for a varying number of S5-like thinkers is the Brouwerian system KTB, the smallest normal epistemic logic satisfying (T) and (B).

The failure of the KK principle for plural knowledge can be generalized. In KTB, for any formula $A, \vdash A \rightarrow \mathbf{K}A$ only in the trivial cases where $\vdash A$ or $\vdash \neg A$.[8] For example, the S5 axiom is not a theorem; not is the formula $\mathbf{K}^n p \rightarrow \mathbf{K}^{n+1} p$, where $\mathbf{K}^n$ is a sequence of n **K**s.

We now turn for the rest of the essay to failures of the KK principle for a single rational individual's knowledge. When such failures occur, the thinker lacks common knowledge with herself.

4. Time Delays

Learning takes time. This is so even if we ignore (as we shall do) the time needed to make inferences. In order to know a fact, we have to react to it, and reaction takes time. This is obvious where learning involves causal interaction with the environment, but there are subtler applications of the same point. We can find one in a puzzle that worried Stoic philosophers. They asked whether the wise man must know that he is wise, and argued that he does not always do so. For consider the very first moment at which he was wise. He did not yet know that he was wise, for he had had no time to react to his wisdom. If he had believed that he was wise, that belief would have been formed in response to a time at which he was not wise; it would be an unwise belief, and fail to constitute knowledge.[9] We might update the example by substituting the word "rational" for "wise," and conclude that there is a time at which the rational man is rational and does not know it. The challenge to the KK principle is clear: at the moment when someone first knows something, how do they know that they know it, not having had time to react to their knowledge?

There is a small mathematical problem with the argument. Suppose that instants of time are ordered like the real numbers. If there is a last instant at which S has never known P, there is no first instant at which S knows P, for between any two instants a third intervenes. Thus S can satisfy the principle that for any time at which S knows P there is an earlier time at which P was true, even if S has not always known that P.[10] This model always gives S some time to react, but it requires S to be able to react in arbitrarily short times. S

does not satisfy the principle that there is a positive length of time δt such that, for any time t, if at t S knows P then P was true at time $t - \delta t$. Yet one might suspect that, for beings who cannot act faster than the speed of light, the latter principle is what is needed.

Those problems can be avoided by a simple model in which time is discrete; instants are ordered like the positive and negative integers. Assume, for simplicity, that S can react to a fact with only an instant's delay. The time delay principle in that case says only that if at time t S knows P then at time $t - 1$ P was true. We also require that if at time t S knows P then P is true at time t, for S knows only what is true (this is axiom (T)). The effect of time delays can best be seen if we idealize away from all other obstacles to knowledge, by imagining a rational thinker who takes in everything, but not instantaneously. This is to assume that it is sufficient as well as necessary for S at t to know P that P be true at both $t - 1$ and t. This amounts to looking at a single frame $\langle W, R \rangle$ with the integers (i.e., times) as worlds, where wRx if and only if either $x = w$ or $x = w - 1$.

Since R is nontransitive, the KK principle fails. For example, if p is assigned the proposition true at all and only nonnegative points, that is, $[p] = \{x: x \geq 0\}$, then $[\mathbf{K}p] = \{x: x \geq 1\}$ and $[\mathbf{KK}p] = \{x: x \geq 2\}$; hence $\mathbf{K}p \to \mathbf{KK}p$ is false at 1. More generally, $[\mathbf{K}^n p] = \{x: x \geq n\}$, so the instance $\mathbf{K}^n p \to \mathbf{K}^{n+1} p$ of the KK principle is false at n. Each instant repairs one failure of the KK principle and introduces a new one at a higher level. Moreover, there is no time at which $\mathbf{K}^n p$ is true for every n, so S never has common knowledge with herself of this proposition. The frame also provides cases in which a proposition is sometimes known but never known to be known. For example, if $[q] = \{0, 1\}$ then $[\mathbf{K}q] = \{1\}$ and $[\mathbf{KK}q] = \{ \}$. More generally, if a proposition is false at a time, then at no later time on this model does S have common knowledge with herself of the proposition.

As already indicated, the failure of the KK principle on the frame has nothing to do with the time needed to make inferences. As soon as the rational thinker in question knows a proposition, she knows all its logical consequences; that is guaranteed by the frame theoretic semantics. On the present picture, its interpretation is simply that, as soon as a fact obtains, so do all its logical consequences; thus the thinker has as much time to react to the consequences as to what they are consequences of.

Because each world has R to at most two worlds, the logic of the frame can be shown to contain the following theorem:[11]

(#) $\vdash \mathbf{K}(p \to q) \lor \mathbf{K}(p \to \neg q) \lor \mathbf{K}p$

The logic of the frame can be shown to be the weakest normal logic containing both (T) and (#), KT#.[12] The failure of the KK principle can be generalized as before. In KT#, for any formula A, $\vdash A \to \mathbf{K}A$ only if either $\vdash A$ or $\vdash \neg A$.[13] A gap between the times at which A is true and the times at which it is known is ruled out only if A must be either always true or always false.

We can avoid the strange principle (#) by using time delays over many instants. For example, we might consider a frame $\langle W, R \rangle$ in which W is the set of real numbers and wRx if and only if $w - 1 \leq x \leq w$. There are many other ways of realizing the general idea that wRx if and only if x is in an interval of fixed length up to w. The logic of such frames is rather sensitive to their mathematical structure. However, in all such frames R will have the property (sometimes known as *connectedness*) that if wRx and wRy then either xRy or yRx (the former disjunct is realized if x is not earlier than y, the latter if y is not earlier than x). A frame has that property if and only if it validates this formula:[14]

(D1) $\vdash \mathbf{K}(\mathbf{K}p \to q) \vee \mathbf{K}(\mathbf{K}q \to p)$

Of course, (D1) will not survive the introduction of obstacles to knowledge beyond time delays.[15]

5. Limited Discrimination

Perfectly rational thinkers need not have perfect eyesight; their powers of discrimination are limited. Detailed examination of a typical case suggests that such limits typically involve failure of the KK principle. The case used here involves a time series, but the point could be made equally well for synchronic discrimination; time delays are no longer the issue.

Our rational thinker is monitoring the growth of a tree. Each morning she goes to see what progress it has made. Her eyesight is not perfect, and it is easiest to imagine that she does not use measuring instruments—but even if she does, they are of limited precision too, and the case is not essentially different. Of course, the tree cannot grow quickly enough for her to see that it is taller than the day before, and on some days it may not grow at all. She is quite aware of this limit to her knowledge. However, she can see that the tree is taller than it was a year ago. Let $h(i)$ be the height of the tree on the ith day after it was planted. There is a small quantity δ (e.g., a millimeter) of which she knows two things: (a) if the difference in height between days is less than δ then she does not know that there is any difference in height at all; (b) the tree cannot grow by as much as δ in one day.

Our thinker's knowledge of the tree's growth itself grows over time. However, this is not the central feature of the example for present purposes. We can regard her as knowing a proposition just in case she knows it from some time or other onwards. Alternatively, the argument to come could be given in terms of what she knows 5000 days after the tree was planted. One could even give it a synchronic form, by imagining the thinker inspecting a series of photographs of the tree, one for each day. Such differences do not affect the argument.[16] Principles (a) and (b) can be symbolized as follows, for any i and j:

$(a_{i,j})$ $\qquad$ $\mathbf{K}[(|h(i) - h(j)| < \delta) \to \neg\mathbf{K}(h(i) \neq h(j))]$

(b_i) $\qquad$ $\mathbf{K}(|h(i) - h(i+1)| < \delta)$

From these two principles we can use the rationality of the thinker to argue for the following conclusion, for any i:

(c_i) $\qquad$ $\mathbf{KK}(h(0) \neq h(i+1)) \to \mathbf{K}(h(0) \neq h(i))$

The argument is as follows. Suppose that $\mathbf{K}(h(0) \neq h(i+1))$, and make two auxiliary assumptions, $|h(0) - h(i+1)| < \delta \to \neg\mathbf{K}(h(0) \neq h(i+1))$ and $|h(i) - h(i+1)| < \delta$. The supposition and the first auxiliary assumption entail $|h(0) - h(i+1) \geq \delta$. By the second auxiliary assumption, $h(0) \neq h(i)$. Now our rational thinker will make this inference for herself, so if she knows the supposition that $\mathbf{K}(h(0) \neq h(i+1))$ and the two auxiliary assumptions then she knows the conclusion that $h(0) \neq h(i)$. But $(a_{0,i+1})$ says that she knows the first auxiliary assumption and (b_i) says that she knows the second. Thus by $(a_{0,i+1})$ and (b_i), if she knows the supposition then she knows the conclusion; but that is just what (c_i) says.

$\qquad$ If the KK principle held, (c_i) would simplify to

(d_i) $\qquad$ $\mathbf{K}(h(0) \neq h(i+1)) \to \mathbf{K}(h(0) \neq h(i))$

Since (c_i) held for all i, so would (d_i). but then we can string (d_0), (d_1), ..., (d_{4999}) together to reach the conclusion $\mathbf{K}(h(0) \neq h(5000)) \to \mathbf{K}(h(0) \neq h(0))$. Since $\mathbf{K}(h(0) \neq h(0))$ is absurd, that yields $\neg\mathbf{K}(h(0) \neq h(5000))$. But that conclusion is absurd too, for it says that our rational thinker does not know that the height of the tree is any different after many years than it was at the beginning. What the argument shows is that the KK principle does not enable us to make sense of situations in which thinkers know of limits to their powers of discrimination.

$\qquad$ So far the argument has been negative. What we need now is a positive account of limited discrimination on which the KK principle fails. To construct such an account, we specify a world w_X for each subset X of the natural numbers. Let $h_X(i)$ be the height of the tree on day i in world w_X. The growth of the tree in w_X is specified recursively:

$$h_X(0) = 0$$
$$h_X(i+1) = h_X(i) \qquad\qquad \text{if } i \in X$$
$$h_X(i+1) = h_X(i) + 2\delta/3 \qquad \text{otherwise}$$

We stipulate that world w_Y is accessible from world w_X if and only if $|h_X(i) - h_Y(i)| \leq 2\delta/3$ for all i (the worlds are too similar to be discriminated). A formula is true at world w_X if and only if the result of subscripting h throughout by X is true.

We can check that schemata $(a_{i,j})$ and (b_i) are true at every world in this frame. (b_i) is easy: For any X and i, $|h_X(i) - h_X(i+1)| < \delta$ by definition of h_X. For $(a_{i,j})$, suppose that $|h_X(i) - h_X(j)| < \delta$, where $i \leq j$. Let $Y = X \cup \{k: i \leq k < j\}$. Now if Y had at least two members not in X, by construction $h_X(j) \geq h_X(i) + 4\delta/3$, contrary to the hypothesis that $|h_X(i) - h_X(j)| < \delta$. Thus X has at most one member not in Y (w_X and w_Y differ at most in that one day the tree grows in w_X but not in w_Y). But then by construction $h_X(k) \leq h_Y(k) \leq h_X(k) + 2\delta/3$ for all k, so $|h_X(k) - h_Y(k)| \leq 2\delta/3$ for all k. Thus w_Y is accessible from w_X. But $h_Y(j) = h_Y(i)$ by construction. In other words, for any world in which $|h(i) - h(j)| < \delta$, there is an accessible world in which $h(i) = h(j)$. Thus $(a_{i,j})$ is true at every world in the frame.

We now need to check that the absurd conclusion $\neg\mathbf{K}(h(0) \neq h(5000))$ is false at some world· in the frame: we want a world at which $\mathbf{K}(h(0) \neq h(5000))$ is true. In fact, we can prove something stronger. There is a world at which for any i, j, k such that $i < j - k$, $\mathbf{K}^k(h(i) \neq h(j))$ is true: that is, the thinker has k iterations of knowledge that the height of the tree on day j is not what it was on day i. For consider $w_{\{\}}$, in which the tree grows every day. Thus $h_{\{\}}(j) = 2j\delta/3$. To prove that $\mathbf{K}^k(h(i) \neq h(j))$ is true at $w_{\{\}}$, we need to prove that $h_X(i) \neq h_X(j)$ for any X such that w_X is within k steps of accessibility of $w_{\{\}}$. Note that for any X, $h_X(i) \leq 2i\delta/3$. By definition of accessibility, if w_X is within k accessibility steps of $w_{\{\}}$, $h_{\{\}}(j) \leq h_X(j) + 2k\delta/3$. Thus if $i < j - k$,

$$h_X(i) \leq 2i\delta/3 < 2(j-k)\delta/3 = h_{\{\}}(j) - 2k\delta/3 \leq h_X(j)$$

Hence $h_X(i) \neq h_X(j)$, as required. Now put $i = 0$, $j = 5000$. The result shows that the thinker can have up to 4999 iterations of knowledge that the height of the tree after ten years is not what it was on day 0. That should be enough for most purposes, although it does not amount to common knowledge with herself of the difference in height.

The KK principle must fail in the frame, for all the other premises of the argument to $\neg\mathbf{K}(h(0) \neq h(5000))$ are true at every world. In fact, the result in the previous paragraph is the best possible, in the sense that if $j < i$, the thinker does not have $j - i$ iterations of knowledge that $h(i) \neq h(j)$ at any world, although she does have every smaller number of iterations at $w_{\{\}}$. To prove that the thinker lacks $j - i$ iterations at world w_X, define a sequence of worlds $w_{X(0)}, \ldots, w_{X(j-1)}$ by $X(k) = X \cup \{m: i \leq m < i + k\}$. Thus $X(0) = X$. Now each $X(k)$ differs from $X(k+1)$ in at most one member; by an earlier argument, it follows that $w_{X(k+1)}$ is accessible from $w_{X(k)}$. Thus one can reach $w_{X(j-i)}$ in $j - i$ accessibility steps from w_X. But $X(j-i) = X \cup \{m: i \leq m < j\}$, so $h_{X(j-i)}(i) = h_{X(j-i)}(j)$. Hence $\mathbf{K}^{j-i}(h(i) \neq h(j))$ is false at w_X. The nontransitivity of accessibility in this frame is no surprise, for one world was defined to be accessible from another just in case they were "not too different." Being not too different is a nontransitive relation, for many small differences can add up to a big one. Of course, there is a huge variety of ways in which differences can be measured, depending on how much weighting is given to the various respects in which the worlds differ; the relevant weights will be determined by the kind of knowledge at issue and other contextual factors.

Being not too different is a reflexive and symmetric relation. The accessibility relation used here is obviously reflexive and symmetric. Thus the logic of the frame is at least as strong as the Brouwerian system KTB—the logic which was seen in Section 2 to be characteristic of plural knowledge for thinkers who are individually S5-like. KTB is indeed the logic for fixed margins for error in the following sense. Let C be the class of frames $\langle W, R \rangle$ such that for some mtric d on W and some $\varepsilon > 0$, for all x, y in W, xRy if and only if $d(x, y) < \varepsilon$ (ε is the margin for error); then L_C is precisely KTB. For any such R is reflexive and symmetric by the definition of a metric; conversely, if R is reflexive and symmetric, we can define a suitable metric d by

$$d(x, x) = 0$$
$$d(x, y) = 2 \quad \text{if } xRy \text{ but } x \neq y$$
$$d(x, y) = 4 \quad \text{if not } xRy$$

Put $\varepsilon = 3$. Thus C is the class of reflexive symmetric frames, so L_C is KTB.

The small differences defining accessibility can be thought of as *margins for error*. Even a rational thinker knows which world she is in only to within a margin for error. She knows a proposition P in a world only if P is true in all sufficiently similar worlds. Every iteration of the knowledge operator requires P to leave a further margin for error. Since P may leave only finitely many margins for error, the KK principle fails.[17]

6. Margins for Error

The examples considered so far have all been characterized by logics with theorems that look too strong when interpreted in terms of rational knowledge: $(**_n)$, (B), (#), (D1). Moreover, if we tried·to combine these axioms, we should find ourselves back with the KK principle. For example, accessibility is symmetric in any frame for (B) and connected (in a sense explained above) in any frame for (D1); but it is easy to show that any symmetric connected relation is transitive, so accessibility is transitive in any frame for both (B) and (D1).[18] Yet the two axioms characterize different realizations of the same underlying intuition about margins for error. Time delays are essentially temporal margins for error, and validate (D1) when they are the only obstacles to knowledge; spatial margins for error like those in Section 4 validate (B) when they are the only obstacles. The question is what logic results from a less restrictive conception of the obstacles to knowledge.

The minimal logic for rational knowledge is KT, sometimes known as T, the weakest normal system containing axiom (T)—that is, the weakest in which knowledge entails truth and is closed under logical consequence. Might there be some additional principle in common between the stronger systems consid-

ered in Sections 2 to 4 that ought to be included in a logic for rational knowledge? We can show that there is no such principle if we assume that rational
knowledge is subject to *variable* margins for error, by showing that KT is the
logic for such knowledge. Thus, in determining the logic for rational knowledge, we need not consider any obstacle to knowledge beyond variable margins
for error, since consideration of them already forces us to the minimal system.

A fixed margin for error principle has the following form: For every proposition P of the relevant kind, P is known in world w only if P is true in every
world x for which $d(w, x) < \varepsilon$. Think of this as a schema, whose instances we
specify by specifying the relevant kind of proposition, the metric d, and the
constant $\varepsilon > 0$. A variable margins for error principle has this form: For every
proposition P of the relevant kind, P is known in world w only if for some
$\delta > 0$ P is true in every world x for which $d(w, x) < \varepsilon + \delta$. A margin ε wide is
just not enough for safety, but anything wider will do.

If one puts $\varepsilon = 0$ in a variable margins for error principle, it says that P is
true at every world in some open neighbourhood of w. This would express the
idea that although the rational thinker's knowledge cannot be perfectly precise,
it can attain any degree of precision short of perfection. This idea is quite
consistent with the KK principle, for if P is true at every world in some
open neighbourhood of w, then for every world x in that neighbourhood, P
is true in every world in some open neighbourhood of x. Thus when a variable
margins for error principle with $\varepsilon = 0$ is the only obstacle to knowledge, the
KK principle holds. However, in many situations a rational thinker's knowledge cannot be made arbitrarily precise. She cannot make her eyesight arbitrarily good just by concentrating hard enough. For situations of this kind we
need $\varepsilon > 0$.

The idea of variable margins for error takes us just beyond the idea of a
standard frame $\langle W, R \rangle$. In effect, we have a family of accessibility relations R_δ,
where $wR_\delta x$ if and only if $d(w, x) < \varepsilon + \delta$; the formula $\mathbf{K}p$ is true at w if and
only if, for some δ, the formula p is true in every world x such that $wR_\delta x$. The
following definition will help:

A *variable margin frame* is a triple $\langle W, d, \varepsilon \rangle$, where W is a set, d is a metric
on W and ε is a positive real number.

A *valuation* [ ] on such a frame is any mapping of formulas to propositions
(subsets of W) such that for all formulas A and B:

$$[\neg A] = W - [A]$$
$$[A \,\&\, B] = [A] \cap [B]$$
$$[\mathbf{K}A] = \{w \in W : \exists \delta > 0 \; \forall x \in W \; d(w, x) < \varepsilon + \delta \Rightarrow x \in [A]\}$$

A formula A is valid on a variable margin frame $\langle W, d, \varepsilon \rangle$ if and only if for
every valuation [ ] on the frame, $[A] = W$. It turns out that a formula is valid
on every variable margin frame if and only if it is a theorem of KT (see

Appendix). Thus KT is the appropriate logic for knowledge subject to variable margins for error.[19]

As usual, the failure of the KK principle can be generalized. For any formula of the KK principle can be generalized. for any formula A, if $A \to \mathbf{K}A$ is a theorem of KT, then either A is a theorem of KT or $\neg A$ is.[20]

Since metrics are by definition symmetric, $(d(x, y) = d(y, x))$, the failure of the (B) axiom in variable margin frames may seem surprising. To see what is going on, consider any example. Let W be the set of real numbers, $d(x, y) = |x - y|$, $\varepsilon = 1$, and $[p] = \{w: w \neq 0\}$. Then $[\mathbf{K}p] = \{w: \exists \delta > 0 \, \forall x | w - x| < 1 + \delta \Rightarrow x \neq 0\} = \{w: w < -1 \quad \text{or} \quad 1 < w\}$. Hence $[\mathbf{K}\neg\mathbf{K}p] = \{w: \exists \delta > 0 \, \forall x | w - x | < 1 + \delta \to -1 \leq x \leq 1\} = \{\ \}$. Thus $0 \notin [\neg p \to \mathbf{K}\neg\mathbf{K}p]$, so (B) is not valid on $\langle W, d, \varepsilon \rangle$.

One obvious issue for further research is the extension of the preceding ideas to probabilistic concepts. The failure of the KK principle may correspond to the existence of cases in which S assigns a probability of 1 to the proposition A, but assigns a probability of less than 1 to the propositions that she assigns a probability of 1 to A. The phenomena discussed here suggest that there need be nothing irrational in such a probability distribution.[21]

Appendix

Theorem
A is valid on every variable margin frame if and only if $\vdash_{KT} A$.

Sketch of proof. (I) *Soundness.* Let $\langle W, d, \varepsilon \rangle$ be a variable margin frame. We need to show that the axioms of KT are all valid on $\langle W, d, \varepsilon \rangle$ and that the rules of inference of KT all preserve validity. Of these, only the axiom $\mathbf{K}(p \to q) \to (\mathbf{K}p \to \mathbf{K}q)$ is worth looking at. Suppose that $w \in [\mathbf{K}(p \to q)] \cap [\mathbf{K}p]$. Then there are δ_1, δ_2 such that $d(w, x) < \varepsilon + \delta_1$ implies $x \in [p \to q]$ and $d(w, x) < \varepsilon + \delta_2$ implies $x \in [p]$. Let $\delta = \min\{\delta_1, \delta_2\}$. Then $d(w, x) < \varepsilon + \delta$ implies $x \in [p \to q]$ and $x \in [p]$, so it implies $x \in [q]$. Hence $w \in [\mathbf{K}q]$. The rest is routine. Thus every theorem of KT is valid on every variable margin frame.

(II) *Completeness.* Suppose that not $\vdash_{KT} A_0$. Since KT is complete for reflexive frames, there is a frame $\langle W, R \rangle$ and a mapping [ ] from formulas to subsets of W such that $[A_0] \neq W$ and for all formulas A and B:

$$[\neg A] = W - [A]$$
$$[A \ \& \ B] = [A] \cap [B]$$
$$[\mathbf{K}A] = \{w \in W: \forall x \in W \ wRx \Rightarrow x \in [A]\}$$

We use $\langle W, R \rangle$ to construct a variable margin frame $\langle W^*, d, \varepsilon \rangle$ on which A_0 is not valid. Put

$$W^* = \{\langle x, y, i \rangle : x \in W, y \in W, yRx, i \in \mathbf{N}\}.$$

$$
\begin{aligned}
d(\langle w, x, i \rangle, \langle y, z, j \rangle) &= 0 && \text{if } w = y, x = z \text{ and } i = j \\
\text{otherwise} &= 1 && \text{if } w = z \text{ and } x = y \\
&= (i + 2)/(i + 1) && \text{if } w \neq z \text{ but } w = y \\
&= (j + 2)/(j + 1) && \text{if } w = z \text{ but } x \neq y \\
&= 2 && \text{if } w \neq z \text{ and } x \neq y
\end{aligned}
$$

d is easily seen to be a metric. Thus $\langle W^*, d, 1 \rangle$ is a variable margin frame. We can define a valuation $[\ ]$ on $\langle W^*, d, 1 \rangle$ by setting $[p_i] = \{\langle w, x, i \rangle \in W^* : w \in [p_i]\}$ for each propositional variable p_i and letting the recursive clauses in the definition of a valuation do the rest.

Lemma

$[A] = \{\langle w, x, i \rangle \in W^* : w \in [A]\}$ *for every formula A.*

Proof. By induction of the complexity of A.

Basis: by definition of $[\ ]$.

Induction step: Suppose $[A] = \{\langle w, x, i \rangle \in W^* : w \in [A]\}$. We must show $[KA] = \{\langle w, x, i \rangle \in W^* : w \in [KA]\}$ (the cases of & and $\neg$ are trivial).

Suppose $\langle w, x, i \rangle \in [KA]$. We must show $w \in [KA]$. Suppose wRy. We must show $y \in [A]$. Now for some $\delta > 0$, $d(\langle w, x, i \rangle, \langle y, w, j \rangle) < 1 + \delta$ implies $\langle y, w, y \rangle \in [A]$ for $j \in \mathbf{N}$.

By definition of d,

$$d(\langle w, x, i \rangle, \langle y, w, j \rangle) \leq (j + 2)/(j + 1) \qquad \text{for } j \in \mathbf{N}$$

For large enough j, $(j + 2)/(j + 1) < 1 + \delta$, so

$$d(\langle w, x, i \rangle, \langle y, w, j \rangle) < 1 + \delta$$

Thus for some j, $\langle y, w, j \rangle \in [A]$. By induction hypothesis, $y \in [A]$, as required. Thus $w \in [KA]$.

Conversely, suppose $w \in [KA]$. We must show $\langle w, x, i \rangle \in [KA]$. The value $1/(i + 1)$ for δ will do. Suppose

$$d(\langle w, x, i \rangle, \langle y, z, j \rangle) < (i + 2)/(i + 1)$$

We must show $\langle y, z, j \rangle \in [A]$. Since $(i + 2)/(i + 1) \leq 2$, the inequality implies, given the definition of d, that either $w = y, x = z$ and $i = j$ or $w = z$. In the former case, note that $w \in [A]$ (since $w \in [KA]$ and R is reflexive), so by induction hypothesis $\langle y, z, j \rangle = \langle w, x, i \rangle \in [A]$. In the latter case $(w = z)$, since $\langle y, z, j \rangle \in W^*$, zRy, that is, wRy. Since $w \in [KA]$, $y \in [A]$, so by induction hypothesis $\langle y, z, j \rangle \in [A]$. Thus $\langle w, x, i \rangle \in [KA]$. This completes the proof of the lemma. ∎

To complete the proof of the theorem, we need to show $[A_0] \neq W^*$, for then A_0 is not valid on all variable margin frames. Now for some $w \in W$, $w \notin [A_0]$. But wRw, since r is reflexive, so $\langle w, w, 0 \rangle \in W^*$; by the lemma $\langle w, w, 0 \rangle \notin [A_0]$, so $[A_0] \neq W^*$.   ∎

Notes

1. Lenzen (1978, 69–77) surveys earlier discussion of the KK principle. Among later work may be mentioned Wiggins (1979) and Sorensen (1988, 242–43 and 313–17).

2. Chellas (1980) and Hughes and Cresswell (1984) give detailed expositions of the possible-worlds semantics for modal logic. The use of similar techniques in epistemic logic goes back at least to Hintikka (1962); for an elementary survey see Halpern (1986).

3. Mathematically, the appearance/reality model is equivalent to the game theoretic model of knowledge by means of information partitions.

4. See Hintikka (1962, 106), Lenzen (1978, 79), Humberstone (1988, 187).

5. The appearance/reality model is not the only source of support for the KK principle. For example, if knowledge were equated with provability from a fixed stock of assumptions, it would satisfy the KK principle, for if a proposition is provable then it is provably provable; (5) is not validated, for unprovability does not entail provable unprovability. For the modal logic of provability in formal systems extending arithmetic, see Boolos (1979) or Smoryński (1985). However, this logic lacks the theorem $\mathbf{K}p \rightarrow p$, and so is not a suitable logic for knowledge; it also has the theorem $\mathbf{K}\neg\mathbf{K}p \rightarrow \mathbf{K}(p \ \& \ \neg p)$. These particular results are avoided if one looks at the logic of "formally provable and true" rather than "formally provable", but even this logic has the theorem $\neg\mathbf{K}\neg(\mathbf{K}p \lor \mathbf{K}\neg p)$, so that it is unacceptable as a logic of knowledge (see Boolos 1979, 160–61 for related results). Thus a concept of informal provability would be needed. The considerations below will undermine this model too. In particular: if someone knows the assumptions in the fixed stock but does not know that she knows them, her knowledge that she has deduced a conclusion from them will not give her knowledge that she knows that conclusion. For connections between common knowledge and the failure of (5) for provability, see Shin (1993).

6. See Aumann (1976).

7. See Littlewood (1953) and Fudenberg and Tirole (1991, 544–48).

8. See Williamson (1992b) for a proof.

9. See Sedley (1977, 94).

10. It may be objected that if a proposition is true at any time then it is true at every time. However, we can speak of a state of affairs (e.g., someone's being wise) obtaining at one time and not at another. The knowledge discussed in Section 3 may be regarded as knowledge of states of affairs. The intuition is that a state of affairs can be known to obtain only if it has been obtaining for some time. This complication is ignored in the text. Note that even if the intuition holds good only for a limited range of states of affairs, the objection to the KK principle remains provided that for each state of affairs X in the range, the range also includes the state of affairs of X's being known to obtain.

11. *Proof.* If (#) is invalid in a frame, there are worlds w, x, y, z and an assignment of propositions to formulas such that wRx, wRy, wRz $p \rightarrow q$ is false at x, $p \rightarrow \neg q$ is false at y and p is false at z. Hence p is true and q false at x, and p is true and q true at y. Hence x, y, and z are distinct.

12. *Sketch of proof.* Let $\langle W, R \rangle$ be the frame described in the text. If $\vdash_{KT\#} A$, A is valid on $\langle W, R \rangle$ for reasons already given. Suppose that not $\vdash_{KT\#} A$. Then A is false at some world w in the canonical model of KT#; this model is based on a frame in which every world can access itself and at most one other world. Now A is false at w in the submodel of the canonical model generated by w, so A is not valid on the frame of this submodel. The latter frame is a p-morphic image of $\langle W, R \rangle$. By the p-morphism theorem, A is not valid on $\langle W, R \rangle$ (for background see Hughes and Cresswell 1984, 16–29 and 70–73).

13. *Sketch of proof:* Let KD! be the smallest normal system having the theorem $\neg Kp \equiv K\neg p$. Define two mappings s and t from formulas to formulas inductively as follows: $sp_i = tp_i = p_i$ for each propositional variable p_i; $s\neg A = \neg sA$; $t\neg A = \neg tA$; $s(A \ \& \ B) = sA \ \& \ sB$; $t(A \ \& \ B) = tA \ \& \ tB$; $sKA = sA \ \& \ KsA$; $tKA = (tA \lor K\neg tA) \rightarrow KtA$. One can show by induction on the length of proofs in standard proof systems for KT# and KD! (with MP and Nec as the only rules of inference) that if $\vdash_{KT\#} A$ then $\vdash_{KD!} sA$ and if $\vdash_{KD!} A$ then $\vdash_{KT\#} tA$. One can also show by induction on the complexity of A that $\vdash_{KT\#} A \equiv tsA$. Now suppose $\vdash_{KT\#} A \rightarrow KA$. Hence $\vdash_{KD!} s(A \rightarrow KA)$. But $s(A \rightarrow KA) = sA \rightarrow (sA \ \& \ KsA)$, so $\vdash_{KD!} sA \rightarrow KsA$. By a result of Williamson (1992b), either $\vdash_{KD!} sA$ or $\vdash_{KD!} \neg sA$, that is, $\vdash_{KD!} s\neg A$. Hence $\vdash_{KT\#} tsA$ or $\vdash_{KT\#} ts\neg A$. But $\vdash_{KT\#} A \equiv tsA$ and $\vdash_{KT\#} \neg A \equiv ts\neg A$, so $\vdash_{KT\#} A$ or $\vdash_{KT\#} \neg A$.

14. See Hughes and Cresswell (1984, 30–31).

15. An argument like that of Section 4 is discussed in more detail in Williamson (1992a), where various objections are rebutted and connections with the paradoxes of the Surprise Examination and Iterated Prisoner's Dilemma are made.

16. The knowledge in question is not restricted to direct perceptual knowledge (otherwise deductive closure would fail even for a perfectly rational subject). It may therefore be objected that our thinker can know that $h(i) \neq h(j)$ even when $|h(i) - h(j)| = 2\delta/3$. For a k can exist such that $|h(i) - h(k)| = 4\delta/3$ and $|h(j) - h(k)| = 2\delta/3$, so that she can directly discriminate $h(i)$ but not $h(j)$ from $h(k)$; why cannot she use this fact indirectly to discriminate $h(i)$ from $h(j)$? The fallacy in this objection is the assumption that the subject is always in a position to know whether she has discriminated successfully or not. Since discrimination between $h(i)$ and $h(j)$ is represented as $K(h(i) \neq h(j))$, the assumption combines special cases of the (4) and (5) axioms. If it were true, a rational subject with terrible eyesight and a terrible memory could work out many years later on exactly which days the tree had grown, by arguments of the above form. For small enough δ, (a) is compelling even for inferential knowledge.

17. One might attempt to restore the KK principle by equating knowledge of p with the infinite conjunction $\wedge_{0 \leq n} K^n p$, rather than with Kp. This corresponds to replacing the original nontransitive accessibility relation by its transitive ancestral. However, the resulting notion is too strong to be of much interest. For example, by what is shown in the text our thinker will not know that $h(i) \neq h(j)$ in the new sense, no matter how much the tree has grown from i to j. The new notion fails to discriminate between relevantly different cases. Nor can one recover the old, discriminating notion of knowledge as true belief of high probability, for the former notion, unlike the probabilistic one, satisfies the principle $(Kp \ \& \ Kq) \rightarrow K(p \ \& \ q)$.

18. Correspondingly, (4) is a theorem of KBD1, the smallest normal logic containing (B) and (D1). For otherwise it would be invalid on the frame of the canonical model for KBD1; but this frame can be shown to be symmetric and connected in the sense defined in the text, and therefore transitive.

19. The remark in the text assumes that every metric can be realized in some possible epistemic situation. This assumption can be weakened to: Every metric on a countable domain can be realized in some possible epistemic situation. For since KT has the finite model property (Hughes and Cresswell 1984, 142–43), the frame $\langle W, R \rangle$ in the completeness leg of the theorem in the Appendix may be taken to be finite, in which case W^* will be countable by construction.

20. See Williamson (1992b) and Chellas and Segerberg (1994).

21. See also Williamson (1992a, 237–39). The approach of Monderer and Samet (1989) to common belief can be generalized to a context in which the KK principle fails as follows. Let $\langle \Omega, \Sigma, \mu \rangle$ be a probability space, I a set of agents, and R_i a (possibly nontransitive) accessibility relation on Ω such that if $\omega \in \Omega$, $\{\pi: \omega R_i \pi\}$ is an event. For any event C, $i \in I$, $\omega \in \Omega$, and $0 \leq p \leq 1$, i p-believes C at ω ($\omega \in B_i^P(C)$) just in case $\mu(C|\{\pi: \omega R_i \pi\}) \geq p$. Now put $E^P(C) = \cap_{n \geq 1} C^n$, where $C^0 = C$ and, for $n \geq 1$, $C^n = \cap_{m < n} \cap_{i \in I} B_i^P(C^m)$. Then C is common p-belief at ω iff $\omega \in E^P(C)$.

References

Aumann, R. 1976. "Agreeing to disagree," *Annals of Statistics* 4: 1236–39.

Boolos, G. 1979. *The Unprovability of Consistency* (Cambridge: Cambridge University Press).

Chellas, B.F. 1980. *Modal Logic* (Cambridge: Cambridge University Press).

Chellas, B.F. and Segerberg, K. 1994. "Modal logics with the MacIntosh Rule," *Journal of Philosophical Logic*, 23: 67–86.

Fudenberg, D. and Tirole, J. 1991. *Game Theory* (Cambridge, Mass.: MIT Press).

Halpern, J.Y. 1986. "Reasoning about knowledge: an overview," in J.Y. Halpern, ed., *Theoretical Aspects of Reasoning about Knowledge: Proceedings of the 1986 Conference* (Los Altos: Morgan Kaufmann): 1–17.

Hintikka, J. 1962. *Knowledge and Belief* (Ithaca: Cornell University Press).

Hughes, G.E. and Cresswell, M.J. 1984. *A Companion to Modal Logic* (London: Methuen).

Humberstone, I.L. 1988. "Some epistemic capacities," *Dialectica* 42: 183–200.

Lenzen, W. 1978. "Recent work in epistemic logic," *Acta Philosophica Fennica* 30: 1–219.

Littlewood, J.E. 1953. *A Mathematician's Miscellany* (London: Methuen).

Monderer, D. and Samet, D. 1989. "Approximating common knowledge with common belief," *Games and Economic Behaviour* 1: 170–90.

Sedley, D.N. 1977. "Diodorus Cronus and Hellenistic philosophy," *Proceedings of the Cambridge Philological Society* 23: 74–120.

Shin, H.S. 1993. "Logical structure of common knowledge," *Journal of Economic Theory*, 60: 1–13.

Smoryński, C. 1985. *Self-reference and Modal Logic* (New York: Springer).

Sorensen, R.A. 1988. *Blindspots* (Oxford: Clarendon Press).

Wiggins, D.R.P. 1979. "On knowing, knowing that one knows and consciousness," in E. Saarinen, R. Hilpinen, I. Niiniluoto and M. Provence Hintikka, eds., *Essays in Honour of Jaakko Hintikka* (Dordrecht: Reidel): 237–48.

Williamson, T. 1992a. "Inexact knowledge," *Mind* 101: 217–42.

Williamson, T. 1992b. "An alternative rule of disjunction in modal logic," *Notre Dame Journal of Formal Logic* 33: 89–100.

CHAPTER 7

How Much Common Belief Is Necessary for a Convention?

Hyun Song Shin and Timothy Williamson

1. Introduction

Coordination problems come in many forms. A case of particular interest to students of norms and conventions is that in which the payoff function of the coordination game depends on the state of nature. In such an environment, the possibility of conditioning one's actions on some signal of the state of nature adds an extra dimension to the coordination problem, and makes it a more accurate representation of the problem of day-to-day interaction in which individuals face a variety of coordination problems determined by the state of nature. In such an environment, the problem becomes one of coordinating on the most advantageous set of rules of action, where each player's rule of action maps a possible realization of his signal to an action.

If the players have perfect information, the problem can be reduced to the solution of each one-shot coordination game for each realization of the state of nature. The equilibrium strategies could then be highly complex in the sense that it prescribes actions that depend very finely on the state of nature. However, if the players have imperfect information, they will not have common knowledge of the game being played. Constraints will be placed on the rules of action that can be sustained as an equilibrium. Nevertheless, the players will have beliefs about their environment, and beliefs about other players' beliefs. Our main question can be posed thus: Given a structure of beliefs between the players about their environment, how complex can a convention be?

The purpose of this essay is to show that for some coordination problems, the optimizing behaviour of individuals eliminates all rules of action except those which are "very simple." To be more precise, equilibrium actions of all players must be common belief with probability 1 at every state. Common belief with probability close to 1 will not do. In other words, a convention can be sustained only if it prescribes actions that do not depend on fine distinctions of the state of nature. Rather, it must be simple enough so that in spite of differential information the equilibrium actions of all players are common belief with probability 1 at every state.

In pointing to this connection between common belief and equilibrium, our result has some bearing on the debate on the robustness of equilibrium to small departures from common knowledge. Rubinstein's (1989) example of the electronic mail game demonstrates in a striking way how equilibrium may change when the hierarchy of iterated knowledge is truncated at some high, but finite degree. For Rubinstein, iterated knowledge of high degree constitutes a situation "close" to common knowledge, and he defends this view vigorously.

An alternative dimension in which to relax common knowledge is to replace knowledge by belief and to restore the unbounded iteration of beliefs. In an important contribution, Monderer and Samet (1989) explore this approach and note its implications for game theory. In particular, they show that if players are boundedly rational in the sense that they are ε-optimizers, then in a large subset of the state space, equilibrium behaviour implied by common belief with high probability approximates behaviour implied by common knowledge. Thus, for Bayesian coordination games, provided that players satisfy the conditions of Monderer and Samet, and provided that they have common belief with sufficiently high probability, they could sustain equilibria which are highly complex.

Our contribution to this debate is to strike a cautionary note for the programme of supplanting common knowledge by common belief. Although Monderer and Samet's result can be seen as a demonstration that this distinction is unimportant for "most" games, coordination games may not fit neatly under this umbrella. For the class of coordination games in this essay, no amount of common belief (short of the maximum) will do as a substitute for common knowledge.

This conclusion places our result on the *simplicity* of equilibrium under sharper focus. On the face of it, we have the somewhat paradoxical result that *full* rationality leads to simple rules, while ε-rationality admits complex ones. As for the question of how reasonable ε-rationality is in this context, the answer must depend on the particular game under scrutiny. However, if behaviour motivated by ε-rationality differs radically from the behaviour motivated by full rationality, then the reasons for this difference ought to be of interest to game theorists. Thus, we may be justified in regarding Monderer and Samet's result as a starting point in the investigation of the role of common belief in games rather than the last word on this subject.

In order to motivate the main questions, we shall begin with an example that brings out the key points in a striking way. A more systematic discussion follows in Section 3 where we state our main result. Section 4 takes a rather different approach to the problem and discusses the problem of convergence to conventions in myopic iterative learning in fictitious play. We begin with our example.

2. An Example

Consider the following pure coodination game. There are two players: player 1 and player 2. The strategy set of both players is given by $\mathbb{R}$, the set of real numbers. There is a set C of *circumstances*, given by the natural numbers:

$$\{0, 1, 2, 3, \cdots\}. \tag{2.1}$$

We use the term "circumstance" rather than "state", because we want to reserve the latter term for a different use. Nature chooses one of the circumstances according to the probability distribution p, where p assigns positive weight to all circumstances, and $p(i) > p(i + 1)$, for all i.

The payoffs of the players are identical, and are given by the negative of a squared loss function. Thus, if we denote by V the action of player 1, and by W the action of player 2, the players' payoff for the pair of actions (V, W) at circumstance i is given by

$$u(V, W, i) = -(V - W)^2 \tag{2.2}$$

For the moment, we will stick to payoffs that do not depend on the circumstance. Our argument goes through with more complex payoffs, and an example is given at the end of this section.

In the absence of any uncertainty concerning the true circumstance, there are many equilibria of this coordination game. Indeed, if we denote by v the strategy of player 1 and by w the strategy of player 2, then any pair of strategies (v, w) where $v = w$ is an equilibrium of this game. We now introduce the following informational assumptions. Both players have signals concerning the true circumstance. Player 1 can observe the true circumstance perfectly. That is, player 1's signal is the function $\sigma^1 \colon C \to C$, where

$$\sigma^1(i) = i \tag{2.3}$$

However, player 2 has a noisy signal. Player 2's signal is denoted by σ^2, and for circumstance $i > 0$ yields

$$\sigma^2(i) = \begin{cases} i & \text{with probability } 1 - \varepsilon \\ i - 1 & \text{with probability } \varepsilon \end{cases} \tag{2.4}$$

where $\varepsilon > 0$. At circumstance 0, player 2's signal has no noise. That is, $\sigma^2(0) = 0$. Thus, for any circumstance other than 0, player 2 learns of the true state with high probability, but there is a small chance (ε) that the signal is inaccurate. We assume that the noise defined in (2.4) is independent of nature's choice of the true circumstance. Player 2's strategy is a function w that maps each realization of the signal σ^2 to an action. We denote by $w(i)$ the action of player 2 given the message i. Player 1's strategy is defined similarly, but with the proviso that her strategy can be written as a function of the true circumstance, since the signal σ^1 is always correct. We denote by $v(i)$ the action of player 1 at circumstance i. The introduction of noise to player 2's signal alters the set of equilibria drastically.

Theorem 1
If (v, w) is an equilibrium, then $v = w$ and v is a constant function.

With noise, the set of equilibria shrinks to the set of constant functions. Only the simplest possible rule of action can be supported as an equilibrium—namely, that which does not depend on the message of either player.

We shall prove Theorem 1 by induction on the set of circumstances. On the assumption that (v, w) is an equilibrium, we first show that $v(0) = v(1)$, and then show that, if $v(i - 1) = v(i)$ then $v(i + 1) = v(i)$.

To see that $v(0) = v(1)$, consider player 1's reasoning given the message 0. Since player 1's signal has no noise, she knows that the true circumstance is 0. Moreover, player 2's signal at 0 has no noise. Hence given the message 0, player 1 knows that player 2 has received the message 0 also. Thus, player 1 sets

$$v(0) = w(0) \tag{2.5}$$

Now, consider player 2's reasoning given the message 0. Refer to Figure 7.1. Given the message 0, player 2 allows two possibilities. Either the true circumstance is 0 and his message is accurate, or the true circumstance is 1 and his message is inaccurate. The probability of the former is

$$p(0)/[p(0) + p(1)\varepsilon], \tag{2.6}$$

while the probability of the latter is

$$p(1)\varepsilon/[p(0) + p(1)\varepsilon] \tag{2.7}$$

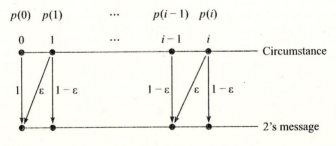

Figure 7.1

We denote (2.6) and (2.7) by $1 - \eta(0)$ and $\eta(0)$, respectively. Thus, given the message 0, player 2 chooses W to maximize

$$(1 - \eta(0))u(v(0), W, 0) = \eta(0)u(v(1), W, 1) \tag{2.8}$$

which yields the decision

$$w(0) = (1 - \eta(0))v(0) + \eta(0)v(1) \tag{2.9}$$

Since $w(0) = v(0)$ by (2.5), we have

$$v(0) = v(1) \tag{2.10}$$

We now demonstrate that if $v(i - 1) = v(i)$, then $v(i) = v(i + 1)$. Consider player 1's reasoning given the message i. Refer again to Figure 7.1. Since player 1's signal has no noise, she knows that i is the true circumstance. However, 2's signal has noise. Player 1 knows that 2 has received one of two messages: namely, i or $i - 1$. Player 2's strategy w yields the actions $w(i)$ and $w(i - 1)$ for these messages. Since 2 receives the messages s and $i - 1$ with probabilities $1 - \varepsilon$ and ε, respectively, player 1 chooses V to maximize

$$(1 - \varepsilon)u(V, w(i), i) + \varepsilon u(V, w(i - 1), i - 1) \tag{2.11}$$

This yields the decision:

$$v(i) = (1 - \varepsilon)w(i) + \varepsilon w(i - 1) \tag{2.12}$$

Now, let us turn to player 2's reasoning. Suppose 2 has received the message i. This leaves open two possibilities. Either the true circumstance is i or the true circumstance is $i + 1$. The latter has probability

$$\eta(i) \equiv p(i + 1)\varepsilon/[p(i)(1 - \varepsilon) + p(i + 1)\varepsilon], \tag{2.13}$$

while the former has probability $1 - \eta(i)$. Thus, given the message i, player 2 chooses W to maximize

$$(1 - \eta(i)u(v(i), W, i) + \eta(i)u(v(i + 1), W, i + 1) \tag{2.14}$$

which gives

$$w(i) = (1 - \eta(i))v(i) + \eta(i)v(i + 1) \tag{2.15}$$

Substituting (2.15) and the analogous expression for $w(i - 1)$ into (2.12), we have

$$[(1 - \varepsilon)\eta(i) + \varepsilon(1 - \eta(i - 1))]v(i) = (1 - \varepsilon)\eta(i)v(i + 1)$$
$$+ \varepsilon(1 - \eta(i - 1))v(i - 1) \tag{2.16}$$

But by the induction hypothesis, $v(i - 1) = v(i)$. Hence, $v(i + 1) = v(i)$. It remains for us to note that (2.15) requires w to be equal to v. ∎

With the particular payoff function chosen for our example, the restriction to constant functions entails no loss of efficiency, since the maximum expected payoff is zero for both players, whether there is noise in the game or not. However, we can construct examples in which there *is* loss of efficiency. Consider the variation of the game in which the strategy set is the interval $[-1, 1]$ and there is an integer $M > 0$ such that player 1's payoff for the action pair (V, W) at the circumstance i is

$$u^1(V, W, i) = \begin{cases} -(V - W)^2 + W & \text{if } i \le M \\ -(V - W)^2 - W & \text{if } i > M \end{cases} \tag{2.17}$$

whereas player 2's payoff function is given by

$$u^2(V, W, i) = \begin{cases} -(V - W)^2 + V & \text{if } i \le M \\ -(V - W)^2 - V & \text{if } i > M \end{cases} \tag{2.18}$$

In the absence of any noise, there is a Pareto dominant equilibrium of this game given by the pair of strategies (v, w), where

$$v(i) = w(i) = \begin{cases} 1 & \text{if } \le M \\ -1 & \text{if } i > M \end{cases} \tag{2.19}$$

These strategies rely on the players recognizing that the true circumstance is to one side of M or the other. On the face of it, this does not seem to be very demanding. However, the induction argument used to prove Theorem 1 can be invoked for this version of our game to conclude that only constant functions can be sustained as equilibria. The formerly Pareto dominant equilibrium in the perfect information case cannot be sustained as an equilibrium in the game with noise. This is a conclusion that echoes the inefficiency result in Rubinstein's (1989) electronic mail game.

The comparison with Rubinstein's example is instructive. In both cases, the inefficiency results from a "small" departure from common knowledge. However, in our example, we shall show that there is common belief with arbitrarily high probability that both players have received the same message. In other words, the departure from common knowledge is in the manner of Monderer and Samet (1989), rather than a truncation of iterated knowledge.

To state these claims more precisely, we turn to a description of belief and common belief in our game. The definitions are those of Monderer and Samet (1989). Because the set of circumstances C does not exhaust all uncertainty, we start by defining the state space as follows. We say that a pair of natural numbers (i, j) is a *state* if $j = i$ or $j = i - 1$. We denote a state by ω and denote the set of states by Ω. In state $\omega = (i, j)$, the true circumstance is i and the message received by player 2 is j. Since player 1's signal is accurate, Ω exhausts all the uncertainty in our game.

Since player 1 knows the true circumstance but does not know the message received by player 2, player 1's information partition over Ω is

$$\{\{(0,0)\}, \{(1,0),(1,1)\}, \{(2,1),(2,2)\}, \cdots \{(k,k-1),(k,k)\}, \cdots\}$$

Similarly, player 2's information partition over Ω is given by

$$\{\{(0,0),(1,0)\}, \{(1,1),(2,1)\}, \{(2,2),(3,2)\}, \cdots \{(k,k),(k+1,k)\}, \cdots\}$$

These information partitions are illustrated in Figure 7.2. The probability distribution p over the set of circumstances and the independent noise in player 2's signal generate a probability distribution over Ω. We denote this distribution by ϕ. We shall be interested in the posterior probabilities obtained from ϕ by conditioning on the players' information partitions.

Denote by $T^1(\omega)$ the element of player 1's partition which contains the state ω. For any event $E \subseteq \Omega$, we denote by $\phi(E|T^1(\omega))$ the posterior probability of E conditional on $T^1(\omega)$. We shall say that *player 1 believes E at ω with degree r* if

$$\phi(E|T^1(\omega)) \geq r. \tag{2.20}$$

In other words, player 1 believes E at ω with degree r if, based on the information at ω, player 1 attaches probability no less than r to the event E. We shall denote by $B_r^1(E)$ the set of states at which player 1 believes E with degree r. That is,

$$B_r^1(E) = \{\omega | \phi(E|T^1(\omega)) \geq r\} \tag{2.21}$$

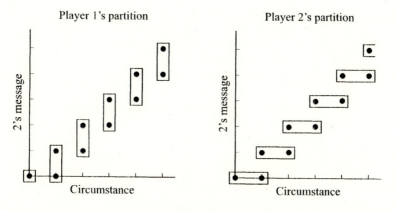

Figure 7.2

$B_r^2(E)$ is defined analogously for player 2. Using this notation, we define common belief in terms of a characterization given by Monderer and Samet (1989, 177). For any event C, define the sequence $C^0, C^1, C^2, \ldots$ as follows. $C^0 = C$, and for $n \geq 1$,

$$C^n = B_r^1(C^{n-1}) \cap B_r^2(C^{n-1}). \qquad (2.22)$$

Definition. Event C is common belief with degree r at ω if $\omega \in \bigcap_{n \geq 1} C^n$.

This definition formalizes the notion of everyone believing C, everyone believing that everyone believes C, and so on, where each layer of belief is to degree r. Notice that the intersection is taken over $n \geq 1$. Thus, C may be common belief even though C is false. This is one important respect in which belief differs from knowledge.

We shall be interested in the common belief between the players of the event that both players have received the same message. Let S be the set of states (i, j) such that $i = j$. S is the set of points on the leading diagonal in Figure 7.2. For player 1, the posterior probability of S at any state ω whose first component is i, where $i \geq 1$, is given by

$$\phi(S|T^1(\omega)) = \phi(\{(i, i)\}|\{(i, i), (i, i-1)\}) = 1 - \varepsilon \qquad (2.23)$$

For $\omega = (0, 0)$, $\phi(S|T^1(\omega))- = 1$. Thus, at every state, player 1 believes S with degree $1 - \varepsilon$. That is,

$$B_{1-\varepsilon}^1(S) = \Omega. \qquad (2.24)$$

For player 2, the posterior probability of S at any state whose *second* component is i is given by

$$\phi(S|T^2(\omega)) = \phi(\{(i, i)\}|\{(i, i), (i+1, i)\}) = 1 - \eta(i) \qquad (2.25)$$

where $\eta(i)$ is the expression defined in (2.13). Since we have assumed that $p(i)$ is decreasing in i, $\eta(i) < \varepsilon$, for all i. Hence $1 - \eta(i) > 1 - \varepsilon$, so that player 2 believes S with degree $1 - \varepsilon$ at all states. In other words,

$$B_{1-\varepsilon}^1(S) = \Omega. \qquad (2.26)$$

Thus, $B_{1-\varepsilon}^1(S) \cap B_{1-\varepsilon}^2(S) = \Omega$. Since Ω has posterior probability of 1 at every state, we have:

Theorem 2
At every state ω, there is common belief of S with degree $1 - \varepsilon$.

As ε becomes small, there is common belief of S with degree arbitrarily close to 1. That is, there is common belief with arbitrarily high probability that the same message has been received by both players. However, the set of equilibria remains the set of constant functions. For $\varepsilon = 0$, the set of equilibria is given by the set of *all* functions. In this sense, there is a failure of lower hemi-continuity of the equilibrium correspondence at $\varepsilon = 0$. We have, therefore, a case where common belief of arbitrarily high probability *cannot* serve as a substitute for common knowledge.

3. Common Belief and Conventions

We now provide a more systematic investigation of the role of common belief. Our investigation centres around the following coordination game. There are n players whose set of actions is given by a closed interval A of the real numbers. We denote by a^i the action of player i, and denote by a the vector of actions $(a^1, a^2, \ldots, a^n)$. The payoff function for player i is given by

$$u^i(a) = -\sum_{j \neq i} (a^j - a^i)^2 \tag{3.1}$$

In our coordination game a player's best reply is to choose a number that is the arithmetic mean of the other players' choices. This payoff function has been chosen for expositional clarity. The argument can be generalized to more general specifications. We shall return to this issue at the end of this section.

Associated with this game is a state space Ω, with a typical element ω. We shall assume that Ω is finite. There is a probability distribution ϕ over Ω which assigns positive weight to all states. Each player has an information partition over Ω. We denote by $\mathcal{T}^i$ the partition of player i, and denote a typical element of $\mathcal{T}^i$ by T^i. The "T" stands for "type" in the sense of Harsanyi (1967). As in Rubinstein (1989), the types belonging to a particular player are distinguished only by the information they possess. The *strategy* of player i is a function

$$s^i \colon \mathcal{T}^i \to A \tag{3.2}$$

that maps each element of i's partition (i.e. each of its types) to an action.

We shall say that the n-tuple of strategies $(s^1, s^2, \ldots, s^n)$ is a *convention* if it is an equilibrium n-tuple of strategies. Given a convention $(s^1, s^2, \ldots, s^n)$, define the equivalence relation $\equiv^i$ on Ω by

$$\omega \equiv^i \omega' \Leftrightarrow s^i(T^i(\omega)) = s^i(T^i(\omega')) \tag{3.3}$$

where $T^i(\omega)$ is the element of i's partition which contains ω. The partition generated by this relation has an important interpretation. This partition consists of those events on which player i's equilibrium strategy can be defined. If this partition is fine, the convention is an intricate one in which player i's action depends on fine distinctions in the states. If this partition is coarse, the convention is a simple one in which player i's action does not vary much over the states. Our question can be posed as follows: Given a set of information partitions, how intricate can a convention be? To give a precise answer to this question, we start with some preliminary definitions.

> **Definition.** An event C is a *conditioning event* for player i in the convention $(s^1, s^2, \ldots, s^n)$ if C is an element of the partition generated by $\equiv^i$.

We shall also carry over the formal definitions of belief and common belief given in the previous section. $B_r^i(E)$ is the event that player i believes E with degree r, and common belief of event C is defined in terms of the sequence $C^0, C^1, C^2, \ldots$, suitably modified to include n players. Since the state space is finite and the distribution ϕ assigns positive weight to all states, belief with probability 1 coincides with knowledge. Accordingly, common belief with probability 1 coincides with common knowledge. Thus, we can help ourselves to the following well-known result. Recall that the *meet* of a set of partitions is the finest partition that is at least as coarse as all the partitions in the set.

Lemma 1
Event E is common belief with degree 1 at ω if and only if there is an event C in the meet of the partitions $\{\mathcal{T}^i\}$ such that $\omega \in C \subseteq E$.

Aumann (1976) and Bacharach (1985) provide proofs of this result. Brandenburger and Dekel (1987) examine common belief with probability 1 in a more general setting. Following Monderer and Samet (1989), we say that an event E is *evident* if E is common belief with degree 1 whenever the true state is in E. We can then state the main result of this section.

Theorem 3
If C is a conditioning event for some player, then C is evident.

This theorem has the following immediate corollary.

Corollary
At all states, the actions of all players in a convention are common belief with probability 1.

Theorem 3 and its corollary provide a precise answer to the question of how intricate a convention can be. In a nutshell, conventions must be simple enough that the actions of all players are common belief with probability 1. Common belief with probability close to 1 will not do. A moment's reflection reveals how stringent this condition is. In order to sustain a rule as a convention, no player can have even a shred of doubt as to what the others will do.

We shall devote the rest of this section to the proof of Theorem 3. Our proof relies on the construction of a Markov chain. Say that an element T^i of the partition $\mathcal{T}^i$ is a *type of player i*. We define the set of *types* to be the union $\cup_i \mathcal{T}^i$, and denote it by $\mathcal{T}$. Consider the following Markov chain. The set of states of the Markov chain is $\mathcal{T}$. The one-step transition probability from type T to type T' is denoted by $P(T, T')$, and is defined as

$$P(T, T') = \begin{cases} \dfrac{\phi(T'|T)}{n-1} & \text{if } T \text{ and } T' \text{are types of different players} \\ 0 & \text{if } T \text{ and } T' \text{are types of the same player} \end{cases} \quad (3.4)$$

wjere $\phi(T'|T)$ is the posterior probability of T' conditional on T. We can verify that the sum of all one-step transition probabilities from type T is 1 since for any player i,

$$\sum_{T^i \in \mathcal{T}^i} \phi(T^i|T) = 1 \quad (3.5)$$

Using received terminology, we say that type T *communicates* with type T' in the Markov chain if there is a positive probability of transition from T to T' in a finite number of steps. The following lemma is central to our argument. Its proof is given in the appendix.

Lemma 2

T communicates with T' in the Markov chain if and only if there is an event E in the meet of the partitions $\{\mathcal{T}^i\}$ such that $(T \cup T') \subseteq E$.

At state ω^*, player i's information is given by the type $T^i(\omega^*)$. Thus, player i chooses a^i to maximize

$$-\sum_{\omega} \phi(\{\omega\}|T^i(\omega^*)) \left[\sum_{j \neq i} (s^j(T^j(\omega)) - a^i)^2 \right] \quad (3.6)$$

which gives

$$s^i(T^i(\omega^*)) = \frac{1}{n-1} \sum_{j \neq i} \sum_{\omega} \phi(\{\omega\}|T^i(\omega^*)) s^j(T^j(\omega)) \quad (3.7)$$

Using the transition probabilities defined in (3.4), this expression can be simplified by dropping the superscripts for the players. Let us denote by $s(T)$ the action of type T. Then (3.7) can be written as

$$s(T) = \sum_{T' \in \mathcal{T}} P(T, T') s(T') \quad (3.8)$$

We thus have a system of linear equations for the action of all types in the convention. At this point, we appeal to Lemma 2. Lemma 2 tells us that for each event E in the meet of the partitions $\{\mathcal{T}^i\}$, the set of types which are subsets of E form an irreducible set of states in the Markov chain. Thus, for each element E of the meet of the partitions $\{\mathcal{T}^i\}$, there is an associated irreducible subchain. Consider one such subchain. We index the set of types in this subchain by $\{1, 2, \ldots, N\}$ and denote by T_k the type with index k. We define

$$s = \begin{bmatrix} s(T_1) \\ s(T_2) \\ \vdots \\ s(T_N) \end{bmatrix} \tag{3.9}$$

Denote by P the associated transition matrix of this subchain—that is, the matrix whose (j, k)th entry is $P(T_j, T_k)$. Then (3.8) implies

$$s = Ps \tag{3.10}$$

We shall argue that any solution of this system takes the form

$$s = \begin{bmatrix} k \\ k \\ \vdots \\ k \end{bmatrix} \tag{3.11}$$

for some constant k. Since P is a stochastic matrix, (3.11) is certainly *one* solution of this system. Suppose that

$$q = \begin{bmatrix} q_1 \\ q_2 \\ \vdots \\ q_N \end{bmatrix} \tag{3.12}$$

is also a solution of (3.10) but that $q_i \neq q_j$ for some i and j. We shall derive a contradiction. Let

$$q_m = \max_i \{q_i\} \tag{3.13}$$

Since q is not a constant vector, there is a component q_k such that

$$q_m > q_k \tag{3.14}$$

Since P is the transition matrix associated with an irreducible Markov chain, there is an r-step transition matrix P^r for which the (m, k)th entry is positive. From the hypothesis that q solves (3.10),

$$q = P^r q \tag{3.15}$$

Denote by $R(i, j)$ the (i, j)th entry of P^r. Then

$$q_m = \sum_j R(m, j) q_j \tag{3.16}$$

From (3.13), (3.14) and the fact that $R(m, k) > 0$,

$$q_m < q_m \sum_j R(m, j). \tag{3.17}$$

Thus $\sum_j R(m, j) \neq 1$. But this contradicts the fact that P^r is a stochastic matrix. Hence q cannot be a solution to (3.10).

We now have all the necessary steps in the proof of Theorem 3. For any event E in the meet of the partitions $\{\mathscr{T}^i\}$, the actions of all types that are subsets of E must satisfy (3.10). However, we have shown that in any solution to (3.10), every type contained in E chooses the *same* action. Thus, the conditioning event for any player must be a union of elements from the meet of partitions. Finally, Lemma 1 tells us that any such union of events is evident. This completes the proof of Theorem 3. ∎

Although quadratic payoffs simplify the argument, Theorem 3 holds more generally. For instance, the following pair of conditions is sufficient for Theorem 3. If we denote by $u^i(a, \omega)$ the payoff function for player i for the game at state ω, and let $a^{-i} = (a^1, a^2, \cdots, a^{i-1}, a^{i+1}, \ldots, a^n)$, the two conditions can be stated as follows:

(A1) For fixed values of a^{-i} and ω, u^i is differentiable and strictly concave in a^i.

(A2) If a^i maximizes u^i given a^{-i} and ω, then a^i can be expressed as a convex combination of $\{a^j | j \neq i\}$, where each a^j receives positive weight.

From these conditions, we can argue as follows. At state ω^*, player i chooses a^i to maximize

$$\sum_\omega \phi(\{\omega\} | T^i(\omega^*)) u^i(a^i, s^{-i}(T^{-i}(\omega)), \omega) \tag{3.18}$$

where $s^{-i}(T^{-i}(\omega))$ is the vector of actions chosen at ω by all players other than i. Define

$$M = \max_{\substack{j \neq i \\ \omega \in T^i(\omega^*)}} \{s^j(T^j(\omega))\}, \qquad m = \min_{\substack{j \neq i \\ \omega \in T^i(\omega^*)}} \{s^j(T^j(\omega))\} \tag{3.19}$$

Since (3.18) is a linear combination of strictly concave functions of a^i, it is also strictly concave in a^i. If $m = M$, then (A2) implies that $a^i = m$ is optimal. If $m < M$, then (A2) and the fact that ϕ assigns positive weight to all states imply that the derivative of (3.18) with respect to a^i at m is positive while the derivative at M is negative, so that the optimal a^i lies in the open interval (m, M). For either case, the optimal a^i can be expressed as a convex combination of

$$\{s(T^j) | \phi(T^j | T^i(\omega^*)) > 0 \text{ and } j \neq i\} \tag{3.20}$$

where each element receives positive weight. In equilibrium, $s(T^i(\omega^*))$ is equal to this convex combination. Thus, there are probabilities $P(T, T')$ defined on pairs of types such that:

(i) $P(T, T') > 0 \Leftrightarrow \phi(T'|T) > 0$ and T and T' belong to different players;

(ii) $\sum_{T'} P(T, T') = 1$;

(iii) $s(T) = \sum_{T'} P(T, T')s(T')$.

The argument then proceeds along identical lines as for the quadratic case. However, it is important to recognize that (A1) and (A2) restrict the applicability of our result. Our result is relevant for those coordination games where the actions can be embedded naturally in some convex set, and the payoff is strictly concave over this set. The coordination of a place or time would fit naturally into this class. Coordination games with a finite number of strategies do not fall into this category.

4. Convergence of Actions

The Markov chain constructed for the proof of Theorem 3 for the quadratic payoff case provides an opportunity to examine the dynamics of belief change. Since the types can be partitioned into irreducible subsets by Lemma 2, we shall conduct our argument in terms of one such irreducible set of types. The belief change we shall examine is that governed by the transition matrix P defined in (3.4), which defines a best-reply function on the actions of all types in this set. For any initial vector of actions s_0, the matrix P defines a sequence $s_0, s_1, s_2, \ldots$, where

$$s_{t+1} = Ps_t \qquad (4.1)$$

This is the sequence generated by fictitious play in which the players start with some common initial hypothesis concerning the players' actions, updating their beliefs by finding the best reply to their initial hypothesis, then finding the best reply to their revised hypothesis, and so on. One of the by-products of our proof of Theorem 3 is a convergence theorem for the sequence (4.1) using the ergodic theorem for Markov chains. There is, however, a twist in the story. For convergence, there must be three or more players in the game. Two is not enough.

With just two players, the Markov chain has a period of two since a necessary condition for a one-step transition from one type to another is for the types to belong to *different* players. Thus, if two types belong to the same player, any transition from one to the other will have an even number of steps. For two types belonging to different players, any transition will have an odd number of steps. Hence, with just two players, the system will exhibit a cycle.

Here is an example. There are two states, ω_1 and ω_2. There are two players. Player 1 has the partition $\{\{\omega_1, \omega_2\}\}$ while player 2 has the partition $\{\{\omega_1\}, \{\omega_2\}\}$. Thus, there are three types. We label the types as follows:

$$T_1 = \{\omega_1\}$$
$$T_2 = \{\omega_2\}$$
$$T_3 = \{\omega_1, \omega_2\}$$

Suppose the prior distribution ϕ attaches equal weight to ω_1 and ω_2. The corresponding transition matrix is given by

$$P = \begin{bmatrix} 0 & 0 & 1 \\ 0 & 0 & 1 \\ \frac{1}{2} & \frac{1}{2} & 0 \end{bmatrix}$$

Then,

$$PP^2 = \begin{bmatrix} \frac{1}{2} & \frac{1}{2} & 0 \\ \frac{1}{2} & \frac{1}{2} & 0 \\ 0 & 0 & 1 \end{bmatrix}, \qquad PP^3 = P = \begin{bmatrix} 0 & 0 & 1 \\ 0 & 0 & 1 \\ \frac{1}{2} & \frac{1}{2} & 0 \end{bmatrix}$$

Thus, in sequence (4.1), for almost all initial action vectors s_0, we have $s_{t+2} = s_t$, but $s_{t+1} \neq s_t$. We therefore have a cycle of period two, and there is no convergence. However, with three or more players, convergence is guaranteed.

Theorem 4
With at least three players, (4.1) converges for any s_0.

The following lemma is instrumental in this result.

Lemma 3
If there are three or more players, P is aperiodic.

Proof. For types T and T' we show that if there is transition from T to T' in k steps, there is a transition in $k + 1$ steps. Let the following sequence be a transition from T to T' in k steps. The arrow denotes one-step transition.

$$T \to T_1 \to T_2 \to T_3 \to \cdots \to T' \qquad (4.2)$$

By the definition of the one-step transition probabilities in (3.4), T and T_1 have a nonempty intersection. Let ω be an element of this nonempty intersection. Since there are at least three players, there is a type T^* which contains ω such that T, T_1, and T^* belong to three different players. Since ω is an element of all three types, any pair of these types has a nonempty intersection. Hence, by the definition of the transition probabilities (3.4), the following transition is possible:

$$T \to T^* \to T_1 \tag{4.3}$$

From (4.2) and (4.3), there is a transition from T to T' in $k + 1$ steps.   ∎

Since we have a finite chain with no transient states, every state is non-null persistent. By showing aperiodicity, Lemma 3 allows us to appeal to the ergodic theorem for Markov chains to conclude that there is a stationary distribution over the set of types, and that P^n converges to the matrix Π whose rows are given by the stationary distribution for this subchain. Thus, the sequence (4.1) converges to Πs_0. Since the rows of Π are identical, the limit is a constant vector. Thus, the actions of the types in the limit exhibit the feature of conventions identified in Theorem 3.

5. Concluding Remarks

There are clear limitations to our argument in this chapter. The class of coordination games for which we have proved the main theorem is rather a restrictive one. The sort of coordination problems for which our framework would be best suited are those in which the actions have a natural mapping into some convex set, such as the coordination of a place or a time. It is less well suited to problems where the choices are discrete.

However, subject to these limitations, our argument may have some explanatory value. When we consider the norms and conventions around us, they tend to be simple relative to the range of possible "sunspots" on which actions can be conditioned. It is perhaps an indication of this simplicity that most discussions of conventions outside the formal game theoretic literature concentrate on one-shot coordination games. Since Lewis's (1969) seminal work on the subject, Ullman-Margalit (1977), Gilbert (1990), Miller (1990), and others have developed the theme of conventions as being equilibrium strategies in coordination games. Given the range of possible signals and sunspots that we could utilize in constructing more complex conventions, the sorts of conventions discussed in these papers are remarkable for their simplicity. In the light of our discussion in this essay, this may not be unduly restrictive.

Appendix

Proof of Lemma 2.   We start with a definition. Define the operator $L^i(\cdot)$ on the subsets of Ω as

$$L^i(E) \equiv \{\omega \mid T^i(\omega) \cap E \neq \emptyset\}. \tag{A.1}$$

$L^i(E)$ is the set of states at which player i allows that E is possible. The following properties of the operator L^i can easily be verified:

(i) $E \subseteq L^i(E)$, for all $E \subseteq \Omega$

(ii) $E = L^i(E)$ if and only if E is a union of elements in $\mathcal{T}^i$

(A.2)

If we denote by $L(E)$ the event $L^1(L^2(L^3(\cdots(L^n(E))\cdots)))$, then (A.2) implies that $E \subseteq L(E)$ for any event E, and $E = L(E)$ if and only if E is a union of elements in $\mathcal{T}^i$ for *every* $\mathcal{T}^i$. Hence, $E = (L(E)$ if and only if E is an element of the meet of $\{\mathcal{T}^i\}$. For a given type T, consider the sequence of events:

$$T, L(T), L(L(T)), L(L(L(T))), \cdots \qquad (A.3)$$

Some term in this sequence is an element of the meet of the partitions $\{\mathcal{T}^i\}$, since otherwise, we would have the strict set inclusions

$$T \subset L(T) \subset L(L(T)) \subset L(L(L(T))) \subset \cdots \qquad (A.4)$$

which violates the finiteness of Ω.

To prove the "if" part of the lemma, suppose $T, T' \subseteq E$, where E is an element of the meet of the partitions $\{\mathcal{T}^i\}$. Then, by the above argument,

$$T' \subseteq L(L(\cdots L(T) \cdots))$$

for some finite number of compositions of L. Then, by the definition of L, there is a finite sequence of types $T_1, T_2, T_3, \ldots, T_k$ such that $T = T_1$, $T' = T_k$, T_i, and T_{i+1} are types belonging to different players, and $T_i \cap T_{i+1}$ is nonempty for all i. Since ϕ assigns positive probability to all states, we have $\phi(T_{i+1}|T_i) > 0$ for all i. Thus, for the transition probabilities defined in (3.4), T communicates with T' in the Markov chain.

To prove the converse, suppose there is no element of the meet of the partitions that contains both T and T'. This implies that T and T' belong to different elements of the meet, so that for any iteration of L, the events T' and $L(L\cdots(L(T)\cdots))$ are disjoint. Hence, there is no finite sequence of types $T_1, T_2, T_3, \ldots, T_k$ such that $T = T_1$, $T' = T_k$, and $T_i \cap T_{i+1}$ is nonempty for all i. For the transition probabilities (3.4), T does not communicate with T'. This completes the proof of Lemma 2. ∎

References

Aumann, R.J. (1976) "Agreeing to Disagree," *Annals of Statistics*, 4, 1236–39.

Bacharach, M.O.L. (1985) "Some Extensions of a Claim of Aumann in an Axiomatic Model of Knowledge," *Journal of Economic Theory*, 37, 167–90.

Brandenburger, A. and E. Dekel (1987) "Common Knowledge with Probability 1," *Journal of Mathematical Economics*, 16, 237–46.

Harsanyi, J.C. (1967) "Games with Incomplete Information Played by Bayesian Players, parts I, II, III," *Management Science*, 14, 159–82, 320–34, 486–502.

Gilbert, M. (1990) "Rationality, Coordination and Convention," *Synthese*, 84, 1–21.

Lewis, D. (1969) *Conventions: A Philosophical Study*, Harvard University Press, Cambridge, Mass.

Miller, S. (1990) "Rationalising Conventions," *Synthese*, 84, 23–41.

Monderer, D. and D. Samet (1989) "Approximating Common Knowledge with Common Beliefs," *Games and Economic Behavior*, 1, 170–90.

Rubinstein, A. (1989) "The Electronic Mail Game: Strategic Behavior under 'Almost Common Knowledge'," *American Economic Review*, 79, 385–91.

Ullman-Margalit, E. (1977) *The Emergence of Norms*, Oxford University Press, Oxford.

CHAPTER 8

Sophisticated Bounded Agents
Play the Repeated Dilemma

Michael Bacharach, Hyun Song Shin,
and Mark Williams

1. Introduction

1.1. Outline

In this essay, we put forward a new solution to the "backward induction paradox" in the theory of the Finitely Repeated Prisoner's Dilemma (FRPD). The paradox is this: An apparently valid argument, the Backward Induction Argument, has the conclusion that if there is common knowledge between the players of the rules of the game and of each other's rationality, then however many rounds there may be both "defect" in all of them. But this conclusion is intuitively implausible.

Our solution is in three parts. We first show that limits on players' abilities to understand long sentences of the type.

1 knows that 2 knows that 1 knows that 2 knows that 1 knows that it is Tuesday (1)

("depth-limits") can confine defection to the last *r* rounds, where *r* is approximately the lower of the two players' depth-limits. Second, we consider the effect of an unfamiliar but important aspect of players' rationality: the ability to understand *game theoretic theorems* ("sophistication"). We show that sophistication lengthens the defection period at the end for any given depth-limits, but that on a natural assumtion about which theorems players understand, it lengthens it only to approximately $r^2/2$ rounds. Third, we show that in any equilibrium of a two-stage game in which unboundedly rational "meta-players" *choose* the depth-limits of players and the players then play a FRPD constrained by these but with sophistication, there is a tight upper bound on the defection period: for example, if the temptation, cooperative, joint defection, and sucker payoffs are $2, 1, 0$ and -1, respectively, the metaplayers choose depth-limits no greater than 3, and in consequence the defection period does not exceed 5 rounds.

1.2. Depth-Limits Can Explain Cooperation

Like that of Kreps et al. (1982), our explanation of cooperation in the FRPD is in terms of bounded rationality. But our work differs from theirs in two ways. Their main result depends on asymmetric information about a special form of boundedness: player i attaches a positive probability to player j's being "hardwired" to play Tit for Tat, while j knows he is not. In our work there is no asymmetry, and the form of boundedness we study is a general limitation of human information-processing.

Consider the Prisoner's Dilemma with the payoff matrix shown in Figure 8.1, where

$$a > 1 > 0 > b \qquad a + b < 2$$

Let it be repeated N times, each player knowing, at each repetition, the history of play to date. Let a player's payoff be the sum of her N stage-payoffs. Call these specifications Model 0 of the FRPD.

The Backward Induction Argument shows that, if there is common knowledge (CK) between the two players P1 and P2 that both are "rational," and know the game they are playing (that is, know Model 0), then both choose D ("defect") in all N rounds. But common knowledge, though sufficient, is not necessary. Index rounds backwards, so that the last round is called round 1, the second last round 2, and so on. Call the players P1 and P2. P1 will defect at round 1 if P1 is "dominance-rational" (obeys the dominance principle) and knows the game. P2 will defect at round 2 if P2 is dominance-rational and knows the game and if in addition P2 knows at round 2 that P1 will defect at round 1. But P2 does know this if P2 knows that P1 is dominance-rational and knows the game. Thus P2 will defect at round 2 if P2 is dominance-rational, knows the game, knows that P1 is dominance-rational, and *knows that P1 knows* the game. We shall describe this last piece of P2's knowledge as "iterated knowledge of degree 2" (IK of degree 2) between P1 and P2 of the game. The highest degree of IK required here is 2. It is intuitively clear (and we shall prove in due course) that IK by each player of degree n that both players know the

	C	D
C	1, 1	b, a
D	a, b	0, 0

Figure 8.1 Payoff matrix of the prisoner's dilemma.

game and of degree $n - 1$ that they are dominance-rational suffices to produce defection in the last n rounds.

By "depth" we mean the ability to understand sentences like (1) containing "nested" *knows that* operators. The more occurrences of "knows that," the greater the "depth" a player needs to understand it. We shall measure a player's depth by a positive integer, her "depth-limit." The basic property of depth-limits is that if a player has depth-limit δ, the greatest degree of IK of which she is capable is δ.

In analysing the FRPD, we have to make "modelling choices" about what to assume players know and iteratively know. That they know certain things, such as the payoff matrix, is part of the very meaning of a FRPD, so no modelling choice is required. But it is less obvious what to assume about the degree of players' *iterated* knowledge when the players have finite depth-limits. Finitely repeated PDs are usually treated as games "of complete information," where this in turn means that there is common knowledge (CK) between the players of its rules and of each other's rationality, that is, IK of these things of every degree; but the latter is impossible for depth-limited players. To preserve as much as possible of the familiar features of FRPDs, we shall assume that there is IK of these things "up to limits." We describe such FRPDs, as games *of boundedly complete information.*[1]

To repeat, the assumption of IK of high enough degree is sufficient for showing ab initio defection by the Backward Induction Argument. The assumption is also necessary, as we shall show in Section 3.5,[2] *for showing it by this argument.* Specifically, to show by the Backward Induction Argument that players defect from round n on, one must use the assumption that they have IK of degree n of the game.

This fact immediately resolves the backward induction paradox for depth-limited players. But it *only* resolves the paradox; it does not by itself give reason to expect cooperation at the start since, even for depth-limited players, it only removes *one* argument for defection, not all arguments. For example, depth-limits or no depth-limits, it is a Nash equilibrium for both players to defect at every round.[3]

Nevertheless, cooperation early on is in fact likely between rational depth-limited players. True, there are no decisive game-theoretic arguments for initial cooperation: that is, no arguments which adduce only game theoretic principles of rationality, and demonstrate that these (and the standard assumptions about what players know) *imply* that rational players defect from the start. But, we shall argue, depth-limits preclude there being any such arguments for initial *defection* either, for all large enough N.[4] In the absence of decisive game theoretic arguments either way, rational depth-limited players, if they are to act, must be guided at the start by a rule based on something else—what we shall call a "default rule." Default rules are likely to be informed by common sense, and so to have such properties as Axelrod's (1984) "niceness" and "provocability." For the sake of concreteness, we shall assume in this study that both players' default rule is Tit-for-Tat.[5]

1.3. Explaining Depth-Limits

There is empirical evidence, both from introspection and formal experiment, that people do have depth-limits, of the order of 4 or 5 or 6 for normal adults in everyday problem tasks.[6] The fact that our theory of cooperation recognizes this phenomenon will appear as a virtue to some. On the other hand, a theory that stipulated particular depth-limits exogenously might seem objectionably ad hoc to many. To defuse this objection, we embed our analysis of the effects of depth-limits in a model of endogenous bounded rationality of the type pioneered by Rubinstein, Abreu and others (Rubinstein 1986; Abreu and Rubinstein 1988).

This type of model takes the form of a two-stage game. The second-stage represents some real economic interaction. In the first stage a "metaplayer" (assumed to be *fully* rational) chooses the level of rationality of a player to whom she will delegate control in the second stage. For instance, in Rubinstein (1986) each metaplayer chooses a mechanical player (mathematically, a finite automaton) with a particular level of "complexity," which she then uses to play an (infinitely) repeated PD for her.

In 1986 Neyman showed that finite automata whose complexity does not exceed an *exogenous* bound *cooperate* in at least some equilibria of the FRPD. This raised the possibility of explaining *both* cooperation *and* bounded rationality by showing that metaplayers for repeated dilemmas choose bounded players. Unfortunately, in the Rubinstein–Abreu model they need not do so. Here, we show precisely this for the case in which the "game proper" is the FRPD and the bound is on players' depth. We not only explain cooperation in terms of rationality bounds, but we also explain these bounds, as equilibrium choices of metaplayers.

There are two main interpretations of the two-stage game model. The first (Abreu and Rubinstein 1988) is the literal one in which the metaplayer and the player of the game proper are two different people, such as a senior manager and a subordinate. A second interpretation, which we ourselves intend, is that the metaplayer is not a person: its "choices" are not really choices but merely the solutions of optimization problems.[7] Showing that they are is meant to show only that it is objectively optimal for the agent to be bounded in the respect in question. On this interpretation, the two-stage game model gives a "functional explanation" of bounded rationality. One version of this is that bounded rationality would be the outcome of an evolutionary process in which successful strategies are selected for (see Binmore 1987).[8]

2. Sophistication

Rationality is not one-dimensional, but a bundle of abilities. Game theory implicitly requires the players to possess a number of quite different ones. In this essay we shall explicitly distinguish some of these. For example, in the next section we shall assume that players are "choice rational" (in a specific way suited to the FRPD), and that they are "deduction-rational" in a certain way. Depth may be regarded as a third dimension of rationality.

"Sophistication" is the name we give to a fourth sort of ability—the ability to discover nonobvious theorems of game theory. It is becoming more common in game theory to make it an explicit postulate that players know the theorems of the very game theory that describes them (see, e.g., Bacharach 1987; Myerson 1991). In this essay we push the investigation of the role of sophistication a bit further than this. We analyse the difference it makes to the effects of depth limits on behaviour in FRPDs for players to be sophisticated.

Sophistication is the ability to discover game theory *by oneself*. The lesser ability to understand it when it is expounded by a game theorist is irrelevant to the analysis of a given game.[9] Sophistication therefore demands the creativity to conceive the theorems in question; the problem-solving ability to prove them; and—crucially—the mastery of the theoretical concepts that figure in them. For serious theorems are often case in terms of non-everyday concepts, such as "perfect equilibrium" or "depth-limit," and it would be difficult or even impossible to formulate or prove the theorems without understanding these concepts.

In this essay we shall first present a specific piece of game theory, which involves the theoretical concepts of *iterated knowledge of degree n* and *depth-limit*, then consider the behaviour of players who are sophisticated with regard to it. Sophistication implies knowledge of the theorems of this theory. It also implies, in the boundedly complete information context that we study, knowledge of the rationality characteristics of the players that appear in the theory—here, their depth-limits. Moreoever, boundedly complete information implies IK up to limits of these things.

The effect of sophistication is to increase the amount of rationally obligatory defection. Say both players have depth-limit 4. Theorem 1 tells us that if both players have depth-limits of n, they defect at least from round n on. If Pi is sophisticated, she knows Theorem 1, and she also knows that both depth-limits are 4. Hence Pi knows that Pj will defect from round 4 on and, being dominance-rational,[10] Pi defects at 5. This is not all: IK of the depth-limits and of Theorem 1 increases defection still further. For example, if Pi knows that Pj knows Theorem 1 and knows that Pj knows both have depth-limits 4, then Pi knows that Pj will defect from 5 on; hence Pi, being dominance-rational, defects at 6. IK of degree 2 of Theorem 1 and of depth-limits has added another round of defection. And this generalizes to higher degrees of IK of Theorem 1 and the depth-limits, until, once again, we reach the degrees of this IK that these very depth-limits prevent players from surpassing.

Some game theorists have seemed to favour an assumption of infinite sophistication: *every* theorem the game theorist proves is taken to be known to the players—and before the theorist proved it! We do not go so far, because we believe that a judicious treatment of bounded rationality maintains proportion between the different dimensions of rationality. Is it not absurd to suppose that players who cannot understand the sentence "He knows that she knows that it is Tuesday" know theorems whose proofs cost us days of hard labour and which the editors of this book see fit to publish?

It is sometimes said that the claim that depth-limits of n are necessary for backward induction reasoning to give n rounds of defection must be mistaken because it reckons without the players' use of mathematical induction. It is felt that players can surely exploit mathematical induction to concertina the backward induction reasoning and so overcome the problem of depth-limits. This intuition receives formal expression in our model of sophisticated play. For sophistication means knowing a theorem (Theorem 1) whose proof is by just such a mathematical induction, and knowing it indeed produces extra defection, depth-limits notwithstanding. However, it is to sophistication, not to induction, that the getting round of depth-limits is ultimately due. We illustrate: Suppose the depth-limits are 4. As long as Pi knows what a depth-limit is, she might come to know Theorem 1 for this special case without using mathematical induction, by grinding out the steps; and Pi would then have as firm knowledge that Pj would defect from round 4 as if she had employed induction.

The rest of the essay is organized as follows. In Section 3, we formalize the notion of depth-limits and we analyse a model of play of the FRPD by depth-limited players in which the amounts of defection are just the amounts that follow from the BIA: Theorem 1 gives these amounts as functions of the depth-limits. In Section 4, we ask what difference "sophistication" makes, and we give (in Theorem 3) the defection periods for this case as functions of depth-limits. In Section 5 we solve the two-stage game for the sophisticated player case to show (in Theorem 4) that there is an upper bound on the depth-limit that a rational player of the FRPD would ever wish to have. In Section 6 we sum up and suggest an extension of the present theory.

3. The Repeated Dilemma with Depth-Limited Players: Model 1

In this section and the next, we add enough specification to Model 0 to give two alternative models of the FRPD in which the extent of cooperation is determined. This section is devoted to the first of these. We begin by a description of the players' rationality characteristics.

3.1. Choice Rationality and Deduction Rationality

By way of *choice rationality* we assume only[11] that

(DOM) P1 and P2 are dominance rational

That is, they always choose an alternative that they know to be strictly dominant. Second, we assume that

(DED) P1 and P2 are deduction rational

By this we mean that players can make "simple deductions." The class of *simple deductions* will be defined as we go along. Its basic element is the set of all one-shot applications of the Modus Ponens rule: that is, inferences in which a player goes from knowledge of *P* and knowledge of *if P then Q* to knowledge of *Q*. A defining feature of simple deductions is that they never carry a player "out of her depth"; that is, they never take her to a piece of knowledge that exceeds her depth-limit.

When a player deduces *Q* from *P* and *if P then Q*, she proves a theorem. But this does not mean that deduction rationality implies sophistication. For the proofs of the theorems established by such deductions are typicaly undemanding as regards structure; and sophistication is therefore needed only if *P*, *Q*, etc. represent propositions that involve esoteric concepts.

3.2. Depth-Limits

The *epistemic degree* of a sentence is defined recursively. A sentence *S* has epistemic degree zero if it contains no knowledge operators (such as "knows that"). For example, *The pistol is loaded* is of epistemic degree zero. *S* has epistemic degree one if its knowledge operators govern subsentences only of epistemic degree zero: thus *Frankie knows that the pistol is loaded* is of degree one. *S* has epistemic degree two if its knowledge operators govern subsentences of epistemic degree at most one; and so on.[12] Thus simple iterated knowledge sentences of the form *Frankie knows that Johnny knows that Frankie knows that . . . knows that S*, where there are *n* "knows that"s, have epistemic degree equal to *n* plus the epistemic degree of *S*.

Real players have a limited capacity ("depth") for dealing with the sort of complexity that consists in the "nesting" of *knows that* operators. To represent this phenomenon, we shall assume that player Pi is characterized by a positive integer δ_i, her "depth-limit," such that the sentence *Pi knows that S* is true only if its epistemic degree is at most δ_i.

Some sentences that players of games have to deal with mix "knows that" operators with other "attitudinal" operators such as "has probability p for the event that," "has utility u for the prospect that," and so on. Since nested mixed operators present the same challenge as nested knowledge operators,[13] we define depth-limit in terms not of epistemic degree but of a generalized notion of degree that treats all attitudinal operators similarly. We call this the *complexity* of the sentence. Let *S* be the sentence *Frankie knows that Johnny knows that Frankie is afraid that Johnny is furious and does not realize that the pistol is loaded.* Then *S* has complexity four, and we write complex(*S*) = 4.

Write $K_i S$ for *Pi knows that S*. By "Pi knows that" we mean, here and henceforth, "Pi knows *throughout* the FRPD that." We call K_i the *knowledge operator of Pi*.

We define "depth-limit" as follows.

Definition. A player Pi *has depth-limit* δ_i if δ_i is a positive integer such that, for all sentences *S*,

(DL) $\mathbf{K}_i S$ only if complex($\mathbf{K}_i S$) $\leq \delta_i$

3.3. Iterated Knowledge

It will be convenient to write, for each nonnegative integer r,

$$\mathbf{K}_1^r S =_{def} \mathbf{K}_1 \mathbf{K}_2 \mathbf{K}_1 \cdots \mathbf{K}_i S \qquad (r \text{ operators})$$

(where $i = 1, 2$ according as r is odd or even) to denote that *P1 has iterated knowledge of degree r with P2 that S*. (To avoid notational clutter, we shall often, as here, state relations for P1 alone, taking as read symmetrical statements in which "P1" and "P2" are interchanged.) Since knowledge is factive (what one knows is true), if P1 knows that P2 knows that S then P2 knows that S, and generally

$$\text{If } \mathbf{K}_1^r S \text{ then } \mathbf{K}_1^q S, \mathbf{K}_2^q S \text{ for } q = 0, 1, \ldots, r - 1 \qquad (2)$$

That is, IK of degree r implies IK of every nonnegative degree up to r.

From the definition of complexity, complex($\mathbf{K}_1^r S$) = complex(S) + r. Suppose complex(S) = 0; then complex($\mathbf{K}_1^r S$) = r and one necessary condition for $\mathbf{K}_1^r S$ is, from (DL), that $\delta_1 \geq r$. But a second necessary condition is imposed by δ_2: $\mathbf{K}_1^r S$ implies $\mathbf{K}_2^{r-1} S$ by (2), which requires that $\delta_2 \geq r - 1$. More generally:

$$\text{If } \mathbf{K}_1^r S \text{ then } \delta_1 \geq \text{complex}(S) + r, \delta_2 \geq \text{complex}(S) + r - 1$$

Hence, there is a maximal degree of IK that P1 can have of S, which depends on both δ_1 and δ_2: $\mathbf{K}_1^r S$ only if $r \leq \min\{\delta_1, \delta_2 + 1\} - \text{complex}(S)$. We shall say that *P1 has iterated knowledge up to her limit that S*, and write $\mathbf{K}_1^{lim} S$, if she has IK with P2 that S of each degree not exceeding this maximal degree. Writing

$$d_1 =_{def} \min\{\delta_1, \delta_2 + 1\}$$

we define

$$\mathbf{K}_1^{\lim} S =_{def} \mathbf{K}_1^r S \text{ for } r = 0, 1, \cdots, d_1 - \text{complex}(S)$$

We shall say that *P1 and P2 has iterated knowledge up to limits* and write $\mathbf{K}^{lim} S$, if $\mathbf{K}_i^{lim} S$ for $i = 1, 2$. Suppose the depth-limits are unequal: $\delta_1 > \delta_j$. Then $\mathbf{K}_i^{lim} S$ means that P_j has IK that S of degree equal to $\delta_j - \text{complex}(S)$, and P$i$ has IK of degree just *one* greater, by however much δ_i exceeds δ_j. This is because for Pi to reach higher levels of IK with Pj, Pj must "keep up with" Pi.

The quantity $d_1 = \min\{\delta_1, \delta_2 + 1\}$ is crucial in what follows. We shall dub it the *effective depth-limit* of P1, for it, not δ_1, is the effective constraint on the degree of P1's IK with P2 of any fact. Note that if d_1 and d_2 differ, they differ by one, since

$$(d_1, d_2) = \begin{cases} (\delta, \delta) & \text{if } \delta_1 = \delta_2 = \delta \\ (\delta_2 + 1, \delta_2) & \text{if } \delta_1 > \delta_2 \\ (\delta_1, \delta_1 + 1) & \text{if } \delta_1 < \delta_2 \end{cases} \qquad (3)$$

3.4. Players' Knowledge in Model 1 of the FRPD

What depth-limited players know and do not know depends on the complexity of sentences describing the facts to be known. To characterize players' knowledge in the FRPD we must ask what are the complexities of sentences specifying "the game," and "players' rationality." These complexities depend on what *attitudes* of players have to be specified in order to describe the game and players' rationality. The description of *the game* (in the sense of Model 0) specifies, about players' attitudes, that: For $r = 1, \ldots, N$, at round r they *know* the choices made at rounds $r + 1, \ldots, N$, and for $i = 1, 2, \pi$ has such and such *preferences* among pairs of act-sequences.[14] It is clear that, if G is a sentence that nonredundantly expresses Model 0,

$$\text{complex}(G) = 1 \qquad (4)$$

Let R denote a sentence saying that *players are rational* in the sense that they satisfy (DOM) and (DED). It is less clear how to assign complexity to this sentence. Generally, given a fact, such as the fact that players are choice rational, the complexity of a sentence expressing it depends on how much "unpacking" is done by the sentence. For example, *Defecting is strictly dominant* has complexity 0, but if we unpack the expression "strictly dominant" in terms of utility attachments we get a sentence of complexity 1. How much unpacking is appropriate is not a cut and dried matter, because it depends on whether we should assume players possess the concept expressed by the "packed" word in question. We credit players with the concept *strictly dominant*, and accordingly assume:[15]

$$\text{complex}(R) = 1 \qquad (5)$$

We assume that the FRPD is a game of boundedly complete information, that is, that the players have IK up to limits of the game and of each other's rationality characteristics. In view of (4)–(5), this implies

$$\mathbf{K}_1^r S \text{ for } r = 0, 1, \ldots, d_1 - 1; \qquad S = G, R \qquad (6)$$

This completes the specification of Model 1 of the FRPD.

3.5. The Backward Induction Theorem

We now have the materials we need to prove our first main result, the Backward Induction Theorem (Theorem 1). We begin with a simple lemma which is the basis for all backward induction reasoning about repeated dilemmas.

Write $a_i(t)$ for Pi's action at round t; thus $a_i(t) \in \{C, D\}$. Also write $A_i(t) = \langle a_i(t), a_i(t-1), \ldots, a_i(1) \rangle$ for Pi's action-sequence from round t on; thus $A_i(t) \in \{C, D\}^t$. We shall say that round t is *endgame for Pi* if Pi defects (plays D) at round t and thereafter. We write

$$e_i = \max\{t | A_i(t) = \langle D, D, \ldots, D \rangle\}$$

That is, e_i is the length of the unbroken sequence of defections by Pi ending with the final round.

Lemma 1
Assume P1 knows the game. Then if P1 knows that t is endgame for P2, $t+1$ is endgame for P1.

Remark. For the assumption and the supposition that P1 knows that t is endgame for P2 to be true, P1 must have enough depth. For the former we need $\delta_1 \geq 2$. Since t is endgame for P2 has complexity 0, this suffices for both.

Proof. Since P1 knows the game (Model 0) and that t is endgame for P2, P1 knows that $A_2(t+1) = \langle C, D, D, \cdots \rangle$ or $\langle D, D, D, \ldots \rangle$, by (DED). For any $A_1(t)$ in $\{C, D\}^t$, P1's payoff from $\langle D, A_1(t) \rangle$ exceeds her payoff from $\langle C, A_1(t) \rangle$ for each of these values of $A_2(t+1)$. P1 knows this, by (DED) and her knowledge of the game. Hence P1 chooses D at round $t+1$, by (DOM). ∎

Theorem 1 (Backward Induction Theorem)
The endgame of P1 satisfies $e_1 \geq d_1 - 1$ $(d_1 = 1, 2, \ldots)$.

Interpretation. Theorem 1 says that P1 confesses from $d_1 = \min\{\delta_1, \delta_2 + 1\}$ at the latest. If the depth limits are equal and equal to δ, then $d_1 = d_2 = \delta$ and Theorem 1 tells us that both are confessing unremittingly by round δ. If they are unequal, suppose that P1 is the shallower; then $d_1 = \delta_1$ and $d_2 = \delta_1 + 1$. Thus the shallower confesses at least from the round with index equal to her depth-limit less 1, and the deeper at least from the round before.

Theorem 1 follows quickly from the following lemma.

Lemma 2
In Model 1, if $\mathbf{K}_1^r G$ and $\mathbf{K}_1^{r-1} R$ then $e_1 \geq r(r = 1, 2, \ldots)$.

Interpretation. Lemma 2 says that if P1 knows the game and if both players are rational, then P1 defects at round 1; if P1 knows that P2 knows the game, and if P1 also knows that both players are rational, then P1 defects at rounds 2 and 1; and so on.[16]

Our proof of Lemma 2 is a formalization of the Backward Induction Argument for the FRPD. The latter receives varied expressions in the literature, but they have a common essence, which we believe our version captures. Though our version is formal, it is not so in the strong sense of "formal" used in logic. For completeness, we also give a version in epistemic logic in

Appendix 1. We note that the proof has the form of a "third-person narrative" of a player's mental process: the succession of statements in it about what Pi knows correspond to the succession of knowledge states Pi goes through as she reasons her way through her problem.

Proof of Lemma 2. It is convenient to rewrite the lemma using "$\cdots \rightarrow \cdots$" for "if . . . then . . .":

$$(H_r) \qquad\qquad (\mathbf{K}_1^r G \text{ \& } \mathbf{K}_1^{r-1} R) \rightarrow (e_1 \geq r)$$

$(\mathbf{K}_1^r G \text{ \& } \mathbf{K}_1^{r-1} R)$ is known as the *antecedent* of the conditional sentence H_r and $(e_1 \geq r)$ as its *consequent*. The proof is by induction on r.

Inductive basis. Assume $\mathbf{K}_1^1 G$ and $\mathbf{K}_1^0 R$, that is, $\mathbf{K}_1 G$ and R. By $\mathbf{K}_1 G$, P1 knows (since by (DED) she can deduce it from G) that D is strictly dominant for her in the subgame starting at round 1, hence by (DOM) she chooses D at round 1. We have shown

$$(H_1) \qquad\qquad (\mathbf{K}_1^1 G \text{ \& } \mathbf{K}_1^0 R) \rightarrow (e_1 \geq 1)$$

Inductive step. We give the step from H_1 to H_2 (for the general step see Appendix 2). Assume the antecedent of H_2, that is, $(\mathbf{K}_1^2 G \text{ \& } \mathbf{K}_1^1 R)$, that is, $\mathbf{K}_1 \mathbf{K}_2 G$ and $\mathbf{K}_1 R$. Then $\mathbf{K}_1(\mathbf{K}_2 G \text{ \& } R)$ by (DED), that is, P1 knows the antecedent of H_1 written for P2. Since H_1 is a theorem (as we have just shown) P1 knows H_1 by (DED); and so, knowing its antecedent, by (DED) she knows its consequent, that 1 is endgame for P2. But since $\mathbf{K}_1 \mathbf{K}_2 G$ implies $\mathbf{K}_2 G$ by (2), it follows from Lemma 1 that 2 is endgame for P1. ∎

The three appeals made here to (DED) deserve comment. The third appeal is to Modus Ponens closure, and the first to the related assumption that if Pi knows two things she knows their conjunction. The second appeal is to the assumption that the agents can deduce a certain theorem. We deem this *not* to be a case of sophistication, for the theorems are easy both in structure (as Appendix 2 shows) and in conceptual content.

Proof of Theorem 1. From (6), $\mathbf{K}_1^r G \text{ \& } \mathbf{K}_1^{r-1} R$ if $r \leq d_1 - 1$. Hence r is endgame for P1 if $r \leq d_1 - 1$ by Lemma 2. ∎

If the players are adequately described by the assumptions of this section, $d_1 - 1$ is the length of the longest endgame for which P1 has decisive game theoretic reasons.[17] Assume that

(TFT)   the default rule of P1 and P2 is Tit-for-Tat

Then the act-pair sequence is $\langle (C, C) \ldots , (C, C), (D, D), \ldots , (D, D) \rangle$ if $d_1 = d_2$, and $\langle (C, C), \ldots , (C, C), (D, C), (D, D), \ldots , (D, D) \rangle$ if $d_1 > d_2$, in each case with $N - d_1 + 1$ plays of (C, C). In the latter case, at round $N - d_1$, when P1 defects for the first time, P2 follows his default rule and plays C. ∎

This completes Model 1.

4. Model 2: The Repeated Dilemma with Sophisticated Depth-Limited Players

4.1. Sophisticated Players' Knowledge in the FRPD

Henceforth we assume that

P1 and P2 are sophisticated with respect to Model 1

Sophistication has not been formally defined. For formal purposes, therefore, we shall simply assume that if P1 and P2 are sophisticated (about Model 1) then they satisfy, in addition to the assumptions made in Section 3, further conditions which impute to them iterated knowledge of certain theorems and assumptions of Model 1.[18] The first two are

$$\mathbf{K}^{lim} D \tag{7}$$
$$(S_1) \qquad\qquad \mathbf{K}^{lim} B_1$$

where D and B_1 express the values of the players' depth-limits, and the Backward Induction Theorem (Theorem 1), respectively.

The key to why sophistication allows extra mileage from given depth is that the extra concepts the sophisticate has carry the same information as certain combinations of non-Model 1 concepts, but at lower expense in terms of depth. The number concept *four* is informationally equivalent to the concept *the successor of the successor of the successor of zero*, but because it is syntactically simpler it is much easier for humans to operate with mentally; our problem-solving abilities are further enhanced by using the *general* concept of a number. Now consider a player with depth-limit 4. One might suppose that a description of her capacity to have iterated knowledge must have complexity 4. There are indeed ways of describing this capacity that do: for example, by listing sentences she can know. But there are other ways that have lower complexity because they take advantage of *number concepts* and the general concept of *complexity*. Our own definition (DL) of depth-limit is of this sort. The reader will observe that there is no "depth-strain" in understanding that definition; once one has the ideas of a natural number, and of the complexity of a sentence, there is little to it. Sophisticated players do, so we assign[19]

$$\text{complex}(D) = \text{complex}(B_1) = 1 \tag{8}$$

Hence, by (7) and (S_1),

$$\mathbf{K}_1^r S \text{ for } r = 0, 1, \ldots, d_1 - 1; S = D, B_1 \tag{9}$$

We also assume that sophisticated players satisfy (DOM), (DED), and (6).

Among the Section 3 concepts are those of *IK of degree 1, IK of degree 2*, and so on. The concept *has IK of degree 3 that* causes essentially no more difficulty than *knows that* (as long as it is manipulated as a whole); thus these attitudes contribute essentially one unit of complexity. The same is true of the corresponding notations: depth-wise, $\mathbf{K}_1^3$ works just like $\mathbf{K}_1$. Mathematicians take advantage every day of such "macros" to boost their limited syntactic powers. This may lead one to conjecture that players can use such macros in conducting a Backward Induction Argument and so economize on depth. But it turns out on scrutiny that the stratagem does not work here. Progress in Backward Induction Arguments—extra "unravelling"—depends on players' tracking each other's conclusions by retracing their deliberations. Chunking is a step in a deliberation. So players must retrace chunkings. But this means knowing the chunker's piece of knowledge in unchunked as well as in chunked form, and nothing is gained.[20]

4.2. The Second Backward Induction Theorem

We now show that sophistication implies defection in excess of the lower bound given in Thoerem 1. Write $d = (d_1, d_2)$ for the pair of effective depth-limits.

Theorem 1.2 (Second Backward Induction Theorem)
If the players are sophisticated then $e_1 \geq F_1^2(d)$, where

$$F_1^2(d) = \begin{cases} 2d_1 - 2 \text{ if } d_1 \text{ is odd} \\ d_1 + d_2 - 2 \text{ if } d_1 \text{ is even} \end{cases}$$

Theorem 1.2 is a special case of Theorem 2, which is proved below.

Interpretation.   Consider the symmetric case $\delta_1 = \delta_2$, and say the common depth-limit is 3. Since the players satisfy (DOM), (DED), and (6), round 2 is endgame for them both by Theorem 1. Since they are sophisticated, they also know the depth-limits and Theorem 1, and so can deduce that it is: for example, P1 deduces that 2 is endgame for P2. Hence P1 chooses D at 3 by Lemma 1. We have extended back one round the lower bound on P1's endgame given in Theorem 1. Now consider P2 deliberating at 4. By P2's sophistication, P2 knows that P1 knows the depth-limits and Theorem 1; so he can figure out that P1 knows that P2 will choose D at 2, and so he can also figure out—since he knows that P1 is rational and knows the game—that P1 will in consequence choose D at 3. So P2 chooses D at 4.

Can we now add a further step of the same form to show that the players choose D at round 5? No. At the last step in the above we used the fact that P2 knows that P1 knows D and B_1. Now we would need the premise that P2 knows that P1 knows that P2 knows D and B_1. But this violates (8).

4.3. The General Backward Induction Theorem and the Sophistication Theorem

Nevertheless, the defection-stretching effects of sophistication do not stop here. The players of Model 2 have all the concepts they need—complexity, iterated knowledge, depth-limits—to discover, just as we have, the *Second* Backward Induction Theorem, Theorem 1.2. We shall assume that they also have the complementary attributes—imagination, and so forth—that one may need to discover it. Since we assume a complete-information setting, they not only know Theorem 1.2 but also have IK up to limits of it. For the same reason, they have IK up to limits of (S_1). Thus we have

(S_2) $\mathbf{K}^{lim} B_2$ & $\mathbf{K}^{lim} S_1$

These items of IK allow the players to argue their way back yet further. For reasons we shall give in a moment, we make the complexity assignments

$$\text{complex}(B_2) = \text{complex}(S_1) = 2$$

We now have

Theorem 1.3 (Third Backward Induction Theorem)
If the players are sophisticated then $e_1 \geq F_1^3(d)$, *where* $F_1^3(d) = 2d_1 + d_2 - 4.$

It is clear that we can generate in the same manner a sequence of theorems of which Theorems 1.2 and 1.3 are the first two members. At this point we shall move straight to the general case.

We assume that, for the same reasons for which P1 and P2 satisfy (S_1) and (S_2), they satisfy the sequence of conditions (S_k) given by

(S_k) $\mathbf{K}^{lim} B_k$ & $\mathbf{K}^{lim} S_{k-1}$ $(k = 1, 2, \ldots)$

(S_0) $\mathcal{T}$

where the B_k are the sequence of theorems to be defined presently, and $\mathcal{T}$ is any tautology. Next we define the functions F_1^r, F_2^r from pairs of positive integers $n = (n_1, n_2)$ to nonnegative integers, thus:

$$F_i^1(n) = n_i - 1 \qquad (i = 1, 2) \tag{10}$$

$$\begin{aligned}(F_1^{r+1}(n) = F_{\Delta(d_1-r)}^r(n) + (d_1 - r) \qquad (r = 1, 2, \ldots, d_1) \\ F_2^{r+1}(n) = F_{\#(d_2-r)}^r(n) + (d_2 - r) \qquad (r = 1, 2, \ldots, d_2)\end{aligned} \tag{11}$$

where Δ, $\#$ are "parity indicators," defined as follows:

$$\#n = 1 \text{ if } n \text{ is odd, 2 if } n \text{ is even}$$
$$\Delta n = 2 \text{ if } n \text{ is odd, 1 if } n \text{ is even}$$

It may be checked that (10) and (11) yield the formulas for F_1^2 and F_1^3 given in Theorems 1.2 and 1.3.

Finally, we assign complexities to the sentences B_k and $S_{k-1}(k = 1, 2, \ldots)$. We assume that for any sentence S

$$\text{complex}(\mathbf{K}^{lim} S) = 1 + \text{complex}(S)$$

That is, we treat *has iterated knowledge up to limits that*, for sophisticates who understand this notion, as a "simple" attitude in terms of its demands on their depth.[21] Together with (8) this gives

$$\text{complex}(B_r) = r, \qquad \text{complex}(S_r) = r + 1 \qquad (r = 1, 2, \ldots) \qquad (12)$$

The general theorem (proved in Appendix 2) is

Theorem 2 (General Backward Induction Theorem)
If the players are sophisticated then, for $r = 1, 2, \ldots, d_1$,

$$(B_r) \qquad\qquad\qquad e_1 \geq F_1^r(d)$$

To illustrate it, consider the symmetric case $\delta_1 = \delta_2 = 3$. We have seen, following Theorem 1.2, that IK up to limits that B_1 extends the players' endgames at least back to 4. What is the consequence of the players' IK up to limits of B_2 and S_1? Putting $r = 3$ we find that $e1 \geq F_1^3(d) = F_{\Delta(3-2)}^2(3, 3) + (3 - 2) = F_2^2(3, 3) + 1 = 5$. Easily, $F_1^4(3, 3) = F_1^3(3, 3)$, and $F_1^r(3, 3)$ is undefined for $r > 4$, so $B_4, B_5, \ldots$ add nothing further to the length of the endgame established by Theorem 2.

Similarly, we find that for $\delta_1 = \delta_2 = 4$, the maximal lower bound on the endgame given by Theorem 2 is 9, and for $\delta_1 = 5, \delta_2 = 3$, it is 7. We shall show in the next theorem that, in the general symmetric case $\delta_1 = \delta_2 = \delta$, Theorem 2 implies that for sophisticated players $e_1 \geq \frac{1}{2}\delta(\delta + 1) - 1$. The asymmetric cases are not quite so simply described.

We show in Appendix 2 (Lemma 8) that $F_1^r(d)$ increases monotonically as r goes from 1 to d_1. Thus the greatest number n for which Theorem 2 establishes that $e_1 \geq n$ is $F_1^{d_1}(d)$. We shall write

$$e_1^* =_{def} F_1^{d_1}(d)$$

the integer e_1^* is the length of the longest endgame for which, if P1 is sophisticated in the sense of Model 2, she has decisive game theoretic reasons.[22] Call it P1's *sophistication bound*. The final theorem (which is proved in Appendix 2) characterizes e_1^* in terms of the two effective depth-limits.

Theorem 3 (Sophistication Theorem)
P1's sophistication bound e_1^* is given by

$$
e_1^* = \begin{cases}
\frac{1}{2} d_1(d_1 + 1) - 1 & \text{if } d_1 = d_2 \\
\frac{1}{2} d_2(d_1 + 1) + (d_1 - d_2) - 1 & \text{if } d_1 \neq d)2, d_1 \text{ odd} \\
\frac{1}{2} d_1(d_2 + 1) - 1 & \text{if } d_1 \neq d_2, d_1 \text{ even}
\end{cases}
$$

It follows easily that $e_1^* = e_2^*$ if $d_1 = d_2$ and $e_1^* = e_2^* + 1$ if $d_1 > d_2$, so that, in analogy with Model 1, if players begin defecting at their sophistication bounds, the deeper defects one round before the shallower. Write $\bar{e}^* = \max\{e_1^*, e_2^*\}$. Using (3), we can obtain $\bar{e}^*$ as a function of δ_1 and δ_2. Defining $\underline{\delta} = \min\{\delta_1, \delta_2\}$, we get

$$
\bar{e}^*(\delta_1, \delta_2) = \begin{cases}
\frac{1}{2} \underline{\delta}(\underline{\delta} + 1) - 1 & \text{if } \delta_1 = \delta_2 \\
\frac{1}{2} (\underline{\delta} + 1)^2 - 1 & \text{if } \delta_1 \neq \delta_2, \underline{\delta} \text{ odd} \\
\frac{1}{2} (\underline{\delta} + 1)^2 - \frac{1}{2} & \text{if } \delta_1 \neq \delta_2, \underline{\delta} \text{ even}
\end{cases} \tag{13}
$$

As an illustration, Figure 8.2 tabulates $\bar{e}^*$ for values of δ_1 and δ_2 up to 6.

Assume that the players' default rule is Tit-for-Tat. Then the act-pair sequence is $\langle(C, C), \ldots, (C, C), (D, D), \ldots, (D, D)\rangle$ if $d_1 = d_2$, and $\langle(C, C), \ldots, (C, C), (D, C), (D, D), \ldots, (D, D)\rangle$ if $d_1 > d_2$, in each cash with $N - e_1^*$ plays of (C, C). P1's payoff in the FRPD is therefore given by

$$
\pi_1(\delta_1, \delta_2) = \begin{cases}
N - \bar{e}^*(\delta_1, \delta_2) + a & \text{if } \delta_1 > \delta_2 \\
N - \bar{e}^*(\delta_1, \delta_2) + b & \text{if } \delta_1 < \delta_2 \\
N - \bar{e}^*(\delta_1, \delta_2) & \text{if } \delta_1 = \delta_2
\end{cases} \tag{14}
$$

This completes Model 2.

		δ_2				
	1	2	3	4	5	6
1	0	1	1	1	1	1
2	1	2	4	4	4	4
3	1	4	5	7	7	7
4	1	4	7	9	9	9
5	1	4	7	12	14	17
6	1	4	7	12	17	20

(δ_1 labels the rows.)

Figure 8.2. The greater sophistication bound in terms of (δ_1, δ_2).

5. The Two-Stage Game

We now turn to the determination of the player's depth-limits. Consider the following two-stage game. In the first stage two "metaplayers" M1 and M2 noncooperatively choose positive integers δ_1 and δ_2. In the second, P1 and P2 play the FRPD of Model 2, in the way described in Section 4, with depth-limits δ_1 and δ_2. In the first stage there is common knowledge between M1 and M2 of all this. These assumptions induce a one-stage game played at stage one by M1 and M2 which we shall call the *Depth Game*.

We assume that the preferences of M1 and M2 are given by the functions π_1, π_2, subject to one refinement. Other things being equal, a lower depth-limit is preferred to a higher one. In other words, the metaplayers have lexicographic preferences over FRPD payoff and depth-limit, with depth-limit secondary: they have "epsilon-aversion" for depth. This means we can interpret our main result as showing that what makes great depth nonoptimal is essentially not its direct cost but its *effect* in making the Backward Induction Argument effective. We record our assumption as

If $\pi_1(\delta_1, \delta_2) = \pi_1(\delta_1', \delta_2)$ and $\delta_1 < \delta_1'$, then δ_1' is not a best reply to δ_2

(15)

This completes the description of the Depth Game.

Our final theorem sets an upper bound to the depth-limits that the metaplayers choose.

Theorem 4
Let Δ be the smallest positive integer greater than $\max\{2a - 1,$ $\sqrt{5 - 2(a + b)}\}$. *Then in the Depth Game every δ_1 greater than Δ is strictly dominated.*

The proof of Theorem 4 depends on two lemmas.

Lemma 3
If δ_1 is a best reply to δ_2, then either $\delta_1 = 1$, or $\delta_1 = \delta_2$, or $\delta_1 = \delta_2 + 1$.

That is, if δ_1 is a best reply to δ_2, then either δ_1 is a *disarming* choice ($\delta_1 = 1$), or a *matching* choice ($\delta_1 = \delta_2$), or a *leap-frogging* choice ($\delta_1 = \delta_2 + 1$).

Proof. Fix δ_2. Then M1's preferences (15) and the function π_i given in (14) imply that $\delta_1 = 1$ is the best reply for M1 such that $\delta_1 < \delta_2$, and that $\delta_1 = \delta_2 + 1$ is the best reply for M1 such that $\delta_1 > \delta_2$. The lemma follows immediately. ■

Lemma 4
If $\delta_2 \geq \Delta$, then

$$\pi_1(1, \delta_2) > \pi_1(\delta_2, \delta_2) \qquad (16)$$

and

$$\pi_1(\delta_2, \delta_2) > \pi_1(\delta_2 + 1, \delta_2) \qquad (17)$$

In words, if $\delta_2 \geq \Delta$, then, in terms of P1's FRPD payoff, disarming is better than matching and matching is better than leap-frogging.

Proof. Since $a > 1, \Delta > 1$ and so $1 < \delta_2$. Hence by (14), (16) holds if $N - \bar{e}^*(1, \delta_2) + b > N - \bar{e}^*(\delta_2, \delta_2)$. From (13), this is true if $N - \frac{1}{2}(1 + 1)^2 + 1 + b > N - \frac{1}{2}\delta_2(\delta_2 + 1) + 1$, which is so if

$$\delta_2 > 4 - 2b - \delta_2^2 \tag{18}$$

Again, by (14) inequality (17) holds if $N - \bar{e}^*(\delta_2, \delta_2) > N - \bar{e}^*(\delta_2 + 1, \delta_2)$ $+ a$. From (13), there are two cases in which this is true. If δ_2 is odd, it is if $N - \frac{1}{2}\delta_2(\delta_2 + 1) + 1 > N - \frac{1}{2}(\delta_2 + 1)^2 + 1 + a$, and so if $\delta_2 > 2a - 1$. If δ_2 is even, it is true if $N - \frac{1}{2}\delta_2(\delta_2 + 1) + 1 > N - \frac{1}{2}(\delta_2 + 1)^2 + \frac{1}{2} + a$, and so if $\delta_2 > 2a - 2$. Thus (17) holds if

$$\delta_2 > 2a - 1 \tag{19}$$

Suppose $\delta_2 \geq \Delta$. Then, first, (19) holds. Second, $\delta_2^2 > 5 - 2a - 2b$, that is, $2a - 1 > 4 - 2b - \delta_2^2$, whence (18) holds, by (19).   ■

Proof of Theorem 4. Let k be any positive integer. We show that $\Delta + k$ is strictly dominated for M1 by Δ.

First, let $\delta_2 = 1, \ldots, \Delta - 1$. Then $\Delta, \Delta + k > \delta_2$, hence $\Delta + k$ is π_1-equivalent to Δ by (14) and (13), and so dispreferred to Δ by (15).

Second, let $\delta_2 = \Delta, \ldots, \Delta + k$. Since $\delta_2 \geq \Delta$, surpassing (choosing $\delta_1 > \delta_2$) is π_i-worse than matching, and matching is π_1-worse than falling short (choosing $\delta_1 < \delta_2$), by (17), (16), (14), and (13). But if $\delta_2 = \Delta, \ldots, \Delta + k - 1$, then $\Delta + k$ surpasses and Δ matches or falls short; and if $\delta_2 = \Delta + k$, then $\Delta + k$ matches and Δ falls short. This in both cases $\Delta + k$ is π_1-worse than Δ.

Third, let $\delta_2 = \Delta + k, \Delta + 1, \ldots$. Then $\Delta + k$ is π_1-equivalent to Δ by (14) and (13), and so dispreferred to Δ by (15).   ■

6. Discussion

6.1. What We Have Shown and What Does the Work

We have found that agents would not choose to be too deep if they knew they were going to have to play Prisoner's Dilemmas. This explains (functionally) low depth-limits in a FRPD-beset world; and in particular, low depth in plays of FRPDs. This in turn explains cooperation for most of the game if players default to a coooperative rule such as Tit-for-Tat.

Why do metaplayers choose low depth? Not, on our analysis, because depth is costly: there is only "epsilon-aversion" for depth. The essential reason is that, if the opponent has more than a certain depth, leap-frogging means losing *many* rounds of (C, C) payoffs. This effect is amplified for sophisticates, since sophistication shifts up the function giving bounds on e_1 in terms of d_1. It also makes it more convex: against anything but tiny values of d_2, increases in d_1 in the neighbourhood of d_2 have powerful effects on the length of the (D, D) phase at the end of the game (see Figure 8.2).

6.2. Supersophistication

It may be asked: "Can't rational depth-limited players unravel yet further by exploiting Theorem 3 just as 'sophisticates' exploit Theorem 1? Understanding Theorem 3, like understanding Theorem 1, imposes no great depth-strain. I have just read it and understood it. As a result, I know that if you and I have depth-limits of 4, say, you will defect at 9. But then I have a game theoretic reason to defect at 10. What is more, this argument may be extended further, just as the earlier one was."

Our answer is that rational depth-limited players *might* unravel further in this way. Moreover, if they did so, this property would be described in another theorem, belonging to a series of which Theorems 1 and 3 are only the first two members. (This series would, however, terminate when the rising complexities of the members made depth-limits bind.) But this possibility depends on the players' having sophistication of a very high order. Such sophistication would be quite disproportionate to the upper bounds on depth-limits implied by Theorem 4 for typical values of a and b, some of which are shown in Figure 8.3.[23]

In the present essay we have in effect hand-set the degree of sophistication at a value commensurate with these. A fuller development of the present theory would take the choice variable of the metaplayers to be a vector of rationality characteristics (depth, degree of sophistication, and so on), perhaps subjected to joint restrictions reflecting the need for some proportion among the dimensions of rationality. It is worth remarking that this method would give solutions in which players have depth-limits no greater than we have found and, in consequence, have no greater sophistication.

a \ b	−0.1	−1	−2	−3	−4	−10
1.1	2	3	3	3	4	5
2	3	3	3	3	3	5
3	–	–	5	5	5	5
4	–	–	–	7	7	7

Figure 8.3. Upper bound on chosen depth-limit.

Appendix 1. The Backward Induction Argument Formalized

For completeness, we sketch a version of the first few rounds of the Backward Induction Argument in the manner of epistemic logic. We assume that the knowledge of P1 and P2 obeys the axioms and rules of the latter. For brevity, we do not cite all the individual axiom-schemas and rules that the argument uses: "RE" indicates an appeal to the Rule of Epistemization (*if T is a theorem then* $\mathbf{K}_i T$ *is a theorem*); otherwise, we write "EL" at each such use. At 7, 12, ... we use the simple theorem $H \rightarrow (\mathbf{K}_i E_j t \rightarrow D_i[t + 1])$, where $D_i t$ means *Pi defects at t*. We write $E_i t$ for *Pi defects at rounds* $1, \ldots, t$, and H for $G \& R$.

1. Assumption	H
2. 1, EL	$E_2 1$
3. 1, 2, EL	$H \rightarrow E_2 1$
4. 3, RE	$\mathbf{K}_1(H \rightarrow E_2 1)$
5. Assumption	$\mathbf{K}_1 H$
6. 4, 5, EL	$\mathbf{K}_1 E_2 1$
7. 1, 6, EL	$E_1 2$
8. 1, 5, 7, EL	$\mathbf{K}_1 H \rightarrow E_1 2$
9. 8, RE	$\mathbf{K}_2(\mathbf{K}_1 H \rightarrow E_1 2)$
10. Assumption	$\mathbf{K}_2 \mathbf{K}_1 H$
11. 8, 9, EL	$\mathbf{K}_2 E_1 2$
12. 1, 11, EL	$E_2 3$
13. 1,5,10, EL	$\mathbf{K}_2 \mathbf{K}_1 H \rightarrow E_2 3$
14. 13, RE	$\mathbf{K}_1(\mathbf{K}_2 \mathbf{K}_1 H \rightarrow E_2 3)$
15. Assumption	$\mathbf{K}_1 \mathbf{K}_2 \mathbf{K}_1 H$
16. 14, 15, EL	$\mathbf{K}_1 E_2 3$
17. 1,16, EL	$E_1 4$

Appendix 2. Proofs of Theorems

Lemma 2: Proof of the Inductive Step

For arbitrary r, assume H_r proved. We derive H_{r+1}. Assume the antecedent of H_{r+1}:

$$\mathbf{K}_1^{r+1} G \ \& \ \mathbf{K}_1^{r-1} R \tag{20}$$

Since H_r written for P2 is a theorem, by (DED) P1 knows it, that is:

$$\mathbf{K}_1(\mathbf{K}_2^r G \ \& \ \mathbf{K}_2^{r-1} R \rightarrow e_2 \geq r) \tag{21}$$

From (20), $\mathbf{K}_1(\mathbf{K}_2^r G \ \& \ \mathbf{K}_2^{r-1} R)$ by the definition of $\mathbf{K}_1^r$ and (DED). Hence $\mathbf{K}_1(e_2 \geq r)$ by (21) and (DED). But since (20) implies $\mathbf{K}_1 G$, it follows from Lemma 1 that $e_1 \geq r + 1$, which is the consequent of H^{r+1}. ∎

Proof of Theorem 2

The functions $F_1^1, \ldots, F_1^r$ are defined recursively in (10)–(11). The next lemma gives formulae for them.

Lemma 5

The functions F_1^r defined by (10)–(11) are as follows ($r = 1$), $\ldots, d_1$):

(a) *If $d_1 = d_2$:*

$$F_i^r = \tfrac{1}{2}r(d_1 + d_2 - r + 1) - 1$$

(b) *If $d_1 \neq d_2$ and d_1 even:*

$$F_1^r(d) = \begin{cases} \tfrac{1}{2}r(d_1 + d_2 - r + 1) - 1 & \text{if } r \text{ is even} \\ \tfrac{1}{2}(r - 1)(d_1 + d_2 - r) - 1 & \text{if } r \text{ is odd} \end{cases}$$

(c) *If $d_1 \neq d_2$ and d_1 odd:*

$$F_1^r(d) = \begin{cases} \tfrac{1}{2}(d_1 + d_2 - r + 1) + (d_1 - d_2) - 1 & \text{if } r \text{ is even} \\ \tfrac{1}{2}(r - 1)(d_1 + d_2 - r) + d_1 - 1 & \text{if } r \text{ is odd} \end{cases}$$

Proof of Lemma 5.   (a) Let $d_1 = d_2 = d$. Then

$$F_i^r = \tfrac{1}{2}r(2d - r + 1) - 1 \quad (r = 1, \ldots, d; i = 1, 2) \tag{22}$$

(22) is true for $r = 1$ by (10). Assume it is true for arbitrary r ($r = 1, \ldots, d - 1$). Then by (11), $F_1^{r+1} = F_1^r{}_{\Delta(d-r)} + (d - r) = \tfrac{1}{2}r(2d - r + 1) + (d - r) - 1 = \tfrac{1}{2}(r + 1)[2d - (r + 1) + 1] - 1$ as required.

(b) Let $d_1 \neq d_2$, d_1 even. Then d_2 is odd, by (3). We have to show

$$F_1^{2q} = q(d_1 + d_2 - 2q + 1) - 1 \tag{23}$$

$$F_1^{2q-1} = (q - 1)(d_1 + d)_2 - 2q + 1) + d_1 - 1 \tag{24}$$

for $q = 1, \cdots, \tfrac{1}{2}d_1$. (23) is true for $q = 1$ by (11). Assume (23) proved for arbitrary $q \leq \tfrac{1}{2}d_1 - 1$.

We have

$$\begin{aligned} F_1^{2q+2} &= F_{\Delta(d_1-2q-1)}^{2q+1} + d_1 - 2q - 1 = F_2^{2q+1} + d_1 - 2q - 1 \\ &= F_{\#(d_2-2q)}^{2q} + d_2 - 2q + d_1 - 2q - 1 = F_1^{2q} + d_1 + d_2 - 4q - 1 \\ &= q(d_1 + d_2) - q(2q - 1) + d_1 + d_2 - 4q - 2 \\ &= (q + 1)[d_1 + d_2 - (2q + 1)] - 1 \end{aligned}$$

by (11) and the inductive hypothesis, which is (23) for $q + 1$. And

$$F_1^{2q-1} = F_{\Delta(d_1-2q+2)}^{2q-2} + d_1 - 2q + 2 = F_1^{2q-2} + d_1 - 2q + 2$$
$$= (q-1)[d_1 + d_2 - 2(q-1) + 1] - 1$$
$$= (q-1)(d_1 + d_2 - 2q + 1) + d_1 - 1$$

by (23), which is (24).

(c) Let $d_1 \neq d_2$, d_1 even. Then d_2 is odd. We show formula (c) for $i = 2$. We have to show

$$F_2^{2q-1} = (q-1)(d_1 + d_2 - 2q + 1) + d_2 - 1 \qquad (24a)$$

and

$$F_2^{2q} = q(d_1 + d_2 - 2q + 1) + d_2 - d_1 - 1$$

for $q = 1, \ldots, d_1/2$. We have

$$F_2^{2q-1} = F_{\#(d_2-2q+2)}^{2q-2} + d_2 - 2q + 2 = F_1^{2q-2} + d_2 - 2q + 2$$
$$= (q-1)[d_1 + d_2 - 2(q-1) + 1] + d_2 - 2q + 1$$
$$= (q-1)(d_1 + d_2 - 2q + 1) + d_2 - 1$$

by (23). And

$$F_2^{2q} = F_{\#(d_2-2q+1)}^{2q-1} + d_2 - 2q + 1 = F_2^{2q-1} + d_2 - 2q + 1$$
$$= (q-1)(d_1 + d_2 - 2q + 1) + 2d_2 - 2q$$
$$= q(d_1 + d_2 - 2q + 1) + d_2 - d_1 - 1$$

by (24a).   ∎

The next lemma we need is

Lemma 6.   *For* $r = 1, 2, \ldots$; $n = 1, 2, \ldots$,

(H_1^n) $(\mathbf{K}_1^n B_r \ \& \ \mathbf{K}_1^n S^{r-1} \ \& \ \mathbf{K}_1^n d \ \& \ \mathbf{K}_1^n G \ \& \ \mathbf{K}_1^{n-1} R) \to [e_1 \geq F_{\Delta n}^r(d) + n]$

(H_2^n) $(\mathbf{K}_2^n B_r \ \& \ \mathbf{K}_2^n S^{r-1} \ \& \ \mathbf{K}_2^n d \ \& \ \mathbf{K}_2^n G \ \& \ \mathbf{K}_2^{n-1} R) \to [e_2 \geq F_{\#n}^r(d) + n]$

Proof of Lemma 6.   We prove (H^n) by induction on n. let $d = d_0$.
Inductive basis.   Assume the antecedent of (H_1^1). The first conjunct, $\mathbf{K}_1 B^r$, may be written $\mathbf{K}_1(S^{r-1} \to [e_i \geq F_i^r(d)])$, by the definition of B^r. Hence the second implies $\mathbf{K}_1[e_2 \geq F_2^r(d)]$ by (DED). Now the third implies $\mathbf{K}_1(e_2 \geq F_2^r(d_0))$ by (DED). But then from the fourth and fifth we have $e_1 \geq F_2^r(d_0) + 1 = F_{\Delta 1}^r(d_0) + 1$ by Lemma 1; this proves (H_i^1) for $i = 1, 2$.
Inductive step.   We derive (H_1^{n+1}) from (H_2^n). Assume (H_2^n) proved. Then P1 knows it, by (DED), $\mathbf{K}_1([\mathbf{K}_2^n B_r \ \& \ \mathbf{K}_2^n S^{r-1} \ \& \ \mathbf{K}_2^n D \ \& \ \mathbf{K}_2^n G \ \& \ \mathbf{K}_2^{n-1} R] \to [e_2 \geq F_{\#n}^r(d) + n])$. Assume the antecedent of (H_1^{n+1}). Then by the definition of

$\mathbf{K}_1^{n+1}$ and (DED), $\mathbf{K}_1(\mathbf{K}_2^n B_r \ \& \ \mathbf{K}_2^n S^{r-1} \ \& \ \mathbf{K}_2^n d \ \& \ \mathbf{K}_2^n G \ \& \ \mathbf{K}_2^{n-1} R)$. Hence $\mathbf{K}_1[e_2 \geq F_{\#n}^r(d) + n]$ by (DED), and so $\mathbf{K}_1[e_2 \geq F_{\#n}^r(d_0) + n]$ by the third conjunct and (DED). But the fourth and fifth conjuncts imply $\mathbf{K}_1 G$ and R, whence, by Lemma 1, $e_1 \geq F_{\#n}^r(d_0) + n + 1 = F_{\Delta(n+1)}^r(d_0) + (n+1)$.   ∎

Proof of General Backward Induction Theorem. It suffices to prove B_r for $r = 2, 3, \ldots, d_1$. For arbitrary r $(r = 1, \ldots, d_1)$, assume S_{r-1}: that is, $\mathbf{K}^{lim} B_{r-1}$ and $\mathbf{K}^{lim} S_{r-2}$. By (12), complex$(B_{r-1}) =$ complex$(S_{r-2}) = r - 1$. Set $n = d_1 - (r - 1)$; then $\mathbf{K}_1^n B_{r-1}$ and $\mathbf{K}_1^n S_{r-2}$ and, by (6), $\mathbf{K}_1^n D, \mathbf{K}_1^n G$ and $\mathbf{K}_1^{n-1} R$. Thus the antecedent of (H_1^n) with $r - 1$ for r is true. Hence, by Lemma 6, $e_1 \geq F_{\Delta n}^{r-1}(d) + n = F_1^r(d)$ by (11).   ∎

Proof of Sophistication Theorem

We now prove the Sophistication Theorem. First we need formulas for $F_i^{d_i}$ for the various cases of parity and symmetry.

Lemma 7
If $d_1 = d_2$ then

$$F_i^{d_i}(d) = \tfrac{1}{2} d_i (d_i + 1) - 1 \tag{25}$$

If $d_1 \neq d_2$ and d_1 is even, then

$$F_1^{d_1}(d) = \tfrac{1}{2} d_1 (d_2 + 1) - 1 \tag{26}$$

$$F_2^{d_2}(d) = \tfrac{1}{2} d_1 (d_2 + 1) + (d_2 - d_1) - 1 \tag{27}$$

Proof of Lemma 7. (25) and (27) are immediate on putting $d_1 = r$ in (22) and $d_1 = 2q$ in (23). For (27), note that from (11) we have

$$F_2^{d_2} = F_1^{d_2-1} + d_2 - d_2 + 1 = F_1^{d_2-1} + 1 \tag{28}$$

Now $d_2 = d_1 + 1$ or $d_1 - 1$, by (3). Suppose the former. Then $F_2^{d_2} = F_1^{d_1} + 1 = \tfrac{1}{2} d_1 (d_2 + 1) + (d_2 - d_1) - 1$ by (28) and (26), as required. Suppose the latter. From (28), $F_2^{d_2} = F_1^{d_1-2} + 1$. But from (23), $F_1^{d_1} - F_1^{d_1-2} = \tfrac{1}{2} d_1 (d_1 + d_2 - d_1 + 1) - \tfrac{1}{2}(d_1 - 2)(d_1 + d_2 - d_1 + 3) = 2$. Hence $F_2^{d_2} = F_1^{d_1} - 1$, as required.   ∎

The Sophistication Theorem is immediate from Lemma 7 and the following fact.

Lemma 8
For each d, $f_1^r(d)$ increases monotonically with r.

Proof. (a) Let $d_1 = d_2$. By Lemma 5, for $r = 2, \cdots, d_1$ we have $F_1^r - F_1^{r-1} = \tfrac{1}{2} r(2d_1 - r + 1) - 1 - \tfrac{1}{2}(r - 1)(2d_1 - r + 2) - 1 = d_1 - r + 1 \geq 0$.

(b) Let $d_1 \neq d_2$ and without loss of generality let d_1 be even. For $q \leq \tfrac{1}{2} d_1$ we have from (11):

$$F_1^{2q-1} = F_{\Delta(d_1-2q+2)}^{2q-2} + d_1 - 2q + 2 = F_1^{2q-2} + d_1 - 2q + 2$$

Hence $\quad F_1^{2q} - F_1^{2q-1} = F_1^{2q} - F_1^{2q-2} - d_1 + 2q - 2 = q(d_1 + d_2 - 2q + 1) - 1 -$
$(q-1)(d_1 + d_2 - 2q + 3) + 1 - d_1 + 2q - 2 = d_2 - 2q + 1$. But $\quad d_1 - 2q + 2$
and so by (3) also $d_2 - 2q + 1$ are nonnegative. $\quad\blacksquare$

Notes

1. This is the appropriate projection of the broad notion of a game of complete information onto a world in which players may be depth-limited. It is appropriate because the circumstances which would produce CK in depth-unlimited players produce IK up to limits in depth-limited ones. What these circumstances are is shown in Bacharach (1992b).

2. Propositions of this kind have also been shown by Bacharach (1992a) and Bicchieri (1992).

3. We ourselves shall give another reason why rational depth-limited players may defect earlier than is implied by the Backward Induction Argument: sophistication.

4. Merely being a Nash equilibrium outcome does not provide such an argument. We shall show later that sophistication brings forward rational defection. However, the number of rounds of extra defection is bounded, independently of N.

5. What default rule the players are likely to use is an empirical question. It might well be some combination of general rules of prudent and decent conduct, culturally inculcated, and these are likely to include refraining from unprovoked aggression (niceness), retaliating (provocability), and so on. Tit-for-Tat is a plausible example of such a rule. Our results would be just the same for any "nice" rule, and essentially the same for a wide range of rules. All that really matters for them is that when both default rules are in force they result in positive average payoffs for each player. If they are symmetric, this is so as long as they give some (C, C)s.

Since our players are assumed to be game theoretically rational, the default rule, though by definition not *determined* by this rationality, must be *consistent* with it: it must not yield actions which are (game theoretically) irrational given the players' initial information. The latter we assume to consist of the usual items, plus the two default rules. Tit-for-Tat satisfies this consistency condition. To see this, note that in our model Pi's default rule cannot be active at the last round, 1 (players' depth-limits are at least 1 and this means it is game theoretically rational to defect at 1), and it is active at t ($t > 1$) only if Pi does not know what Pj will do at round $t - 1$. Let $N = 2$. If Pi does not know at 2 what Pj will do at 1, it cannot be irrational for Pi to cooperate at 2, as Tit-for-Tat requires, for Pi might rationally believe that this will lead to Pj's cooperating at 1. This argument generalizes by induction.

6. See Wimmer and Perner (1983) for evidence that most children do not have thoughts of degree 2 before the age of 5 years, or of degree 3 until nearly 10 years old. Degree 4 ones are reached only after age 16 (Barenboim 1978), and adults' depth-limits in speech events are probably at most 6 (Harder and Kock 1976).

7. "Optimality" must be understood here game theoretically, as that which is a best reply to the "choice" of another metaplayer.

8. A third interpretation is as a though-experiment which amounts to a reductio ad absurdum of the view that economic agents should be modelled as unboundedly rational. The hypothesis of unbounded rationality is self-refuting, since if there were an unboundedly rational chooser, and she had the choice, she would choose to be otherwise. Unbounded rationality is unboundedly rationally rejected: it fails Nozick's test (Nozick 1981).

9. It would be relevant only if we amended the assumption about the players' given knowledge to make this include not only the rules and the rationality of the players but also the fact that the eminent game theorist Sperk has spoken thus and so; and this would change the game.

10. A full version of the argument of this paragraph adds "if Pi is dominance-rational," "if Pi knows that Pj is dominance-rational," etc., at appropriate points.

11. These are enough for our "positive" results. We note that our negative claims—that, without assumptions of sufficient depth, defection can *not* be proved—would not be affected by strengthening the choice rationality assumptions.

12. For further details see Hughes and Cresswell (1968).

13. There is some evidence that nestings of mixed operators are a little easier to cope with than relentless nestings of a single operator, but we shall ignore this.

14. Expressing preferences (over events of complexity zero) in terms of the attitude *attaches utility u to the event that* shows that they have complexity one.

15. The assumption (DED) is of complexity 1 because the sentences describing the various deductive abilities are. One example is the Modus Ponens closure ability described above.

16. What matters for defection at r is, in truth, only that the player knows *at r* that the other knows *at r − 1* that the first knows *at r − 2* that . . . . The condition in the theorem concerns game-long knowledge, and so is overstrong; but it is simpler.

17. We have not quite shown this: it is, rather, the longest one for which we have proved she has reasons, from our assumptions. But it is clear that there is no longer one entailed by them.

18. Not all, on pain of inconsistency. Sophisticates could not know anything that entails that they are not sophisticated, such as that their endgames are $d_1 − 1$ when $d_1 = d_2$.

19. In making these assignments we have chosen to "unpack" the phrase *has depth-limit δ* into the form *knows a sentence only if its complexity is not more than δ − 1*.

20. Suppose that P2 reaches (i) $\mathbf{K}_2(\mathbf{K}_1\mathbf{K}_2 H \to E_1 2)$ and (ii) $\mathbf{K}_2\mathbf{K}_1\mathbf{K}_2 H$, and by Modus Ponens gets to $\mathbf{K}_2 E_1 2$ and so to a defect at 3, as in Appendix 1. To retrace this and reach $\mathbf{K}_1 E_2 3$ and a defect at 4, P1 must know (i) and (ii), which requires depth-limit 5. Say P2 uses the macro $\mathbf{B}_1 =_{def} \mathbf{K}_1\mathbf{K}_2$; then it seems P1 need only know $\mathbf{K}_2(\mathbf{B}_1 \to E_1 2)$ and $\mathbf{K}_2\mathbf{B}_1 H$, for which a depth-limit of 4 suffices. However, in order to know that $\mathbf{K}_2\mathbf{B}_1 H$, P1 must know that a moment earlier $\mathbf{K}_2\mathbf{K}_1\mathbf{K}_2 H$.

21. This is of a piece with our assumption that *P2 has depth-limit δ* has complexity 1, not δ.

22. We have not quite shown this: it is the longest one for which we have proved she has reasons in Model 2, not that there is no longer one for which she has. But it is clear that there is not: see Section 6.

23. It will be noticed that most of the figures seem empirically reasonable. Those for high values of a may not, but it should be remembered that these are only *upper bounds* on the *supoorts* of mixed strategies of the metaplayers.

References

Abreu, Dilip and Rubinstein, Ariel (1988), "The Structure of Nash Equilibrium in Repeated Games with Finite Automata," *Econometrica* 56, 1259–82.

Axelrod, Robert (1984), *The Evolution of Cooperation*, New York: Basic Books.

Bacharach, Michael (1987), "A Theory of Rational Decision in Games," *Erkenntnis* 27, 17–55.

Bacharach, Michael (1992a), "Backward Induction and Beliefs about Oneself," *Synthese* 91, 247–84.

Bacharach, Michael (1992b), "The Acquisition of Common Knowledge," in C. Bicchieri and M. L. Dalla Chiara (eds.), *Knowledge, Belief, and Strategic Interaction*, New York: Cambridge University Press.

Barenboim, C. (1978), "Development of Recursive and Nonrecursive Thinking about Persons," *Developmental Psychology* 14, 419–20.

Bicchieri, Cristina (1992), "Knowledge-Dependent Games: Backward Induction," in C. Bicchieri and M. L. Dalla Chiara (eds.), *Knowledge, Belief, and Strategic Interaction*, New York: Cambridge University Press.

Binmore, Kenneth (1987), "Modelling Rational Players II," *Economics and Philosophy* 4, 9–55.

Harder, P. and Kock, C. (1976), *The Theory of Presupposition Failure*, Copenhagen: Akademisk Forlag.

Hughes, G. E. and Cresswell, M. J. (1968), *An Introduction to Modal Logic*, London: Methuen.

Kreps, David, Milgron, Paul, Roberts, John and Wilson, Robert (1982), "Rational Cooperation in the Finitely Repeated Prisoner's Dilemma," *Journal of Economic Theory* 27, 245–52.

Myerson, Roger (1991), *Game Theory*, Cambridge, Mass.: Harvard University Press.

Neyman, A. (1986), "Bounded Complexity Justifies Cooperation in the Finitely Repeated Prisoner's Dilemma," *Economics Letters* 19, 227–29.

Nozick, Robert (1981), *Philosophical Explanations*, Oxford: Oxford University Press.

Rubinstein, Ariel (1986), "Finite Automata Play the Repeated Prisoner's Dilemma," *Journal of Economic Theory* 39, 83–96.

Wimmer, Heinz and Perner, Josef (1983), "Beliefs about Beliefs: Representation and Constraining Function of Wrong Beliefs in Young Children's Understanding of Deception," *Cognition*, 103–28.

CHAPTER 9

Can Free Choice Be Known?

Itzhak Gilboa

1. Introduction

The last two decades have witnessed a proliferation of attempts to formalize the notions of knowledge, choice, and rationality, especially in interactive situations. Two, admittedly related, types of problems arise in this context: the substantial philosophical questions that have a couple of millennia of experience in tormenting innocent minds, and the more modern formal questions. Among the former, the essence of rationality, choice, and knowledge may lead one to causal decision theory, self-referential paradoxes, and the age-old problem of determinism and free will. Among the latter, it seems that even when we have a very clear idea of some notion of rationality, a satisfactory formulation of it may be extremely evasive. At times, the formulation problem would indeed be rooted in a much more fundamental philosophical quandary.

The main goal of this essay is to address a question of the second type. We highlight a problem in the formal modeling of rational choice and suggest a way to deal with it. The discussion seems to lead one inevitably to dangerous areas shadowed by ominous problems of "the first type." On our retreat from these areas to a safe haven, we will naturally watch the ogres carefully and relate their size and ghastliness as seen from our viewpoint, though we will not tackle them directly.

We start by presenting a well-known argument, according to which rational agents who play a one-shot Prisoner's Dilemma should choose to cooperate if they know they are identical. We then argue that, regardless of how convincing this type of reasoning is, it cannot be dismissed without refining our definition of rational choice. We propose a solution that consists of two main points. The first, more technical one, involves the "synchronization" of proof steps. The

163

second point is that one should ignore any self-knowledge of free choice when attempting to model the latter. After discussing this solution in general, we briefly relate it to causal decision theory and to the problem of determinism versus free will.

2. Motivating Example

Consider the classical "Prisoner's Dilemma" game:

		Player 2	
		C	D
Player 1	C	(3, 3)	(0, 4)
	D	(4, 0)	(1, 1)

As customary, player 1 chooses a row and player 2 chooses a column. The choices can be thought of as simultaneous. The payoff matrix above gives, for each pair of choices of the two players, the utility of player 1 and that of player 2, respectively. These utility functions are assumed to be derived from past observed choices, so that the model implicitly assumes that, in a one-person decision problem under certainty, each player would maximize his or her utility by definition. (In general, the utilities are taken to be von Neumann-Morgenstern utilities (1944), which also reflect each player's decision under a situation of risk, but this additional assumption is not needed here.)

It is implicitly assumed that the game is played exactly once by rational agents. Furthermore, the game and the players' rationality are assumed to be common knowledge between the players. (For the definition of common knowledge, see Lewis (1969) and Aumann (1976). The notion of rationality will remain vague for the time being and, alas, probably also at the end of this chapter.) By the behavioral definition of the utility function, it already incorporates all psychological and sociological payoffs, altruism considerations, and so forth.

We will not discuss the Prisoner's Dilemma at length here. (See, for instance, Aumann (1987b).) Let us only point out that, if one of the players, say player 1, had only one possible choice, player 2 would choose D by definition of the utility function. This claim implicitly assumes that the mere existence of player 1 does not change player 2's behavior, that is, she still views the decision problem as a single-person one. However, there is nothing in the definition of the utility function above, nor in that of von Neumann–Morgenstern's utility function, which implies that player 2 would choose D in this game, where player 1 is not a "dummy" player. (This would follow, however, from the stronger assumptions used in subjective probability models as by Savage (1954) and Anscombe and Aumann (1963).) Yet the noncooperative choice (D) does follow from a very weak assumption of rationality, namely that a player would choose a strictly dominating strategy if such existed. (D is such a strategy since for every choice of the other player it guarantees a strictly higher utility level.)

Using this additional assumption one therefore concludes that both players would choose the noncooperative outcome. (This has been a source of puzzlement and agony to the profession since (C, C) Pareto dominates (D, D), i.e., both players would have been better off had they decided to play C.)

In particular, one may impose an additional assumption at the outset, stating that the players are identical in some sense. The game is symmetric, and the players may follow identical reasoning to conclude they should play D, that is, make identical choices.

However, with the same assumptions one may suggest the following reasoning: "Suppose I am player 1. Knowing that player 2 is identical to me, she would end up making the same choice. That is, if I play C, so does she, and the same applies to D. To be precise, if I choose C, the outcome is (C, C) and my payoff is 3. If I choose D, the outcome is (D, D) and I get 1. Thus, using my information I conclude that C dominates D. To be precise, you could deduce that I will choose C over D by the mere definition of my utility function."

Thus, the argument goes, if identical rational players, who are aware of their identicality, play the Prisoner's Dilemma, they will choose to cooperate (C).

3. Modeling Free Choice

3.1. A Paradox

Most game theorists would reject the above reasoning as nonsensical, ignoring the independence of different players' choices.[1] They would argue that it actually corresponds to the following one-player game, which we will refer to as "the identical prisoners' choice", and which already incorporates the identicality of the two players, but it does not make any sense in the original game, even if the players in it end up making identical choices.

$$
\text{Player 1} \quad \begin{array}{c|c} C & 3 \\ \hline D & 1 \end{array}
$$

Further, they would continue, the fact that the players are identical does not mean that in their reasoning process they cannot conceive of situations in which they differ. Thus, the off-diagonal outcomes are *conceivable*, even if not *possible*, and, indeed, they are the distinction between the two games above. Moreover, in the process of rational decision making one has to consider the conceivable states of the world, even if the decision theory will end up ruling them out as "impossible." (See Gilboa 1990, 1991.) Finally, rationality in the context of independent decision makers has to be applied in such a way that a player compares states of nature (possible or merely conceivable) that differ only in his or her own decision.

While we agree with all these claims, we find that they fail to pinpoint the flaw in the argument of Section 2. To be more specific, consider some formal model of the game describing players' knowledge and choices. (See, for example, Kaneko (1987), Bicchieri (1988a, 1988b, 1989, 1993), and Kaneko and Nagashima (1989).) Suppose that in such a model the following assumption of rationality is assumed to be common knowledge: if a player is faced with finitely many conceivable choices, and knows the payoff derived from each of them, then the player would choose an act that maximizes the payoff function. (This was dubbed the "common sense" assumption in Gilboa and Schmeidler (1988).)

Notice that this assumption does *not* follow directly from the definition of the utility function, since it involves the player's knowledge, which will turn out to be a crucial issue. Note also that, as formulated, this axiom does not imply the choice of a dominant strategy in the presence of uncertainty, say, about other players' choices. We may either strengthen it to say that an action will be chosen by a player whenever it is known (by that player) to guarantee a higher payoff than all other actions, whatever other players may do, or we may additionally impose a separate axiom stating that dominant actions be chosen. The second option does not allow for iterative elimination of dominated strategies, but it simplifies exposition. Let us therefore refer to the conjunction of the "common sense" axiom and the "domination" axiom as "the rationallity assumption."

For clarity of exposition, let us further impose the identicality assumption (we will later see that it is actually redundant). Its exact meaning may be problematic: to say that the players are identical typically means that for a certain class of predicates Ψ, ψ (player 1) holds if and only if ψ (player 2) does, for all ψ in Ψ. Obviously, this may be hard to formulate in first-order-logic models. However, for our purposes, "identicality" may simply mean that "player 1 chooses C iff player 2 chooses C."

As explained above, there seems to be no reason for classical game theorists to reject this assumption in the Prisoner's Dilemma case, since it has a unique dominant strategy—indeed, the same one—for both players.

Yet, equipped with this assumption, we can now follow the reasoning of Section 2 in a formal proof: If identicality is known to both players, each knows that "I play C implies the other player plays C," and the rationality assumption concludes that each player would choose C. On the other hand, it also implies that each player would choose D (by the domination argument). In other words, the model is inconsistent even though the identicality assumption itself does not contradict the implication of the other assumptions (namely, the conclusion that the players would play D.)

3.2. Synchronization of the Proof

The reader may claim that the identicality assumption is unwarranted. Indeed, one may argue that there seems to be no compelling reason to believe that two (or more) players will choose the same strategies even if the game is symmetric, unless this conclusion is derived from more primitive assumptions. (Consider, for instance, a game in which both players have two equivalent strategies that dominate all others.) According to this view, the assumption "If I play C, the other player does the same" may be imposed at the outset only if there is some direct ("causal") relationship between the players' choices. For instance, assume that player 2 is the image player 1 sees in a mirror. In this case, player 1 actually faces the "identical prisoners' choice," a game in which he will play C both by the common sense and by the domination axioms. Differently put, the very formulation of the game (in its normal form) presuppses that no conditional statement "If A then B" may be imposed where A and B relate to different players' choices.

In the next subsection we provide another argument by which the identicality assumption should be rejected. However, in the prisoners' dilemma case, the identicality assumption is not necessary for an inconsistency to occur: since rationality implies a unique choice for each player, one can prove that the players' choice will be identical. To be precise, after having proven that each player will play D, both statements "If I play C, the other player will play C" and "If I play D, the other player will play D" would be logically correct for and known by both players. But then they may be used, in conjunction with the rationality assumption, to derive the contradiction.[2]

There seems to be a problem with the synchronization of the proof in the above reasoning. After the choice C is ruled out at some stage, vacuously true statements beginning with "If I play C" come back to haunt us and derive various unwarranted conclusions.

At this point the similarity to the backward induction problem is rather evident. It has been commonly believed for quite some time that if rationality is common knowledge (whatever that may mean), a backward induction solution is the only consistent one in finite extensive form games with perfect information. However, this belief has been challenged. Reny (1988) pointed out that common knowledge of rationality cannot hold at all nodes of the game tree, and Bicchieri (1988a, 1988b, 1989) further argued that common knowledge (of the game and of all behavioral axioms) and rationality are incompatible axioms.

Gilboa (1990) and Ben-Porath (1997) attempted to provide formulations of these axioms that will be consistent (at least as long as the backward induction solution is actually played). The solution proposed by Gilboa (1990) deals with "synchronization" of the proof in such a way that proven impossibilities will not be allowed to be used again in later derivation.

It seems that a similar idea may be adopted here, and it would roughly run as follows: We first introduce a set of "possible" states of the world as a formal entity of the model.[3] The rationality assumption is qualified to hold only for a player's actions that are "possible," and it is used to conclude that some of them are "impossible." Put differently, the axioms are viewed as an operator, ascribing to each set of states of the world a subset thereof, with the interpretation that if the argument of the operator is known to include all possible states, so does its value.

A set is said to be "possible" if it is a fixed-point of this operator, and there exists a chain of applications of the operator, starting with the set of all states of the world and leading to it. (Gilboa (1990) and, in a different formulation, Ben-Porath (1997) note that the fixed-point requirement alone will not do for derivation of the backward induction solution. It seems that dropping the "chain condition" would result in unintuitive conclusions in our context as well.)

Note that for all finite games there exists a unique possible set according to this definition. However, it may well be empty if the behavioral axioms happens to be inconsistent.

In a way, then, this solution concept imitates the reasoning of the players or of an outside observer. Following this solution in our case, one first has to conclude that choosing C is impossible for both players, whence the identicality assumption follows. But then one cannot use it to show that rationality implies the choice C, because the rationality assumption has no bite after C is dubbed "impossible."

As described here (and in Gilboa 1990), this "solution concept" is imposed from outside the model, and only implicitly may one assume that the players indeed follow the reasoning implied by the chain of operator applications. One may well wish to formally include this "proof" in the model, using a three-place predicate such as "Player i considers state ω possible at step t" where the steps are a well-ordered set (say $\mathbb{N}$) corresponding to steps of the proof. Then one may formulate the claim that all players start out by considering all conceivable states of the world, and the rationality assumption would allow us to conclude that some states previously deemed possible wil no longer be so.

There is one rub, though: in this case one also needs an axiom stating that whatever was deemed possible would continue being so unless otherwise proven. (This is close to the "Frame Axioms" in the artificial intelligence literature.) That is, something along the lines of "For all i, ω, and t, if i does not have a t-stage proof that ω is not possible, then i considers ω as possible at stage $t + 1$." It is not clear to us at this point whether there are satisfactory formulations of such a system that are also consistent.

At any rate, if we avoid this problem and leave the "proof" steps in the definition of the solution concept, we obtain a consistent model that seems to capture our basic game theoretic intuition.

3.3. Two Kinds of Knowledge

We can therefore hope that there is a way to resolve the paradox, at least as long as the identicality assumption is ruled out. Notice, however, that the "synchronization" solution does not suffice in the presence of the identicality assumption, since in this case the reasoning leading to the cooperative outcome may be carried out immediately, and it need not "wait" for the classical reasoning to first conclude that the noncooperative solution will be played.

However, we will argue that the identicality assumption cannot be known by the players to begin with, for reasons that have nothing to do with the paradox discussed above. Ruling the identicality assumption out on theoretical grounds, coupled with the "synchronization" argument of the previous subsection, will complete the resolution of the paradox.

Let us first analyze a simpler example. Consider the following one-person decision problem: Sir Isaac Newton is standing in a room, considering the possibility of jumping out of the window. If he decides to do so, there are two possibilities (or should we write "conceivabilities"?). He may hover in the air, possibly enjoying the view, or he may fall down to the ground. The latter outcome is assumed highly undesirable.

Now let us assume Newton knows two facts about the world: that the law of gravity holds and that he is rational. The first implies that he may practically ignore the possibility of hovering in the air. The second one, by the same token, means that he is not going to jump out of the window.

This decision is certainly made in accordance with Newton's free will. Indeed, the rationality assumption attempts to model precisely these choices that are intuitively referred to as "free." Yet there is something rather troublesome in this formulation: if he "knows" that he is rational in the same way he "knows" that gravitation works, then prior to making up his mind Newton will rule out the possibility of jumping out of the window just as he rules out the possibility of hovering in the air if he does jump. In this case, then, the preliminary analysis he conducts in order to make a "rational" decision leaves him with no choice whatsoever.

The problem here is not logical consistency. Even a "naive" formulation of the axiom of rationality does not seem to lead to any inconsistencies in this simple decision problem. However, we feel that this could hardly be counted as an intuitive modeling of "free choice." Treating one's knowledge of the outside world (which may include other players as well) and one's knowledge of oneself in the same way (formally) does not seem to correspond to our first-hand experience of "making a choice."

Thus, regardless of the problem discussed in Section 3.1, we are tempted to suggest the following principle: When analyzing a (possibly interactive) decision problem from the subjective viewpoint of one individual, one should ignore that individual's knowledge regarding himself/herself. To be precise, one may assume that the individual "knows" his/her tastes and beliefs in the same sense he/she "knows" rules of nature but does not "know" any behavioral assumptions that he/she may satisfy. (Note that we use here the term "taste" rather than "utility." For clarity of exposition, we refer to one's tastes derived from direct introspection and *not* to utility, which is a theoretical construct one uses to explain and predict other players' observed behavior. However, these tastes can still be behaviorally defined, as long as they relate to past choices and not to the choice that is about to be made. To be precise, there is no distinction in this respect between reasoning about others and about oneself. The distinction is that, regarding others, one may "believe" or even "know" that they make choices in a consistent way with past ones, so that their utility functions may be used for prediction. As for one's own self, however, no similar consistency axiom can be known or believed. We will come back to this point in Section 4.)

Formally speaking, an individual may "know" conditional statements of the type "If I choose . . . then . . . "; indeed, these statements are essential for the formalization of rational choice. But then he or she may not have any non-trivial belief, let alone knowledge, regarding the conclusion of such a statement.[4] In particular, the latter may not be a strict subset of other players' (or nature's) normal form strategies.

With this interpretation in mind, Newton's decision not to jump out of the window is the result of his free choice, which relies on his knowledge of gravity as well as on his preference not to be smashed on the ground. Yet neither while making this decision nor afterwards does he "know" that he satisfies the rationality assumption in general or that he always follows his preferences. He may know that his beliefs satisfy certain axioms (such as the system S5), and he may know all about his tastes now or in the future, but he never "knows" anything about a choice while making it.

A similar interpretation problem was raised and discussed in Aumann (1987a) regarding the assumption that a state of the world specifies all players' actual choices. Our solution is similar to his. Gilboa (1991) further elaborates on this point in the same spirit.

Considering the paradox of Section 3.1 again, we first note that the "knowledge" referred to in the rationality assumption should be more carefully defined as the player's knowledge about all but his or her choices. (Other players' "knowledge" about our player is to be interpreted as their beliefs, which may be known to the player.)

Thus, the identicality assumption, even if incorporated in the model, cannot be used in the proof in conjunction with the rationality assumption: a player cannot know, nor use in any further reasoning, the identicality assumption, since it involves the player's own choices and relates them to events about which she or he may have beliefs.

There are several ways to formulate this intuition. One may introduce, for each player, two knowledge designators (which may be characters, operators on propositions, operators on sets, prediates, or whatever entity they are in a formal model of knowledge). One of them will refer to the "outside" world, which, broadly understood, includes not only other players and "nature" but also results of introspection such as tastes and beliefs. The other knowledge designator will refer to an agent's knowledge of her own behavior. Alternatively, one may parametrize the knowledge operator by time and allow the agent to know her choices only after they were actually made. Yet another solution is to keep only one knowledge designator but to assume that it does not apply to propositions involving the player's choices, where these are given by a formal choice function. (As opposed to a player's utility, which may be known by the player—interpreted, say, as taste—and by others—interpreted as observed behavior—the player's actual choice in each state of the world can only be known by others.)

While the precise way one chooses to formalize this distinction may not be of paramount importance, it seems that some formal distinction between these two types of knowledge is needed for consistency and for more intuitive modeling of "free choice."

4. Causal Decision Theory

Causal decision theory distinguishes between "two kinds" of expected utility (See Gibbard and Harper 1978). One would assume independence of beliefs from choices, while the other allows for a decision maker to have beliefs regarding his or her own choices and update beliefs regarding states of the world given a certain choice. Thus the decision maker may, indirectly, choose what to believe.

In the spirit of the above discussion, we find the second "kind" of expected utility problematic. This is so not only because it robs decision theory of one of its most cherished assets, namely, the theoretical dichotomy between states of the world (which cannot be controlled) and choices (regarding which there are no beliefs), but also because a choice about which the chooser has beliefs does not seem to comply with our intuition of "free" choice.

We see no problem with decision maker who has beliefs regarding his or her own tastes, or "action tendencies," as well as states of the world and updates the beliefs regarding the latter given some information about the former. (This approach is discussed in Lewis (1981), but it is there rejected as a substitute for learning-from-one's-own-choices.) Indeed, Savage's (1954) classical approach would incorporate the uncertainty about one's tastes into that about the state of the world to begin with. However, we are generally happier with a model in which one cannot be said to have beliefs about (let alone knowledge of) one's own choice *while making this choice.*

One may legitimately ask: Can you truly claim you have no beliefs about your own future choices? Can you honestly contend you do not believe—or even know—that you will not choose to jump out of the window? And is such a model really more intuitive?

The answer to these questions is probably a resounding (or reluctantly muttered) "No." But the emphasis should be on the timing: when one considers one's choice tomorrow, one may indeed be quite sure that one will not decide to jump out of the window. However, a future decision should actually be viewed as a decision by a different "agent" of the same decision maker. One's beliefs about one's behavior tomorrow probably derive from knowledge of one's past choices as well as past and present introspection. These, however, cannot rule out the possibility of evolving into a different person, as in the changing preference literature. Almost all authors who addressed these problems, of which the classical one (with "constant" preferences) is but a special case, seem to agree that the best way to conceptualize them is by considering different "agents" as separate players. (See Peleg and Yaari (1973), Hammond (1976), and Ferreira et al. (1995), which also includes additional references.)

Thus, when asked about his suicidal choice, Newton is not actually making the choice. (Perhaps he makes a different choice—namely, which answer to give.) He may therefore have beliefs about the future choice without leading to any inconsistency, nor undermining the notion of "free choice." It is only at the time of choice, within an "atom of decision," that we wish to preclude beliefs about it.

In the same vein, one may relate the introspection into tastes and beliefs to the behavioral approach. That is to say, their separation from the actual decision need not necessarily leave them at the mercy of direct intuition or subject them to the risk of being considered "metaphysical nonsense" by the decision maker. The latter may ask herself or himself hypothetical questions about a variety of choice situations. As long as these are not the actual choices being made at present, our approach allows the individual to have very strong intuition regarding such choices. If these turn out to satisfy, say, the Savage axioms, the individual may elicit her or his own tastes and beliefs.

When introspection is considered, one may assume that hypothetical choices are the primitives about which a decision maker has intuition, and from which tastes and beliefs are derived, or vice versa, or even claim that the two are inextricably interrelated. All of these views (and probably many others as well) are consistent with our view of "free choice" as long as no beliefs about a choice are assumed to exist while it is actually made.

5. Determinism and Free Will

It would seem an outrageous cowardice to get that close to the problem of determinism versus free will and avoid even glancing at it. Let us therefore try to look at it from our viewpoint for what it is worth.

The traditional problem arises as a conflict between the undeniable intuition people have of making choices freely and the belief that this choice is known or could in principle be known. The latter may arise from belief in a superbeing, or from monism coupled with the assumption that physical laws completely determine the future given present data, or from many other beliefs.

The common feature seems to be, therefore, that an individual, while making a seemingly "free" choice, also knows that someone else knows or could in principle know what this choice will end up being. Thus formulated, it is indeed very similar (though not identical) to the problem discussed in Section 3.

True to our arguments above, we should therefore contend that when modeling "free will" in a careful but intuitive way, one should make sure not to assume any knowledge, or knowledge of knowledge, of one's choice.

There is, of course, no problem if one is happy with this assumption. Indeed, the problem discussed in Section 3, which dealt only with the modeling of choice, ends here. However, the problem does not seem to have changed if the above has to be reconciled with the inutitive feeling that the choice *is* known. (We here interpret "predetermined" as "known" or "knowable" by some entity.)

While no resolution of this contradiction is to be expected from this essay, let us just carry the reformulation of the problem one step further. It can be argued that "free will" or "free choice" refers to this very well-known feeling one has while making a choice and having the clear impression that the choice is not knowable. If one generally believes that impression is false, one may treat it as an illusion, perhaps similar to the phenomenon of *déja-vu*. (Admittedly, the free will illusion happens more frequently than the *déju-vu* one and, alas, has weightier implications.)

Obviously, many other suggested reconciliations of determinism and free will are consistent with our notion of "free choice." For instance, one may argue that as long as the choice is knowable only in principle, rather than in actuality, it does not contradict free choice. Thus, as long as Newton does not know whether he is going to jump out of the window, his "free" choice is nicely modeled even if he realizes that "in principle" it could be deduced from data that are "in principle" available. (The qualification "in principle," however modeled, may suffice to distinguish the knowledge of his choice from the knowledge that gravity works.) Similarly, if one believes that one's choice can only be known by a superbeing and not by oneself and, in particular, that one will never know what exactly the superbeing knows of one's choice (apart from the very fact it knows it), there may already be a qualitative distinction between knowledge of choice and of other facts so as to satisfactorily model "free choice."

Needless to say (partly because this has already been said too often), this chapter does not attempt to suggest a resolution to the age-old problem of determinism and free will, nor even to make a claim regarding the existence of such a solution. We do hope, however, that a clearer understanding of what is meant by "free choice" may help thinking about this problem, which people continue to address either because they choose to or because they are preordained to do so (or possibly both).

Notes

Acknowledgments—I am grateful to Andy Fano, Eva Gilboa, Shlomo Gilboa, Eric Jones, Ehud Kalai, and Eitan Zemel for the discussions that motivated this work, as well as for comments and references.

1. That is a result of an informal small survey. In fact, most first-year graduate students are already enlightened/indoctrinated enough to reach the same conclusion.

2. As noted by Ehud Kalai, a similar inconsistency may arise also in a one-person decision problem.

3. The distinction between "conceivable" and "possible" states of the world was earlier suggested by Hintikka.

4. By "nontrivial" we would like to exclude statements such as "If he chooses not to jump, $1 = 1$," which may be known simply because "$1 = 1$" is known.

References

Anscombe, F. J. and R. J. Aumann (1963), "A Definition of Subjective Probability," *Annals of Mathematical Statistics*, 34, 199–205.
Aumann, R. J. (1976), "Agreeing to Disagree," *Annals of Statistics*, 4, 1236–39.
Aumann, R. J. (1987a), "Correlated Equilibrium as an Expression of Bayesian Rationality," *Econometrica*, 55, 1–18.
Aumann, R. J. (1987b), "Game Theory," in *The New Palgrave: Game Theory*, J. Eatwell, M. Milgate and P. Newman (eds.), New York: W. W. Norton, pp. 1–53.
Ben-Porath, E. (1997), "Common Belief in Rationality in Extensive Form Games," *Review of Economic Studies*, 64, 23–46.
Bicchieri, E. (1988a), "Strategic Behavior and Counterfactuals," *Synthese*, 76, 135–69.
Bicchieri, C. (1988b), "Common Knowledge and Backward Induction: A Solution to the Paradox," in *Proceedings of the Second Conference on Theoretical Aspects of Reasoning About Knowledge*, M Vardi (ed.), Los Gatos, CA: Morgan-Kaufmann, 318–93.
Bicchieri, C. (1989), "Self-Refuting Theories of Strategic Interaction: A Paradox of Common Knowledge," *Erkenntnis*, 30, 69–85.
Bicchieri, C. (1993), *Rationality and Coordination*, New York: Cambridge University Press.
Ferreira, J.-L., I. Gilboa and M. Maschler (1995), "Credible Equilibria in Games with Changing Utility," *Games and Economic Behavior*, 10, 284–317.
Gibbard, A. and W. L. Harper (1978), "Counterfactuals and Two Kinds of Expected Utility," *Foundations and Applications of Decision Theory*, 1, 125–62.
Gilboa, I. (1990), "A Note on the Consistency of Game Theory," in *Proceedings of the Third Conference on Theoretical Aspects of Reasoning About Knowledge*, R. Parikh (ed.), Los Gatos, CA: Morgan-Kaufmann, 201–8.
Gilboa, I. (1991), "Rationality and Ascriptive Science," mimeo.
Gilboa, I. and D. Schmeidler (1988), "Information Dependent Games: Can Common Sense Be Common Knowledge?" *Economic Letters*, 27, 215–21.
Hammond, P. J. (1976), "Changing Tastes and Coherent Dynamic Choice," *Review of Economic Studies*, 43, 159–73.
Kaneko, M. (1987), "Structural Common Knowledge and Factual Common Knowledge," RUEE Working Paper No. 87-27, Hitotsubashi University.
Kaneko, M. and T. Nagashima (1990), "Game Logic I: Players' Deductions and the Common Knowledge of Deductive Abilities," Virginia Polytechnic Institute Working Paper No. E90-03-1.
Lewis, D. (1969), *Conventions: A Philosophical Study*, Cambridge: Cambridge University Press.
Lewis, D. (1981), "Causal Decision Theory," *Australian Journal of Philosophy*, 51, 5–30.
Peleg, B. and M. E. Yaari (1973), "On the Existence of a Consistent Course of Action when Tastes are Changing," *Review of Economic Studies*, 40, 391–401.
Reny, P. (1988), "Rationality in Extensive Form Games," *Journal of Economic Perspectives*, 6, 103–18.
Savage, L. J. (1954), *The Foundations of Statistics*, New York: Wiley.
von Neumann, I. and O. Mortenstern (1944), *Theory of Games and Economic Behavior*, Princeton: Princeton University Press.

CHAPTER 10

Symmetry Arguments for Cooperation in the Prisoner's Dilemma

Cristina Bicchieri and Mitchell S. Green

1. Introduction

A variety of philosophers, decision theorists, and game theorists have advanced arguments according to which rational agents who play a one-shot Prisoner's Dilemma (PD) should choose to cooperate if they know either that they are in identical circumstances, or are in some sense identical twins (Brams 1975; Lewis 1979; Davis 1985). The reasoning in favor of the cooperative solution raises the question whether the PD with the appropriate "Identicality" assumption is inconsistent, since there is a separate argument employing dominance reasoning that favors noncooperation. We argue here that the question can only be answered relative to a clarification of the Identicality assumption. There turns out to be only one interpretation of the Identicality assumption that justifies cooperation, but this interpretation may be controversial. On another interpretation of this assumption the description of the PD game is indeed inconsistent, while on the remaining interpretations of that assumption the argument for the cooperative solution is unsound. Seeing the inconsistency teaches us a lesson concerning the kinds of postulates that can be added to the description of a game. Seeing the unsoundness will motivate a more careful treatment of the relation of modal concepts to the notion of rational choice, and will help us to illuminate the relevance to game theory of technical tools developed by logicians.

From G. Holmstrom, J. Hintikka and R. Tuomela (eds), *Contemporary Action Theory*, Vol. II, pp. 229–49. Copyright © 1997 by Kluwer Academic Publishers. Reprinted by permission of the authors and publisher.

2. Motivating Example

Consider the classical "Prisoner's Dilemma" game (Figure 10.1). Player 1 chooses a row and player 2 chooses a column. Furthermore, it is assumed that the players' choices are causally independent of one another, in that one player's choice does not influence the other player's choice or beliefs. The payoff matrix above gives, for each pair of choices of the two players, the utility of player 1 and of player 2, respectively, where 4 is the highest utility and 0 the lowest.[1] We assume players' utilities to encompass all the relevant psychological and social characteristics that might influence their choices, such as altruism, envy, the pursuit of some moral or political goal, and so forth. We also assume that the game in Figure 10.1 is played exactly once by the players and that they believe this to be the case.

Player 2

		C	D
	C	(3, 3)	(0, 4)
Player 1	D	(4, 0)	(1, 1)

Figure 10.1

The informal characterization of the game given above can be expressed more rigorously with explicit postulates concerning players' payoffs and actions as well as their rationality and beliefs.[2] One such postulate is that each player's act is causally independent of the other player's act, as expressed below:

> *Independence*: For each player i and each strategy s_i available to i, if i plays strategy s_i, then for each player i' and each strategy $s_{i'}$, available to i', it is causally possible for i' to play $s_{i'}$.[3]

Independence implies that if player 1 chooses C, it is causally possible that player 2 plays C and causally possible that player 2 plays D. The same holds for player 1's choice of D. The situation is symmetric as between the two players.[4]

We also employ a Rationality assumption according to which a player will choose a strictly dominant strategy if one exists, provided that the Independence postulate holds.[5] As formulated, only in the presence of a dominant strategy does the Rationality assumption predict a choice under uncertainty.[6] If a player does not have a dominant strategy, the Rationality assumption does not predict any choice. We could strengthen our Rationality assumption by saying that whenever a player is in a situation of uncertainty, she will choose the action that maximizes her expected utility. This further requirement is unnecessary, however, in treating the PD, since in this game both players have dominant strategies. Finally, we postulate that the full description of the game, as well as the assumptions of Rationality and

Independence, are common belief among the players.[7] These postulates jointly imply that the players' choice will be (D, D). This conclusion has, nevertheless, been a source of puzzlement since (C, C) Pareto dominates (D, D), that is, both players would have been better off had they decided to play C.[8]

On the other hand we now also see how one might formulate an argument in favor of joint cooperation. The proponent of the cooperative solution may add to our description of the PD game a postulate according to which the players are qualitatively identical in some sense. Although the exact meaning of such "Identicality" assumption is far from clear, for present purposes we shall take it as saying that, necessarily, player 1 chooses $C(D)$ iff player 2 chooses C (D), leaving open for the moment the interpretation of 'necessarily'. As we shall see later, a great deal turns on whether we construe this modality in a causal or doxastic sense.

There would appear to be no immediate reason for game theorists to refuse to allow the Identicality assumption to be added as a postulate governing the PD. After all, the game has a unique dominant strategy—indeed, the same one—for both players, and given that Identicality appears to be consistent with Independence, the Rationality assumption will still imply that both players will play D. However, with these same assumptions one may also suggest the following reasoning:

> Suppose that I am player 1. Since player 2 is identical to me, she will end up making the same choice as I do. That is, if I play C, so will she, and the same applies to D. In particular, if I choose C the outcome is (C, C) and my payoff is 3. If I choose D, the outcome is (D, D) and I get 1. Thus C dominates D, and since I am rational I will play C.

Thus, so the argument goes, if identical rational players, who are aware of their identicality, play the PD, they will choose to cooperate.

There seems, then, to be a paradox. If both players believe in Identicality, then each of them believes that "My playing C implies that the other player plays C" is true, and the Rationality assumption appears to entail that each player will choose C. On the other hand, we also argued with the help of the Rationality assumption that each player will choose D. In other words, barring our finding a flaw in one of these two lines of reasoning, we should conclude that our description of the game is after all inconsistent. This is the case even though the Identicality assumption itself does not contradict the implication of the other assumptions (namely, the conclusion that the players will play D).

3. The Identicality Assumption: Doxastic Interpretations

Many game theorists would reject the reasoning favoring the cooperative solution on the ground that such reasoning ignores the causal independence of different players' choices.[9] The game theorists would contend that the choice situation presented in the argument for cooperation is best represented by the

$$
\begin{array}{c|c}
 & \overline{} \\[-4pt]
\text{Player 1} & \begin{array}{c|c} C & 3 \\ D & 1 \end{array}
\end{array}
$$

Figure 10.2

following one-player game (where $i = 1, 2$), to which we will refer as the "Mirror's Choice" (Figure 10.2).

This matrix incorporates the identicality of the two players by not leaving room for the possibility of their doing different things. According to this representation each player is facing a single-agent decision problem in which he has two possible choices, C or D, the outcome of each of which is certain. The game theorist would argue that Figure 10.2 should not be used to represent the original game, even if the players in it end up making identical choices. The reason is that even though the players in the originally described scenario make identical choices, and believe that they will do so, it does not follow that they could not behave differently from one another. Yet the Mirror's Choice representation of their situation presupposes exactly this.

Even adhering to the original representation of the PD, however, it is not clear that the argument in favor of the cooperative solution is sound. For unless it can be proved that the postulates defining the PD together with the Identicality assumption imply that the Mirror's Choice correctly characterizes the PD, each player is in a position to reason as follows: "The other player will in fact choose as I do and she is going through the same reasoning and will reach the same conclusions that I will. In these circumstances, playing C seems to be an acceptable choice, but what would happen were I to choose D instead?" For all we have said so far, even with the Identicality assumption each player might find that the answer to this question leads him to opt for D. We therefore do well to treat the question with some care.

Consideration of subjunctive conditionals such as the foregoing is central to deliberation.[10] In deliberation, one typically considers several scenarios that differ from one another only with respect to the action chosen and evaluates the consequences of the alternative feasible actions. Deliberation of this sort may also involve the provisional settling upon one course of action and exploration of what would happen were one to deviate from that course. It may involve, for example, deliberation about what would happen were one to choose irrationally. Having arrived at the provisional conclusion that her best choice is, say, to play strategy s_1, the player may ask what would happen were she to choose an alterative strategy s_2 instead. If the expected outcome of s_2 is preferable to that of s_1, then a rational player will give up her provisional commitment to perform s_1.

In order to represent alternative possibilities, as well as players' deliberation processes, it will be helpful to provide a model theoretic framework within which we can perspicuously represent what a player believes and how possibilities are entertained. The usual description of a strategic form game G is a triple $\langle N, S_{i \in N}, u_{i \in N} \rangle$, where N is the set of players and, for each player $i \in N$, S_i is the set of pure strategies available to i, and u_i is player i's utility function.[11]

The description of G is, however, only a partial specification of the decision problem faced by the players, since it gives players' utilities and feasible actions but does not specify players' beliefs about one another or about the game, nor what the players are actually going to do. A model of a game G then represents a completion of the partial specification of the decision problem given by the definition of G.[12] A *model M of game G* is a quadruple $\langle W, w^*, C, \langle s_i, R_i \rangle_{i \in N} \rangle$, where

(i) W is a nonempty set (the set of "possible worlds", each of which is a realization of exactly one complete play of the game G);

(ii) $w^* \in W$ (w^* is the "actual world");

(iii) $C \subseteq W^2$ is a binary relation of nomic accessibility such that $w \, C \, w'$ iff w' is consistent with the laws of nature that hold at w;

(iv) (a) for each $i \in N$, s_i is a function from W to S_i;

(b) R_i is a binary relation defined on W that gives, for each world $w \in W$, a subset W' of W each member of which is consistent with what i believes at w.

A few comments on the model M and how it applies to our game are now in order. The set W represents all the things that could happen in a given game. When a game G is represented in the strategic form, for each cell in the matrix there will be at least one member of W.[13] Moreover, clause (iv)(a) gives, for each $w \in W$ and each player i, a pure strategy played by that player in that world. Each model of a game G thus represents a complete play of that game.

R_i is a relation of doxastic possibility, giving the set of possible worlds that are consistent with what i believes at w^*. To refer to this set we write $\{w: w^* R_i w\}$. This is the set of states of affairs that, for all that player i believes at w^*, could be actual. In order to impose certain intuitive conditions on players' beliefs, we must further specify the properties of the accessibility relation R_i. For example, R_i might not be reflexive, because our concern is beliefs, which might be false. To ensure that i has coherent beliefs in each world, R_i must be serial, that is, for any world w there must exist at least one world w' such that $w R_i w'$. Also, to ensure that players know their own minds, we require that R be transitive and Euclidean.[14]

In a model of the sort just defined, it is natural to construe a proposition as a subset of the set of possible worlds.[15] For example, the proposition that player 1 plays D is identified, in a given model M, with the set of possible worlds w' of M for which $s_1(w') = D$. Because the set W is constrained by the definition of G, what a player can believe in a given model is limited by the description of the game she is playing. We say that a proposition p is *doxastically necessary* at world w for agent i in model M if and only if p is true in all worlds w' that are doxastically accessible to i at w in M (i.e., iff p is true in all w' such that $w R_i w'$ in M). We also say that a proposition p is *doxastically possible* at world w for agent i in model M if and only if its negation is not doxastically necessary for i at w in M.[16]

We have interpreted the accessibility relation R_i as a relation of doxastic possibility, but we have also defined a model for a game as containing a relation of causal possibility. C is a binary relation defined in W that gives, for each world $w \in W$, a set of possible worlds that are consistent with the laws of nature that hold at w. Thus we say that a world w' is causally possible relative to w just in case everything that occurs at w' is consistent with the laws of nature that hold at w. Since a proper description of a game must list all the possible outcomes that may result from all the possible combinations of players' strategies and we are modeling games in which players have common beliefs about the structure of the game (i.e., all the available strategies and payoffs), we must assume that every outcome in a game is causally possible, even if some of them are ruled out by rationality considerations. Thus, for the games we are considering, it is the case that $\cup_{i \in N} R_i \subseteq C$, that is, for all w, w' in W, if $w R_i w'$, then $w C w'$.[17]

The primary aim of incorporating a relation of causal possibility into our models is to ensure the satisfaction of the Independence assumption. We may do so by stipulating of the C relation that:

> For each player i, and each $w \in W$, if i plays strategy s at w, then for each $i' \in N$ (where $i \neq i'$) and each $s' \in S_{i'}$, there is a world $w' \in W$ such that wCw' and $s_{i'}(w') = s'$.

Observe that an action may be doxastically impossible for a player at a world w and yet be causally possible relative to w.[18] For example, given that John has made up his mind what he will do next week, his gambling away all his money in Las Vegas will be doxastically impossible for him, but doing so would not violate any law of nature. If he wanted to, he could go to Las Vegas and fritter away his savings.

With causal independence thus guaranteed, we may stipulate the satisfaction of the Rationality assumption by requiring that if M is a model of game G then the actual world, w^*, of M is one in which no player plays a dominated strategy. In conjunction with the requirement of causal independence, this stipulation has the consequence that although in each model of a game no player acts irrationally in the actual world of that model in the sense of playing a dominated strategy, in each such model it is causally possible that some player plays such a strategy.

Following Stalnaker (this volume), common belief is here defined as the transitive closure R^* of the set of all the R_i relations. That is, $w R^* w'$ if there exists a finite sequence of worlds $w_1, \ldots, w_n$ such that $w = w_1$ and $w' = w_n$, and for each k from 1 to $n - 1$, there is some j such that $w_k R_j w_{k+1}$. For any proposition p, p is common belief at w just in case $\{w' : w R^* w'\} \subseteq p$. We require that in any model of the PD game the structure of the game and the Rationality and Independence assumptions are common belief among the players. As we are about to explain, one can give several interpretations of the identicality assumption, but for each such interpretation we shall take it that the assumption is common belief among the players.

An advantage of providing a class of models for a game G is that it is only with reference to a model that we can meaningfully represent a player's deliberation process. Each model for G represents a particular play of G and completes the partial specification of the decision problem defined by G in a way that is compatible with the conditions imposed by G's definition. Each model of a game will contain many possible worlds, since we need to represent not only what happens in a particular play of the modeled game, but also what would happen in alternative situations compatible with the description of the game. To ensure that a model M represents all the options that the definition of G says are open to the players, we have required that for every possible world $w \in W$, every player i and every strategy choice s open to i, there is a causally accessible world w' in which i has the same beliefs about the game as she has in w and in which she plays s' (where $s \neq s'$).[19] For example, when a player is considering what would happen were she to choose, say, a dominated strategy, she is not thinking of an alternative game in which she has different beliefs from those she has in the actual world of the model. What the player is contemplating is a situation in which she makes what is by her lights an irrational choice, and we want to represent a situation such as this with a possible world in which such an action is taken. The possible world in which a rational player chooses a dominated action may not be doxastically accessible to the player in the actual world, because that player may believe that she will not choose a dominated strategy. Such a world is nevertheless causally possible. Finally, we want to stress that because a player's beliefs can differ in different models of a given game, strictly speaking it is only relative to a model that we can ask what it is rational for a player to do. In what follows we shall always raise questions of rationality with respect to a given model of a game.[20]

Consider now what it is rational for players to do in models of the PD game in which both players believe that they will necessarily do the same thing. This question admits different answers depending upon what kind of necessity is being invoked. Suppose first that the Identicality assumption is understood to mean that in the actual world of the model players believe that they will act alike (and it is common belief that they will). Thus for each player, "The players make the same choice" is true in all worlds that are doxastically accessible to that player from the actual world.[21] On such an interpretation, player 1 will believe that if she plays C, player 2 will play C, and if she plays D, player 2 will play D. Analogously for player 2. A model of the game incorporating the Identicality assumption so construed is one in which in the actual world of that model it is doxastically necessary for both players that they do the same thing. In such a model it can still be the case that off-diagonal outcomes (i.e., those outcomes that result from a play of (C, D) or (D, C)) are causally possible, and that players are aware of this.

Now players may not believe that an off-diagonal outcome is causally possible. If they do not, then as we shall explain in Section 4 it may be rational for them to cooperate. Our question is instead whether just by virtue of being in a situation in which it is doxastically impossible for both players that an off-diagonal outcome is played, the players can reason to a cooperative solution.

One might argue that since player 1, for instance, believes that either (C, C) or (D, D) will be played, then given that the payoff of the former outcome is greater than that of the latter, the cooperative outcome is the rational choice. Player 2 may reason in the same way and conclude in favor of playing C. Moreover, the players' conclusions will be common belief.[22]

This reasoning is fallacious. It depends upon the false premise that if two actions, x and y, are the only doxastically possible options, then if the payoff of x is greater than that of y, it is rational to choose x. To see that this premise is false, suppose that an agent i has, and believes she has, three actions open to her: x, y, and z, where her preference ordering is $x > y > z$, and ' $>$ ' represents a strict preference relation. Imagine now that what i believes to be a seer tells her that she will not choose x—not that it is causally impossible for her to do so, but just that she will not do so. She continues to believe that her choice of x is causally possible, but she now believes that she will not choose x. As a result there are only two doxastically possible actions for i, namely the choices of y and of z. It does not, however, follow that it is rational for her to choose y. The rational thing to do is still to take x. This would not be the case if i came to believe that the choice of x was not causally possible, since it is reasonable to ignore what one takes to be causally impossible actions in one's deliberation. So long, however, as she does believe that x is causally possible, her believing that she will not take x does not make it rational for her to do something else.[23]

Not only is the above reasoning in favor of the cooperative solution fallacious, but the conclusion—that it is rational in the envisioned model for both players to play C—appears to be false. The reason is that a provisional commitment to perform a certain action is rational only if that commitment is stable under consideration of alternative possibilities, and player 1's provisional commitment to play C, were she to make one, is not stable in this way. To see this, suppose that player 1 has formed the plan to play C, and takes it that player 2 will play C as well. If player 1 now asks herself what would happen were she to play D instead, the answer would appear to be that player 2 would nevertheless play C. For on a familiar semantical construal of subjunctive conditionals, 'Were A the case, then B would be the case', is true at world w iff in the world most similar to w in which A is true, B is true as well. In the world now in question, both players play C. Because by assumption there is no causal interaction between the two players, the most similar world to w in which player 1 plays D (and has the same beliefs and utility function he has in w) is one in which player 2 continues to play C.[24] Since, however, (D, C) nets player 1 more than does (C, C), it follows that player 1's provisional commitment to perform C is not rational. Because the cooperative choice is not robust under consideration of alternative possibilities, both players will reach the conclusion that D is the only rational choice. We conclude that models of the game incorporating a doxastic version of the Identicality assumption are not, as such, ones in which it is rational for players to cooperate.

4. The Identicality Assumption: Nomic Interpretations

Having considered a model of the PD game that incorporates a version of the Identicality assumption, and finding it unable to support an argument for the cooperative solution, let us contemplate a second model, in which players believe that it is causally necessary that both do the same thing. Specifically, this is a model in which both players believe there is no possible world consistent with the laws of nature in which they do different things.[25] The reasoning in favor of the cooperative solution might go as follows. Since player 1, for instance, believes that the set {(C, C), (D, D)} contains all and only causally possible outcomes, then given that the payoff of the former outcome is greater than that of the latter, the cooperative outcome is the rational choice. Player 2 will reason in the same way and conclude in favor of playing C. Moreover, the players' conclusions will be common belief.

The premises of this reasoning conflict with the fact that players have common belief in the Independence assumption,[26] which requires that off-diagonal outcomes are causally possible. On the present interpretation of the Identicality assumption, however, players must also believe that off-diagonal outcomes are *not* causally possible. This pair of beliefs is ruled out by our requirement that the doxastic accessibility relation is serial, that is, that players' beliefs are internally consistent. There would appear, then, to be no model of the PD in which we construe the Identicality assumption in terms of causal necessity.

One can, however, distinguish two notions of independence, each one corresponding to a different conception of causal dependence. For just as the notion of causation itself admits of importantly distinct elucidations,[27] so too may the notion of causal independence. Moreover, on one account of causal independence, we find that the Independence assumption is consistent with the nomic interpretation of the Identicality assumption. To see this consider the following construals of independence:

I_1: No matter what one player does, it is causally possible that the other plays either C or D.

I_2: No matter what one player does, that choice has no causal influence on the choice of the other player.

I_2 requires that there be no causal interaction between the players' actions, so that if these two actions are spacelike separated then I_2 will be satisfied. On the other hand, as we shall see presently there may be indeterministic point-events that, in spite of being spacelike separated, are such that it is not causally possible that they both occur. I_1 therefore implies I_2, but not vice versa.

The nomic version of the Identicality assumption is inconsistent with I_1, since according to I_1 it must be causally possible that (C, D) occur and causally possible that (D, C) occur. Independence interpreted according to I_2, however, is consistent with this version of Identicality. For on this nomic construal of Identicality there need be no causal influence between the acts of the two players since we may take the two choice-events to be spacelike separated. Yet in such a case it might nevertheless be causally impossible that the two players do different things, and this would be so in spite of the fact that the action of neither one has any effect on the action of the other.

Our question is thus whether there could be an example in which although it is causally necessary that the acts of the two agents are the same, their actions are nonetheless causally independent in the sense of I_2. The answer depends upon whether there could be an agentive analogue to the Einstein–Podolsky–Rosen phenomenon in quantum mechanics.[28] The phenomenon involves a pair of particles, #1 and #2, each of which could either go spin-up or spin-down. For each particle neither outcome is causally determined by states of affairs in its light cone. However, in the EPR situation it is causally necessary that if #1(#2) is spin-up, then #2(#1) is spin-down, and if #1(#2) is spin-down, then #2(#1) is spin-up, even though there is no causal interaction between the two particles in that no light ray could connect either point-event to the other.

An agentive analogue of EPR in the context of the PD would be a model of this game played by players 1 and 2, and satisfying the following conditions:

(i) Given that player 1 chooses C, it is causally necessary that player 2 chooses C, and given that player 1 chooses D, it is causally necessary that player 2 chooses D.

(ii) Given that player 2 chooses C, it is causally necessary that player 1 chooses C, and given that player 2 chooses D, it is causally necessary that player 1 chooses D.

(iii) The choice events are causally independent, in that the choice events are spacelike separated.

(iv) Neither agent's choice is causally determined by antecedent states of affairs.

(v) The above four conditions are common belief among the players.

We shall not try to construct such a model here, since doing so would require building enough spatiotemporal structure into each possible world in the model to capture some basic features of relativity and quantum indeterminacy. Yet we see no reason why such a construction could not be carried out.[29] Further, we readily grant that any case satisfying the above five conditions would be mysterious. Were we ever confronted with what seemed to be a case of this kind we would be justified in searching for a "hidden variable" that explains the correlation between the actions of the two players. Our contention, however, is only that a case of this kind, an "EPRPD," is for all we know a possibility.[30] Indeed, it appears to be the only kind of case in which Identicality (causally interpreted) and Independence are jointly satisfied.

Now although such an EPRPD does violate Independence construed as I_1, it does not violate that assumption construed as I_2. Yet we know of no good reason for preferring the first construal of the Independence postulate over the second. For this reason we are in no position to assert that the PD version of the EPR involves a violation of causal independence. We shall therefore treat the EPRPD as a case that does not violate the Independence assumption. Let us imagine, then, a model that satisfies the above five conditions. Such a model may be graphically represented by means of what in Section 3 we called the

Mirror's Choice. Since the only two causally possible outcomes in this model are (C, C) and (D, D), and the players are aware of this fact, Rationality implies that each agent will choose C.

There appears to be no separate argument for the conclusion that the rational choice for each player in the model in question is to play D. Such an argument requires the premise that each of the off-diagonal outcomes is causally possible, and this premise is false in the present model. For while one of the off-diagonal outcomes is preferable to each of the players, neither is causally possible in at least one sense of 'causally possible', and it is reasonable to ignore what one believes to be a causally impossible outcome in one's deliberation. Observe further that a provisional commitment to play C is robust under consideration of alternatives. The reason is that because the actions of the two players are causally correlated, each player is able to see that were he to play D instead, the other player would play D as well. It would thus seem that if there can be a model of the PD satisfying the five postulates that we have used to characterize the EPRPD, then in such a model it is rational for agents to cooperate.[31]

5. Does the Symmetry of the Game Imply Identicality?

Proponents of the argument for cooperation will perhaps now urge that we have misconstrued their aim. Their reason might be that one need not treat Identicality as a postulate that is satisfied only in certain models of the PD. Rather, Identicality, appropriately construed, is just the product of symmetry and rationality and so holds for all models of the PD. Thus Rapoport writes

> . . . because of the symmetry of the game, rationality must prescribe *the same choice to both* [players]. (Rapoport 1966, 142)

In the most detailed formulation of this approach to date, Davis (1977) largely follows Rapoport, replacing rationality with common knowledge thereof. Speaking of one player's belief that the other player's choice will be a "mirror reflection" of his own, Davis says,

> To the contrary, it seems an obvious entailment of the assumption that each knows that each knows that each is rational, together with the symmetry of the situation. (Davis 1977, 322)

Now rationality, even when it is common knowledge, does not alone imply that two players endowed with it will make the same choice, even if they are playing a symmetrical game.[32] A game may be symmetrical and each player may have two equivalent strategies that dominate all others, with the result that they could end up choosing different rational strategies. Symmetry and rationality (or common knowledge of rationality) alone do not entail that players will make the same choice. In the PD, however, symmetry and rationality entail the same choice for both players because there is a unique rational choice for both.

How, then, might one reason from the premise that both players will do the same thing to the conclusion that the rational action for each player is to play C? Further, we must consider whether this reasoning reveals a fallacy in the standard argument for the (D, D) solution, or whether it shows that there are models of the PD in which it is *both* rational to play D and to play C.

In the passage from which the above quotation is drawn, Rapoport reasons in favor of the cooperative solution:

> . . . because of the symmetry of the game, rationality must prescribe *the same choice* to both. But if both choose the same, then (C, C) and (D, D) are the only possible outcomes. Of these (C, C) is clearly the better. Therefore I should choose C.[33]

Rapoport might mean by 'possible' here either causally possible or doxastically possible. Suppose that he intends causal possibility. Then if Rapoport is correct in concluding that (C, C) and (D, D) are the only causally possible outcomes, the PD reduces to the Mirror's Choice discussed above, in which C is indeed the rational choice. It does not seem, however, that symmetry and rationality could conspire to imply that (C, C) and (D, D) are the only causally possible outcomes of the game. For as we have remarked, a given player could do something irrational even if we theorists are confident that she should not. On the other hand, Rapoport might intend to pick out doxastic possibility in his use of 'possible'. As we have seen, however, there is no good inference from the premise that it is doxastically necessary for both players that both play C, to the conclusion that the rational choice for each of them is to play C. There are, then, two interpretations of Rapoport's claim that (C, C) and (D, D) are the only possible alternatives. On the first interpretation (in terms of causal necessity) the claim is unjustifed, while on the second interpretation (in terms of doxastic necessity) the claim does not imply that the rational choice for both agents is to cooperate.

Assuming that we have exhausted the relevant alternatives for interpretation of Rapoport's notion of possibility, we must conclude that this author's argument for cooperation is defective. We turn therefore to a consideration of Davis's more detailed argument for cooperation.[34] In preparing to argue that the rational choice is for players to cooperate, Davis contends first that it will be the case that the players do the same thing. Both players are rational, and both rationality and the structure of the game are common knowledge. Further, the game is symmetrical, so that players have the same number of strategies, and the payoff to player 1 of (C, D) = payoff to player 2 of (D, C). As we have seen, a game may be symmetrical with each player having two equivalent strategies that dominate all the others; in such a case the players could end up choosing different strategies with no violation of their rationality. However, in the PD game there is only one dominant strategy for each player, and it is the same for both. Hence the symmetry of the PD game, together with the rationality of both players, implies that both players will do the same thing, that is, that the outcome will be an element of the set $\{(C, C), (D, D)\}$. Let us agree as well that both players know that the outcome will be an element of the set $\{(C, C), (D, D)\}$. Davis now argues that the rational solution to the game is (C, C). Abbreviated, his argument runs as follows:

1. An alternative x is rationally prescribed for an agent i if i knows that there are just two possible outcomes m and n, such that if i takes x then the outcome is m, if i does not take x then the outcome is n, and m is better (in i's judgment) than n.
2. Each player knows that the set $\{(C, C), (D, D)\}$ includes the only possible outcomes, and that if he takes C, then the outcome is (C, C), and that if he does not choose C, then the outcome is (D, D).
3. Each player knows that he judges (C, C) to be better than (D, D).

Davis infers from (1), (2), (3) that

4. C is rationally prescribed for each player.

We follow Davis in treating the conditionals in (1) and (2) as material rather than as subjunctive conditionals,[35] since if read as subjunctive, one of the conditionals contained in premise (2) would be false in all but EPR-style models of the PD. Furthermore, unlike what we found in Rapoport's discussion, there is no ambiguity in Davis's use of "possible" in steps (1) and (2) of his argument; he makes it clear that the notion in question is one of epistemic possibility:

The desired sense is *epistemic*, and *relative*: the outcomes (C, C) and (D, D) are said to be alone possible relative to each agent's *relevant information*.[36]

Davis's argument explicated in terms of material conditionals and epistemic possibility is thus

1*. An alternative x is rationally prescribed for an agent i if i knows that there are just two epistemically possible outcomes m and n, such that if i takes x then the outcome is m, if i does not take x then the outcome is n, and m is better (in i's judgment) than n.
2*. Each player knows that the set $\{(C, C), (D, D)\}$ includes the only epistemically possible outcomes, and that if he takes C, then the outcome is (C, C) and that if he does not choose C, then the outcome is (D, D).
3*. Each player knows that he judges (C, C) to be better than (D, D).
4*. C is rationally prescribed for each player.

The difficulty is that, even if the inference to (4*) is valid, premise (1*) interpreted in terms of material conditionals is implausible. Observe that the expression "just two" can here mean only " at most two" rather than "exactly two"; but thus disambiguated premise (1*) leads to an absurd consequence. For suppose an agent can choose either $10 or $100, and that she knows that rationality prescribes choosing the $100, and that she will do what rationality prescribes. Suppose the agent also knows that no one will give her $1,000, whatever she chooses. So it follows that she knows that either she chooses the $100 and no one will give her $1,000, or she chooses the $10 and someone

gives her $1,000. She knows this since this disjunction is an obvious conse-
quence of what she knows. So all the agents' epistemic possibilities are included
in the set {choose $100 and get $100, choose $10 and get $1,000}. The agent
prefers the latter, so rationality prescribes that she chooses $10.[37]

Premise (1*) would become plausible only if the conditionals appearing in it
were interpreted as subjunctive conditionals. But if (1*) and (2*) were interpreted in terms of subjunctive conditionals, premise (2*) would be false. We
must therefore conclude that the argument is unsound, no matter how it is
interpreted.

Notes

Acknowledgment—We are grateful to R. Stalnaker for comments on an earlier draft of
this paper, as well as to N. Belnap, I. Gilboa, W. Harper, D. Hubin, P. Humphreys, A.
Margalit and B. Skyrms for helpful discussions of many of the issues treated here.

1. The utilities are taken to be von Neumann–Morgenstern (1944) utilities, which
also reflect each player's decision under a situation of risk, but this additional assumption is not needed here.

2. Examples of formal models are Kaneko (1987), Bicchieri (1988a, 1988b, 1993),
and Kaneko and Nagashima (1990).

3. Note that in extensive form games of perfect information, our Independence
assumption would be violated. Consider a game in which player 1 moves first, and
player 2 can observe player 1's move. All choices available to player 2 at her decision
node are causally possible once player 1 has made his choice, and hence player 2's choice
at her decision node is not causally necessitated by player 1's choice, even if player 1's
choice may give player 2 a reason to choose a particular action at her decision node.
However, player 1's choice has restricted player 2's choice-set by cutting off some
initially possible paths along the decision tree. Thus, although player 2's choices are
causally independent of player 1's choices at every (local) decision node at which player
2 is called upon to play, player 2's initial choice-set as defined by the game (i.e., player
2's initial strategy-set) is not causally independent of player 1's choices. If we construe
causal independence as applying to choice-sets, then Independence as we define it is not
satisfied in extensive form games of perfect information. It is easy to verify that it is
always satisfied in strategic form games.

4. We shall presently consider the Independence postulate with greater care, for one
can distinguish between Independence as we have formulated it and a version of that
principle according to which two acts are independent of one another just in case neither
event influences the other. Which of these two construals of independence we adopt will
affect our assessment of certain symmetry arguments.

5. We are here referring to games in strategic form, where Independence as we define
it applies. It might be objected that our formulation of Independence is too weak to
guarantee the rationality of a dominant strategy, since a player's choice may alter the
probability of another player's choices. To answer this objection, we need to distinguish
between a player believing that her choice is evidence that the other player is making a
similar choice, and her belief that her choice is *causing* the other player to make a similar
choice. Causal decision theory allows us to make this distinction, whereas evidential

decision theory does not. As will be clear from the following discussion, we side with causal decision theory (Gibbard and Harper 1978).

Savage's classical formulation of decision theory does not allow beliefs that make an agent regard his choices as evidence about which of the states, on which the outcome depends, obtain. For Savage, acts are not even in the algebra of propositions for which his model provides subjective probabilities (1954, 8–17). Jeffrey (1965, 2d edition 1983) introduced a decision theory in which acts are in the algebra of propositions that the beliefs are defined for. His theory allows for the expression of the belief that other agents probably made the same choice as you did, and it makes such beliefs relevant to deliberation.

In a PD, the so-called evidential expectations $E(C)$ and $E(D)$ of C and D are thus:

$$E(C) = p(C|C)u(C, C) + p(D|C)u(C, D)$$
$$E(D) = p(C|D)u(D, C) + p(D|D)u(D, D)$$

If one is convinced that what one does counts as evidence that the other player will do the same thing, then one's personal evidential expectation for C could be higher than one's evidential expectation for D. The dominance built into the Savage expectation, where for each action (C or D) of your opponent the same probability multiplier is used in the expectation for C as in the expectation for D (i.e., $p(C|C) = p(C|D) = p(C)$; and $p(D|C) = p(D|D) = p(D)$), can be broken up in the evidential expectation if $p(C|C)$ favors low defection (thus, it is greater than $p(D|C)$) and $p(D|D)$ favors high defection (thus, it is greater than $p(C|D)$). In the latter case, one could assign conditional probabilities that make the evidential expectation for C higher than the evidential expectation for D.

According to evidential expectation, sure thing reasoning can lead to fallacies unless the probabilities of the states are the same no matter which act is performed. There are two ways in which a player's probability of choosing a given strategy might be altered by another player's choice. One is the case in which players move sequentially, and player 2 can observe what player 1 did. Another is a situation in which a player believes her choice to be evidence of what the other player's choice is going to be. We want to argue that in both cases sure thing reasoning applies, even if in the first case Independence (as we define it) is violated.

Here is an example (suggested to us by Harper) of what is considered a fallacious application of Savage's sure thing principle: player 1 is deciding which of two offers to make to player 2, who will then have the options to either accept or reject the offer. The extensive form may be represented as in Figure 10.3.

Player 1 can offer a good (G) or a bad (B) contract, and player 2 can accept (a) or reject (r) the offer. If the states on which the outcomes of the acts depend are whether or not player 2 accepts the offer, the decision matrix for player 1 would be:

	a	r
G	2	0
B	3	0

If this were a correct formulation of the states, then Savage's sure thing principle would recommend offering the bad contract, B. For according to the sure thing principle (Savage 1954, 21–26), states on which the acts have the same outcome can be ignored

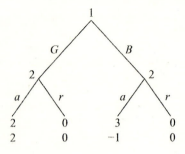

Figure 10.3

so that preference between them goes by conditional preference given the states in which they differ. However, this application of sure thing reasoning would be fallalcious. It ignores the fact that an offer of *G* would be accepted, whereas an offer of *B* would be rejected (as can be seen in the extensive form with perfect information). Evidential decision theory would represent this by having $p(a|G)$ close to 1 and $p(a|B)$ close to 0. According to our formulation of Independence, player 2's choices are not causally independent of player 1's choices, as player 1's move does restrict player 2's choice-set. Note, however, that player 2 has four, not just two, strategies available, thus *a* and *r* are not the correct representations of the states on which the outcomes of player 1's decision depends. If we give the correct representation of player 2's strategies, then Savage's theory also avoids the fallacy. The correct strategic form for the above extensive form representation is: .

	a	*r*	*a* if *G*/*r* if *B*	*r* if *G*/*a* if *B*
G	2, 2	0, 0	2, 2	0, 0
B	3, −1	0, 0	0, 0	3, −1

These are the correct Savage states, based on the structure built into the tree (Harper (1988) calls it the tree's "causal structure"). If we correctly specify the strategic form corresponding to the above extensive form, there is no sure thing fallacy. Player 1's fallacious sure thing argument for *B* has been rejected by adding the new states corresponding to the strategies for conditional choices available to player 2. In the new matrix, sure thing reasoning applies to make "*a* if *G*/*r* if *B*" the unique rational choice for player 2.

Let us now consider the second case, in which player 1's choice is taken to be evidence of another player's choice, and where Independence (as we define it) holds. In the PD, choices are causally independent, in the sense that each player chooses in isolation, no previous communication is possible, and each knows that his choice is not going to influence the way the other chooses. Causal independence, however, does not prevent a player from regarding his choice as evidence that the other will probably choose similarly. Now, evidential decision theory would recommend cooperation to any player who regarded his choice to cooperate as better evidence that the other will cooperate than the choice to defect would be. According to causal decision theory, the argument from such an assignment of probabilities to cooperation is a fallacy if the states are causally independent of the acts. One can have evidential relevance and causal independence together. Choosing *C* might count as evidence that the other player chooses C, but in no way influences his choice. Causal decision theory (CDT) argues that an agent's epistemic conditional probabilities are not always sufficient to represent the relevant beliefs about what his choices can or cannot influence. Following Stalnaker's idea of using subjunctive conditionals to represent deliberation, CDT considers the following conditionals in the PD game:

"If I were to do C, you would do C", . . . and so on.

Agents in CDT assess unconditional probabilities of conditionals, that is, they assess the probability of conditionals such as "If I were to do C, you would do C". Player 1's belief that whether the other player does C or D is not influenced by player 1's choice makes the probabilities of the conditionals equal the probabilities of their consequents, so that the causal expectation reduces to the Savage's expection:

$$U(C) = p \text{ (If I were to do } C, \text{ you would do } C) \, u(C, C) + p \text{ (If I were to do } C, \text{ you would do } D) \, u(C, D)$$

which is turn reduces to:

$$U(C) = p \text{ (you would play } C) \, u(C, C) + p \text{ (you would play } D) \, u(C, D)$$

This supports the sure thing argument for D. According to CDT, the argument in favor of playing C because $p(C|C)$ is greater than $p(D|C)$ is akin to deciding to play C to bring about evidence that the desired outcome (C, C) obtains even though one knows that this can in no way help to bring it about. To reiterate the above point: if you believe that the other player's action is causally independent of your choice, then your evaluation of the probabilities of the conditionals will go by your evaluation of the probabilities of their consequents. Thus: p (If I were to do C, you would do C) $= p$ (you would do C) $= p$ (If I were to do D, you would do C).

6. A strategy s for player i is strictly dominant iff, for all combinations of other players' strategies, the payoff of s is strictly better than the payoff of any other strategy s' available to i.

7. Common belief may be defined in a way that is analogous to that for common knowledge, which has been characterized by Lewis (1969) and Aumann (1976).

8. Outcome x Pareto dominates outcome y just in case the payoff for each player in x is strictly better than the payoff for each player in y.

9. See, for example, Binmore (1994, 204–205).

10. See Hubin and Ross (1985) for an elaboration of the point.

11. In a strategic form game a pure strategy for player i is an action tht i may choose. In an extensive form game a pure strategy for player i is a function that assigns an action to each information set of player i. For a fuller account see Fudenberg and Tirole (1992, 4 and 83).

12. In what follows we will employ a slightly modified definition of a model for a game provided by Stalnaker (this volume).

13. Note that a two-person strategic form game is always represented by a matrix.

14. R is a Euclidean relation iff for any x, y, z, if $x R y$ and $x R z$ then $y R z$. Transitivity and euclidity each correspond to reflection principles, namely that if a player believes that p, then she believes that she believes that p (transitivity), and if a player does not believe that p, then she believes that she does not believe that p (euclidity). Stipulating that R be transitive and Euclidean implies that a player's beliefs in any world w are the same as they are in any other world w' accessible to w.

15. There are well known difficulties with such a "coarse grained" construal of propositions, but the idealization is adequate for our purposes, and one wishing to do so may replace propositions as we conceive them with more fine grained entities.

16. We use the expression 'doxastic' as opposed to 'epistemic' because we are considering beliefs and not knowledge.

17. Note that we are referring here to so-called games of complete information. In such games, there is no uncertainty as to the other players' strategies or payoffs. If a player were uncertain, say, about the strategies available to the other players, they might not be playing the same game and in such a case it would be appropriate to assume that a player can falsely believe some outcome to be causally possible.

18. On the present treatment of C, the converse is not true. If a proposition is causally impossible relative to a world w then it will be doxastically impossible for all players in that world as well.

19. For more on this point see Stalnaker (this volume). A player's belief is *about the structure of the game* just in case it is a belief she holds in every model of that game.

20. This way of speaking may be unfamiliar, for there are some games for which the question of what it is rational to do is well posed independent of any model for that game. For instance, in a game that has a unique Pareto optimal Nash equilibrium in dominant strategies, it is natural to say of a player to whom that equilibrium strategy is available that it is rational *simpliciter* for her to follow that strategy. Thus in the following game:

		Player 2	
		left	*right*
	top	2, 2	3, 3
Player 1			
	bottom	1, 1	0, 2

{*Top, Right*} is the unique Nash equilibrium in which the two players play dominant strategies, and it is also Pareto optimal. It is obviously rational for each player in the above game to follow her dominant strategy in *all* models of this game.

21. Robert Stalnaker has suggested to us that the doxastic version of the Identicality assumption might also be interpreted as the assumption that players "necessarily" believe that they choose alike. That is, in all possible worlds players believe that they choose alike. This assumption would be inconsistent with the Independence assumption, since the latter implies that there is a possible world w' in which one player chooses differently from the other player, and is aware of it. Consequently, this strengthened version of the doxastic form of the Identicality assumption is not one that we employ.

22. The reasoning here resembles an argument considered, but not endorsed, in Nozick (1974, 131).

23. Our contention—that even if a player believes that he and his opponent will cooperate, it does not follow that rationality precludes the consideration of an off-diagonal outcome—runs afoul of arguments presented by Schick (1979) and Levi (1992) aiming to show that once one has made up one's mind as to how to act, one no longer has any choice to do otherwise. Although consideration of these arguments would take us too far afield, we would suggest that these arguments depend upon conflation of causal and epistemic modalities.

24. The worlds in which player 1 plays D that are most similar to the world in which both players play C will keep the laws of nature constant. Because the Identicality assumption is not here being construed to be a law of nature, it need not be held

constant in worlds similar to the actual one. Instead those features of player 2's psychology that result (though perhaps not deterministically) in her playing C in the world in which both players play C should be held fixed in considering the world in which player 1 plays D.

25. That is, this is a model in which in the actual world w^*, for each player i, and each world w' such that $w * R_i w'$, there is no w'' where players do different things and $w' C w''$. Each player might, for instance, believe that her action has a causal propensity to "trigger" the same kind of choice in the opponent. Whether such a belief is justified is a matter that goes beyond the present discussion.

26. Analogous reasoning for an inconsistency in "perfect predictor" versions of the Newcomb problem may be found in Hubin and Ross (1985).

27. See Skyrms (1984) for a list of seven of them.

28. See Skyrms (1984) for a philosophical treatment of the phenomenon. In private conversations both W. Harper and A. Margalit reported having considered giving an agentive analogue to the EPR phenomenon in treating the so-called "paradox of the twins" in the Prisoner's Dilemma context.

29. The tools for such a construction have, in fact, been provided in Belnap (1992).

30. Sobel (1988) asks us to consider a version of the Newcomb problem according to which the predictor is *in principle* incapable of error. He argues that any agent who is aware of the infallibility of the predictor could not have a choice between taking one box and taking both. For Sobel holds that it is a necessary condition of the agent's having a decision problem that he be sure, of at least two actions, that he can do either of them; and he argues that this condition does not hold in the infallible predictor version of the Newcomb problem. Even though the case that Sobel considers involves conceptual necessity whereas the EPRPD involves only causal necessity, one might wonder whether Sobel's reasoning, or an appropriate variation thereon, could undercut the intelligibility of the EPRPD. It might seem on the face of it that each player in the EPRPD only *appears* to be making a choice when in fact her hand is in some sense tied by the act of the other player. There is, however, a crucial difference between the EPRPD nd the infallible predictor version of the Newcomb problem. In the latter there is a moment *prior to the moment of choice* (or putative choice), such that as of that moment there is only one action that the agent can perform. Further, the agent in the Newcomb problem is (or at least can come to be) aware of this fact. By contrast, in the EPRPD there is no such pre-choice moment. There is no moment prior to the moment of choice (or putative choice) as of which it is even causally necessary that, say, player 1 do either C or D. For we have stipulated that the two point-events of choosing are spacelike separated. Because of this, each agent in the EPRPD can be sure that as of every moment leading up to that of his making his choice, he can either perform C or perform D. This, in turn, seems to be enough to show that each agent in this scenario can be sure that there will be two actions open to him when it comes time to choose between C and D.

31. Note that if we were to cast the EPRPD in terms of causal decision theory, we would have to conclude that each player would maximize her causal expected utility by cooperating if her probabilities for conditions of the form "If I were to play C, the other player would play C as well" are high enough for each player's choice of C to be a ratifiable alternative in the sense of Harper (1988).

32. In a symmetric game, the players have the same number of pure strategies, and the payoff to player i of (a_i, b_j) = payoff to j of (a_j, b_i). In other words, a symmetric game is one that looks the same no matter which player one is. In the PD, if both players do the same thing, they get the same payoff. If they choose differently from each other,

the *D*-chooser gets 4 and the *C*-chooser gets 0. So the payoff is determined by what a player does, not by who she is.

33. Other authors who have endorsed reasoning along similar lines are Gauthier (1974), Watkins (1972), and Hardin (1982).

34. Pettit (1986) has shown the fallacy in his reconstruction of Davis's argument while leaving open the question whether every reconstruction of the argument is fallacious. We here consider another such version of the argument, perhaps closer to Davis's intent.

35. Davis (1977, 325).

36. Davis (1977, 325).

37. We are grateful to R. Stalnaker for suggesting this example to us in correspondence.

References

Aumann, R.J. (1976), "Agreeing to Disagree," *Annals of Statistics* **4**, 1236–39.

Belnap, N. (1992), "Branching Space-time," *Synthese* **92**, 385–434.

Belnap, N. and M. Green (1993), "Indeterminism and the Thin Red Line," in J. Tomberlin (ed.), *Philosophical Perspectives VII: Logic and the Philosophy of Language*. Atascadero, CA, Ridgeview, pp. 365–88.

Bicchieri, C. (1988a), "Strategic Behavior and Counterfactuals," *Synthese* **76**, 135–69.

Bicchieri, C. (1988b), "Common Knowledge and Backwards Induction: A Solution to the Paradox," in M. Vardi (ed.), *Theoretical Aspects of Reasoning about Knowledge*. Los Altos, CA, Morgan Kaufmann, pp. 381–93.

Bicchieri, C. (1993), *Rationality and Coordination*. Cambridge, U.K., Cambridge University Press.

Bicchieri, C. and M. Dalla Chiara (eds.) (1992), *Knowledge, Belief, and Strategic Interaction*. Cambridge, U.K., Cambridge University Press.

Binmore, K. (1994), *Playing Fair: Game Theory and the Social Contract*, Vol. I. Cambridge, MA, M.I.T. Press.

Brams, S. (1975), "Newcomb's Problem and Prisoners' Dilemma," *Journal of Conflict Resolution* **19**, 597–612.

Campbell, R.K. (1989), "The Prisoner's Dilemma and the Symmetry Argument for Cooperation," *Analysis* **49**, 60–65.

Campbell, R. and L. Sowden (eds.) (1985), *Paradoxes of Rationality and Cooperation: Prisoner's Dilemma and Newcomb's Problem*. Vancouver, University of British Columbia Press.

Davis, L. (1977), "Prisoners, Paradox, and Rationality," *American Philosophical Quarterly* **14**, no. 4, 319–27.

Davis, L. (1985), "Is the Symmetry Argument Valid?" in Campbell and Sowden (1985), pp. 255–62.

Fudenberg, D. and J. Tirole (1992), *Game Theory*. Cambridge, MA, M.I.T. Press.

Gauthier, D. (1974), "The Impossibility of Rational Egoism," *Journal of Philosophy* **71**, 439–56.

Gibbard, A. and W. Harper (1978), "Counterfactuals and two kinds of expected utility," in C.A. Hooker, J.J. Leach, and E.F. McClennen (eds.), *Foundations and Applications of Decision Theory*. Dordrecht, D. Reidel, pp. 125–62.

Hardin, R. (1982), *Collective Action*. Johns Hopkins University Press.

Harper, W. (1988), "Causal Decision Theory and Game Theory: A Classic Argument for Equilibrium Solutions, a Defense of Weak Equilibria, and a New Problem for the Normal Form in Decision, Belief Change, and Statistics," in W.L. Harper and B. Skyrms (eds.), *Causation in Decision, Belief Change, and Statistics.* Dordrecht, Kluwer Academic Publishers.

Hubin, D. and G. Ross (1985), "Newcomb's Perfect Predictor," *Nous* **19**, 439–47.

Jeffrey, R. (1965, 2d edition 1983), *The Logic of Decision.* Chicago, University of Chicago Press.

Kaneko, M. (1987), "Structural Common Knowledge and Factual Common Knowledge," *RUEE Working Paper* no. 87–27, Hitotsubashi University.

Kaneko, M. and T. Nagashima (1990), "Game Logic I: Players' Deductions and Knowledge of Deductive Abilities," E90-3-1, VPI-SU.

Levi, I. (1992), "Feasibility," In Bicchieri and Dalla Chiara (1992), pp. 1–20.

Lewis, D. (1969), *Convention.* Cambridge, MA, Harvard University Press.

Lewis, D. (1979), "Prisoners' Dilemma is a Newcomb's Problem," *Philosophy and Public Affairs* **8**, 235–40.

Nozick, R. (1974), "Newcomb's Problem and Two Principles of Choice," in N. Rescher et al., *Essays in Honor of Carl G. Hempel.* Dordrecht, D. Reidel, pp. 114–46.

Pettit, P. (1986), "Preserving the Prisoner's Dilemma," *Synthese* **86**, 181–84.

Rapoport, A. (1966), *Two-Person Game Theory.* Ann Arbor, University of Michigan Press.

Savage, L.J. (1954), *The Foundations of Statistics.* New York, John Wiley and Son.

Schick, F. (1979), "Self-knowledge, Uncertainty, and Choice," *British Journal for the Philosophy of Science* **30**, 235–52.

Skyrms, B. (1984), "EPR: Lessons for Metaphysics" in P.A. French, T.E. Uehling, and H.K. Wettstein (eds.), *Midwest Studies in Philosophy IX: Causation and Causal Theories.* Minneapolis, University of Minnesota Press, pp. 245–55.

Sobel, J.H. (1988), "Infallible Predictors," *Philosophical Review* **97**, 3–24. "Dilemma," *Synthese* **55**, 347–52.

Stalnaker, R. (1994), "On the Evaluation of Solution Concepts," *Theory and Decision* **37**, 49–73.

von Neumann, J. and O. Morgenstern (1944), *Theory of Games and Economic Behavior.* Princeton, NJ., Princeton University Press.

Watkins, J. (1972), "Imperfect Rationality," in R. Borger and F. Cioffi (eds.), *Explanation in the Behavioral Sciences.* Cambridge, U.K., Cambridge University Press.

Printed in the United States
704500003B

9 780195 117158